Don't Trust Anyone Over Thirty

Books by Howard Smead

Blood Justice: The Lynching of Mack Charles Parker
The African-Americans
The Redneck Waltz
Kak Drenner
My Name is Zed

Don't Trust Anyone Over Thirty

The First Four Decades of the Baby Boom

Howard Smead

Writers Club Press
San Jose New York Lincoln Shanghai

Don't Trust Anyone Over Thirty

Writers Club Press
an imprint of iUniverse.com, Inc.

For information address:
iUniverse.com, Inc.
5220 S 16th, Ste. 200
Lincoln, NE 68512
www.iuniverse.com

ISBN: 0-595-12393-7

Printed in the United States of America

To my three millennials:
Julius, Leah and Xander

Scenes and sayings from the formative years

From wooden puppets to the World Wide Web.

From Woodstock to woodstoves.

From "Say, kids, what time is it?" to "Up Against the Wall, Motherfucker."

From "Non-negotiable Demands" to "Have a Nice Day."

From fallout shelters to Internet service providers.

From Hula-Hoops to cell phones.

From "Can't Buy Me Love" to IRAs and 401Ks.

From free love to free range chickens.

From LSD to Lattes

From Days of Discord to Disco Nights.

From Freedom Rides to Drive-by shootings.

From poppers to poopie

From coddled babies to baby coddlers.

From cocaine to Rogaine.

From "A Day in the Life" to "Life's a bitch and then you die"...

"What a long, strange trip it's been."
                                        —The Grateful Dead

Contents

Foreword

As a baby boomer intrigued by his self-absorbed generation, I have long wondered what, besides our big numbers, makes us so distinctive. How did we become a crew of such motley iconoclasts? Why are we such an anxious generation? Why are we so driven? Once I started asking, it didn't take long to find out that other boomers shared these questions, as well as the intrigue—and pride. The Web, for example, is loaded with boomer sites of varying degrees of relevancy. As I looked for ways to characterize our wild and arrogant cohort, I searched for a hook on which to hang our yearnings—and our peccadilloes.

One seemed obvious: Our undiminished emphasis on "youth" and "youthfulness," concepts which, in our own inimitable way, we have glorified beyond all sense of proportion. Pride in being young during times of change is nothing new. Long before there was a baby boom or a twentieth century, William Wordsworth in remembering the French Revolution wrote: "Bliss it was in that dawn to be alive. But to be young was very heaven."

Boomers—blissfully immortal for most of our young lives— knew just how heavenly it was. We never got over it. Today, although we're all pretty much middle-aged, being young continues somehow to define us. The cult of youth in all its permutations has become the elastic clause in our generational constitution.

Beyond that, other things keyed the idealism and the outrage as well as the angst and psychodrama that has made up so much of our history on this planet. Baby boomers were the first generation to stand at the confluence of mass culture, mass advertising and mass annihilation. It was like the union of mighty and beautiful rivers, magnificent in their turmoil. Those currents swept us along with their wonders as well as their fears.

From an early age, we were carpet-bombed with aphorisms, jingles, marketing phrases, and warnings. As we got older we came up with our own, many of them chanted in the streets. Others we repeated with, we thought, Confucius-like wisdom until we often became walking, talking clichés. As I began assembling a short list of them—one or two for each year since 1946, I found I was having trouble limiting their number. Then it came to me that all these phrases, quotations and snatches of lyrics described my pop culture-soaked generation in a novel and compelling way. So rather than winnowing, I began harvesting every scene and saying I could find.

It wasn't enough simply to cite a catchy phrase: that phrase had to have special meaning for baby boomers. If it meant something to others, that was fine, so long as it mattered to us. (An utterly boomeresque point of view in itself.) I left out items that may have received wide play if, in my opinion, it wasn't special to boomers. (For example, "If you got it, flaunt it.") Throughout, the criterion, like the song, remained the same. I was searching for anything that helped define my generation. It wasn't always easy—although it was always a lot of fun. The project turned into a labor of love. The result, I hope, is not boring. That's the last reaction I would want from my compatriots. I'm sure I excluded a few things. But then, our long, strange trip is far from over.

This book covers its first four decades.

Introduction

Welcome to the most egocentric generation in the history of humankind.

This is its story, told through the vignettes, sayings, slogans and quotations that shaped and characterized an era. Baby boomers witnessed a lot of history, made some of it and, along the way, produced a pop culture treasure trove of aphorisms to explain it all. So many slogans, sayings and quotations that, when laced together, paint a striking portrait of growth and change. But these are not mere slogans. Our history lies in our music and albums, books, TV shows and movies, and in remarks by people prominent or infamous.

Beginning with the placid 50s ("Awl, gee, Wally"), charging through the idealistic stirrings of the 60s ("Ask not what your country can do for you..."), only to experience the disillusionment and despair that came a few years later ("Up against the wall, motherfucker"), and the reaction ("There you go again") and counter-revolution it engendered ("The era of big government is over" and "Soccer moms"), our story is as fascinating as it is rich.

It's impossible to deny the distinctiveness of the 76,441,000 million American babies born during the post-World War II baby boom. What are we to make of our anxious generation? We grew up the most affluent generation ever, protected in suburbs and small towns, enjoying greater health and expecting longer, fuller lives than our predecessors. We are more idealistic than the Founding Fathers and as zealous as abolitionists.

All the attention we've received, you'd think we were born with life in our hip pocket. We lived through the longest and greatest period of national prosperity, the nation's first losing war, and its most culturally eccentric period only to end up gazing at the world we inherited with a sense of longing, unfulfilled promise, and self-doubt. We grew by turns more idealistic, less realistic, and, when our dreams didn't pan out quite the way we wanted, more disillusioned with our country and its government and alienated from it than seems possible given the privileged lives bestowed upon us. We're as immature as Peter Pan and as arrogant as Napoleon.

From our infancy, the fertile fields of opportunity lay beneath our feet, offering all their wonders, asking that we use them to the fullest. Hoping to create a generation free from the fear and deprivation they suffered, our parents pampered and protected us. In doing so they inadvertently gave birth to two separate waves of self-absorbed activists—one on the left, the other on the right—that have produced a continuing series of cultural revolutions and counterrevolutions. And none of us may live to see the ultimate consequences of all this protest and transformation. After all, we only set out to save the world, twice.

*   *   *

What exactly is the Baby Boom Generation? And where did it get its Olympian ego? First things first. Why is it called the *baby boom*? Simple, because of a boom in babies. Seventeen million extra babies in fact. That's how many more babies were born than would have been had *our* mothers paid any attention to the fertility rates of *their* mothers. Why didn't they? The experts were predicting a continuing decline in the birth rate. But young husbands had just gotten back from World War II and wanted to settle into the old and safe routine of hearth, home and children, lots of children. Their wives, our mothers, were in full agreement. The amorous burst that followed World War II became a freak occurrence caused by the conjunction of youthful optimism, material affluence, victory in one war and fear of loosing another. You want to blame the baby boom on one person? Blame Adolf Hitler. His activities in Europe distorted the family cycle in America. To that you might add a dash of Stalin. Because in the 50s, the Cold War with its emphasis on family strength—Mom at home, pregnant and in the kitchen—sustained the boom into the 1960s.

VE Day came in May 1945. VJ Day followed in August after Hiroshima and Nagasaki. Sixteen million GIs came home a short time later and got down to business. Nineteen years later when the birthing boom subsided, there were 76 million more natural born Americans. Three demographic trends coalesced to bring this about. Older women who waited during the war started having kids. Women started having babies at a younger age. Women started having more babies.

During the first year of the boom 3.4 million babies arrived—at the time a record number for one year. Our mothers were popping out kids at the rate of 338,000 a month, 100,000 more a month than the previous year. In 1947 the number increased over 1945 by one million. From 1954 on, over four million little boomers appeared on the scene each year, peaking at 4.3 million in 1957, finally exhausting itself in 1965, when births fell below four million, where they have stayed.

All those born during the demographic bulge between 1946 and 1964 are baby boomers. According to the 1990 census, our ranks included 38,503,000 women and 38,038,000 men. Sixty one million of us are white. Nine million black, and about six million Hispanic, Asian and Indian. At century's end, counting deaths and 8 million foreign born boomers, our generation reached almost 78 million and may continue to increase for a few more years. Almost as many of us are dying these days as are immigrating. We account for 31% of the population, a figure that will drop to 20% in a few decades as we start dropping out for good and baby boomer babies take their place in the sun.

We appeared at the right time, in sufficient numbers, and under the most auspicious economic circumstances imaginable. We're the best-informed generation ever, and are likely to remain so. Vietnam prompted many of us to go to college if for no other reason than to avoid the draft. Black boomers were the first generation in most black families to go to college. The move toward racial equality also opened the campus door to women. The money was there for all of us, thanks to NDEA '58, which granted low-cost college loans, no questions asked. Because of Vietnam we're much more preoccupied with and pessimistic about world problems and our involvement in them than Generation X (1965—1981), The Silent Generation (1925—1945) or the G.I. Generation (1901—1924). Most of the Millennial Generation (Generation Y) (1982—2000) is still too young to know or care.

The oldest are turning fifty at the rate of one every seven seconds. The youngest are looking at the thirties with the cold realization that they're no longer kids. The majority of us went to elementary and secondary school in the 50s and college in the 60s and 70s. For the most part we were old enough to serve in Vietnam or have friends who did. Most boomers entered the working world, adulthood that is, during the 70s. At the same time, while some of us were getting married and starting families, many of us, especially women, held off in favor of careers until the mid-80s.

Those born after 1957, members of the second wave, don't feel nearly as strong a generational identity as the first wave. The feeling of specialness that gave rise in the 60s to the mistrust of our elders known as the Generation Gap largely preceded them. Many boomers born in the 60s have more in common with our successors (and antagonists) in Generation X, who were born between 1965 and 1981. Think of it this way: first wave boomers became hippies, second wave punks. Both expressions of dissatisfaction with the world came from our generation, even though they were often at polar opposites within the legions of misfits.

Pity the second wave. Those who came of age in the 70s feel excluded from the endless self-adulation among baby boomers. They suffered when the sexual revolution hit the mainstream. *Their* parents practiced wife swapping and open marriages. *Their* parents went to sex clubs. *Their* parents smoked dope. *Their* parents tried to let their thinning hair grow long, wore striped bell-bottoms and love beads. *Their* parents got divorced. Parents of the first wave stayed straight, married and at home. That made a huge difference because those boomers born on the down slope are even more cynical than their older peers.

There is also a group of pre-boomers who share the era with us. They were born between 1941 and 1945. This leading edge was very much part of the generation that came of age in the 1960s— the Vietnam Generation. Or, the under-twenty-five generation that became *Time* magazine's 1966 "Man" of the Year. That would include Newt Gingrich, Bob Dylan, Tom Hayden, Oliver North, Joni Mitchell, Angela Davis and Bill Bradley and H. Rap Brown— and the Beatles. Technically they're not boomers. But they were shaped by the same forces.

The leading edge and the first wave came of age under the influence of the Civil Rights Movement, the war in Vietnam, and profound economic prosperity. The second wave arrived in the 70s during Watergate, the oil embargo, gas lines, runaway inflation, and vastly lowered economic expectations. No wonder some became punks. Unlike early boomers, second wavers, now in their 30s, learned that they probably won't achieve the same standard of living as their parents or the same degree of economic security as older boomers. For them the American Dream assumed entirely different dimensions. And if they haven't already, some day soon they might be forced to rely on their parents for financial support and perhaps a place to live until they get themselves together.

As a result of years of protest ferment, our generation is considered to be socially and politically liberal. We think of ourselves that way. But we're not. In 1975 46% of those boomers old enough to be surveyed called themselves liberal. Ten years later that percentage fell to 29%. Now it's below 20%. Besides that and contrary to commonly held assumptions, the second wave tends to be more liberal than the first wave and leading edgers. Time might prove this simply a factor of age. Early boomers are firmly in their 40s, a time of creeping conservatism. The second wave will be there soon enough and might change when it gets there.

Despite thousands of hairy-headed hippies in the streets protesting against the War, most of us supported the American effort in Southeast Asia at least through the Cambodian Incursion and the Kent State Massacre. And we damn sure supplied the bulk of the one million GIs that served there. Although not everyone who crossed the pond did so willingly, for the most part those who went did their duty as they believed it should be done—and, if they lived, suffered the consequences from their wrathful peers and neglectful elders.

On the whole, we disliked LBJ and his Great Society, even though we grew to embrace its programs. The first two times we voted, we voted Republican: for Nixon twice; then Carter once. We loved the Gipper and gave him our votes. In fact, Ronald Reagan is *the* boomer president. The Reagan Era's emphasis on self-centeredness and living for today made him just our sort of guy. (Disposable income became the marijuana of the 80s.) A plurality favored Bush over Dukakis. We voted for Clinton even though we have a negative fixation on the first boomer president. But then, who doesn't? Put simply, a whole lot of us hate both him and his smart, successful wife Hillary. Possibly it's because they're such super-achievers. More probably it's because Bill Clinton's white trash origins destroyed any notions the rest of us might have that we lack the wealth and status to become president. We find it hard to forgive him for surpassing us. The Silent Generation that came of age in the 50s has failed so far to produce a president. He's surpassed them as well.

Despite our dislike of Clinton, the most revealing vote remains the 1972 election, where we supported Tricky Dick over George McGovern, who was supposed to be the candidate of the young. Our candidate! Still, our radical and reformist politics gives us our cachet. And for good reason. We grew up in a bigoted society and helped change it to a fairer, more equitable place. An activist minority shortened the war in Vietnam and made the plight of the less fortunate and the condition of the environment urgent national issues.

But it doesn't end there. The activist beat goes on. Today we make up a substantial portion of the shock troops of the Radical Right. These neo-radical boomers are no less committed, no less zealous in their political and cultural beliefs than their counterculture brethren, and manifest the exact same generational arrogance: our way or no way at all. If it indeed turns out that our generational legacy is revolutionary change, that change may well be conservative/right wing not liberal/leftist. Some of the same people who took part in street demonstrations now attend conservative fundraisers. Many others, though, are new to the business of activism.

Anyway you look at it, the effects are the same. We're the cohort that revolutionized society. Where we once sat cross-legged in black-lighted rooms sharing bong hits, we now share anti-drug literature at public forums. We did more than Just Say No. We became crusaders. Where we once mocked religion as hypocritical, many of those same boomers now embrace enthusiastic, fundamentalist Christianity and look down their pious noses at those who don't. Now it's the non-believers who are "off the bus." Once upon a time, if it felt good we did it—naked, in groups, in the road, "where ever the spirit say go, do whatever the spirit say do." Now we jerk our children out of R-rated movies at the local cineplex. No way they're going to see sex scenes. We did it, but we're not letting them even watch it. At the same time, our alarm over "hate speech" and pornography has led to the most significant of our many value shifts. Where we once championed free speech, free expression and the right to "do your own thing in your own time," we now seek to limit free speech on computer networks and on college campuses. Both are conservative attitudes even if the cult of "political correctness" comes straight out of the left and radical feminism.

Although we suffer from a conservative-liberal split perhaps as sharp as the North-South or pro-and anti-slavery split before the Civil War, we remain a cohort. What other generation has been treated as an entity unto itself, breathing the fires of its identity into every national nook and cranny? What other generation has received so much special attention? Pampered? Self-righteous? You betcha.

We invented a new stage of life—youth—and the culture that surrounds it. Because of us, teenagers aren't expected to grow directly into adulthood. They learn to spread things out a little, to enjoy their youthful vigor, daring and optimism into their early 30s...sometimes much later. The Peter Pans among us introduced yet another age group that has been called "mid-youth," over thirty men and women whose outlook on life remains youthful, who enjoy the idiosyncrasies of being young. They loved Seinfeld and the X-Files; they buy lots of rock CDs. They have a bevy of 30-something actors to serve as role models.

We've retained our deep skepticism of authority to the point of exaggerated informality. Compare Bill Gates to J.P. Morgan, for example. Imagine J.P. Morgan conversing via e-mail. Listened to talk radio lately? We insist on first names. Our generation is on a first name basis with the entire world. We continue to reject or at least disparage authority at every turn. That will change in a few decades when we're all in our 50s and 60s. Then we'll be in full power and will exercise commanding influence over business, politics, religion, media and culture.

Although we question authority, we specialize in authoritative moral wisdom right down to how-to books on just about every-thing. Although our antipathy extends to lawyers, banks and credit cards, we continue to be free-spending, heedless over-age mall rats, playing the grasshopper to the parental ant. We save less. We buy more. And we put it all on our credit cards. We love to buy things. From catalogues or glittery malls. We're the mall mavens for whom those palaces of shopping splendor were built.

We're fools for natural foods, or at least anything without artifi-cial flavors or chemical additives. In this we stand alone among the four or five generations with whom we share the earth. This love for things green and organic most likely stems from our craving for the authentic. Remember that line from *The Graduate*? "Just one word, Benjamin. Plastics." We took it to heart, although not the way it was intended. We abhor anything plastic or phony. Whether it be food, people, or products. Ironically, we have surrendered one generational mantle. The ecology movement is no longer ours. GenXers are much more concerned about the environment than we are. Hey, we have children to raise.

We are more than likely to insist upon strict discipline for them—a reaction no doubt from the amazing leniency we experi-enced. We like to rise early because we are hard workers, and we have no fear of hi-tech. Quite the opposite. We wholeheartedly embrace it. We're responsible for home computers and the Internet and Web which are re-inventing the world. We're more likely to own and use one at home than either pre-boomers or GenXers. We were young when computers appeared. And once R2D2 and C3PO helped us get over our antipathy for Hal 9000, we embraced them fervently—just like everything else we embrace. Nothing halfway about us. Never has been, never will be.

As a consequence of the fast pace we keep, we feel stress more than our parents and let *everybody* know it. Did you think we'd keep it to ourselves? Our high divorce rate and delayed marriages have run their course. These days most of us are married, including second wavers. You'll find us in a family with kids, most of which are under eighteen. Over six million of us are already grandparents. Half of us have been through a divorce. And most of our children have seen their parents get divorced.

Besides glutting the political market place with radical ideas, we also glutted the job market: seventy-five percent of baby boom women have entered the labor force. Our numbers caused a major building boom that drove up housing prices. Our parents had to pay for more schools and teachers. Now, as we send our kids off each morning, the decline in births (the baby bust) means there are too many schools. In our fear that our kids might be getting an inadequate education, we're withdrawing them and teaching them at home, over-raising them, over-coddling, over-organizing their lives, over-protecting, over-coordinating everything they do, and then complaining we don't spend enough "quality time" with them. With schedules like ours, who has time?

Where our parents merely indulged us, we are freaking out about our children. It's led to an Anxiety Gap where the burden of caring for them has destroyed our highly prized sense of individualism and personal freedom. We have group activities for everything from playing to pooping. Over half of first wavers pull down over $40,000 a year and own a home similar to the one in which they grew up. Most husbands and wives work. The peak of earning power will come as boomers fall between forty-five and fifty-four.

Each of us has held about ten jobs, is healthy and in fairly good shape. Although we're facing heart-disease, high blood pressure, hearing and sight impairment, all of which become a real danger after age forty-five, most of us are not quite there yet. In fact, now that we've got some age on us, we have the money, the time, and the will to join a gym and work out. As for sexual appetite, we're all old enough to be concerned about its decline. And young enough that it remains merely a concern.

Only twenty-three percent of us participated in the counterculture. We smoked or were exposed to marijuana. Some went beyond that to other drugs, but not nearly as many as we think. For most of us, drugs were something we did in college. The real significance of illegal drugs was that we took them at all. Many who did, did so to separate themselves from their parents for whom drugs was a bigger social taboo than sex. Fewer still actually dropped out of society and lived in communes. Most boomers enjoyed—and benefited in various ways—from the sexual revolution. We renounced the double standard and aggressively, for a while, sought to remove it from our lives. However, it's the younger boomers who streaked across college campuses and were ultimately more relaxed about sex and sexuality.

Let us not kid ourselves, overall we've had it pretty good. We've made our mark. We began our lives as the indulged "Little Emperors and Empresses" of our households. We emerged from our protected neighborhoods intensely idealistic and so ill-disciplined we expected social change to come as easily as ordering from an F.A.O. Schwartz catalogue. We became rooted in time—the Sixties—rather than in region or place, and we hated hypocrisy and injustice. If we didn't get our political way, we threw a public tantrum until we got tired of that and tried something else—such as eastern mysticism, spiritual cults, fundamentalist Christianity. And finally, conservative politics.

We just can't leave things alone, as though we're still reacting to our parents yelling at us to sit down and be quiet. We've seen our ideas, reforms and lunacy become mainstream and commonplace. Not only freer sex, but such widely shared concerns as environmentalism, consumerism, and a belief in egalitarian democracy. Our mistrust of institutions has become a traditional value.

Many of us now reject the ideas we once touted. Some of us have created a contra-culture that looks to the past, the 50s in particular, for an approach to the future. The contra culture is in many ways counterrevolutionary. It seeks to stamp out all vestiges of the Sixties. It blames that era as others of us once blamed our parents and their parents for the country's social ills. In any case, it's possible that when the contra-culture gets finished, the 1990s will have as radically influenced the country as the 60s. All because we are still blessed with the calling to better ourselves and the world around us.

PART I

In the Beginning...

"A generation of idealistic children"

—Dr. Benjamin Spock

1945-1949. Fifty million people died in World War II, 405,399 of them Americans. The causes they died for were real; the enemies evil and aggressive; the celebratory relief at war's end well deserved. GIs came home to a grateful country that awarded them one of the most ambitious and effective pieces of social legislation in the country's history—the GI Bill of Rights, which offered money for college and a new home in the suburbs.

The GIs yearned to settle down and start families—to live life. And they did so prodigiously. The year after the Japanese surrendered to the Allies on the Battleship Missouri, a birthing spree began that would not peak until 1957. When it finally ended in 1964, 76 million babies had been born into a booming economy with limitless possibilities.

But new fears threatened the optimism. Terrible weapons of war, more destructive than any in history, darkened the sky with promises of a very hard rain. The land thundered with fears of espionage and subversion, drawing an ominous edge along our mighty clouds of joy. Parents didn't know whether to giggle with delight at their wealth and power or shudder with foreboding at the world's new perils. The tough years of depression and war left them determined to make a better life for their kids, to raise them in a better way, in a more tranquil world.

Chapter 1

The Radiance of a Thousand Suns

1945. Twin cataclysms ended one era and started another, two nuclear attacks. The issue was not that "Hiroshima was a blunder and Nagasaki a crime," as one Manhattan Project scientist put it. The issue was nuclear annihilation, instant vaporization. It told us life had no meaning; life was so impermanent, so transitory we meant nothing and served no purposed by being here. For kids at least the Bomb bred selfishness. For as much as boomers played guns among the neighbor's box elders, they never played Armageddon. We would come to dream about it in the terms uttered in reaction to the first nuclear test at Trinity Site near Alamogordo, New Mexico, at 5:29:45AM on July 16, 1945. For the new generation, this was a day that would also live in infamy.

> *"If the radiance of a thousand suns were to burst into the sky, that would be like the splendor of the Mighty One...I am become Death, destroyer of worlds."*
>
> **—J. Robert Oppenheimer quoting the Bhagavad Gita**

The first substantial thing most kids come to fear is the death of their parents. For legions of boomers the loss of their parents was secondary to their own extinction. It's a tough thing growing up optimistic and self-confident while looking over your shoulder at a whimsical God.

Much of the outrage that appeared decades later grew from resentment at the world our fathers created, a world characterized by the rarefied madness of nuclear weapons. Is it any wonder boomers became so self-indulgent? We grew up less certain about our fate than any other generation in human history. Our generation would come into being caught between the good victory over tyranny on one side and the potential evil of nuclear devastation on the other. They were like squabbling parents.

A wise General Douglas MacArthur warned of the potential for massive destruction brought forth by the Bomb. "We have had our last chance. If we do not devise some greater and more equitable system, Armageddon will be at our door."

*   *   *

But for the time being his warning went unheeded.

"These proceedings are closed."

—General Douglas MacArthur

The entire world breathed a sigh of relief on September 2 as MacArthur stood before the morning-suited representatives of Imperial Japan on the Battleship Missouri in Tokyo Harbor and closed the formal declaration of surrender of the remaining Axis power. The most destructive war in human history was over. For Americans it ended fifteen years of economic deprivation, fear, and loss. They knew, whether they were entrenched along the hedgerows of Europe, in the foxholes of Tarawa, or on the streets of New York City, GIs soon would be coming home. Good had prevailed. God had prevailed. America had prevailed. The green felt expanse upon which lay the documents of surrender seemed to be the cupped hand of providence protecting our destiny. To John Winthrop's children—and boomers came to believe they were precisely that—America could at long last finish building her City on the Hill and release her shining light for all the world to behold.

Chapter 2

Baby and Child Care

1946. President Harry S Truman could not have known when he invited the ex-British prime minister to speak at Westminster College in Fulton, Missouri, on March 5 that the speech by the Allies' strongest leader would set the tone for the global strife that was already underway. This new war fought by proxy between former allies became a duel to the death of competing ideologies.

> *"From Stettin in the Baltic to Trieste in the Adriatic an Iron Curtain has descended across the continent."*
>
> **—Winston Churchill**

Welcome to the Cold War, World War III by another name: a bloody, forty-year world-wide conflict. Considering the twenty-plus million who would die and the trillions of dollars pumped into this for-keeps version of Mortal Combat, Quake and Jedi Force, peaceful co-existence was a mutually agreed upon fiction. Both sides knew there would ultimately be a triumphant victor and a devastated loser.

Only no one knew who it would be. And you couldn't hit reload and start the game again. Meanwhile, prospective parents were entering the national raise-a-family sweepstakes, in which the contest was its own reward. On every nightstand lay a book containing the contest rules.

*   *   *

This unassuming and at first somewhat disreputable paperback sold four million copies by 1952 and one million a year for eighteen straight years. That came to over 50 million copies, translated into 39 languages including Urdu and Catalan. Beginning in June of '46 parents could buy it for 35 cents.

The Pocket Book of Baby and Child Care
—Benjamin Spock

To a generation of expecting mothers, Dr. Spock's book (originally titled *The Common Sense Book of Baby and Child Care*) took the place of the Holy Bible on the nightstand and at the breakfast table. His message was new then and so obvious now. "Trust yourself. You know more than you think you do." Above all, said Spock, "Hug your children." Spoil, flatter, and indulge your adorable babies. Spock also counseled to be friendly rather than stern, encouraging rather than didactic. If they were successful, the result would be a generation of "idealistic children."

> *"...I think that more of our children would grow up happier and more stable, if they were acquiring a conviction, all through childhood, that the most important and the most fulfilling thing that human beings can do is to serve humanity in some fashion and to live by their ideals...If you raise a child who has idealism he will have no lack of opportunities to apply it."*

Our parents took these optimistic ideas to heart. They'd won a war. They'd survived the Great Depression. They had reason to believe "[We] are in this world not for [our] own satisfaction but primarily to serve others." He told them their job was to create a generation of dreamers that would originate new designs for life that might free our countrymen from economic turmoil and destructive wars. He wanted this new generation of babies to be reformers with a feel for the past and an eye to the future. To do that he urged our mothers to nurture us towards our full potential. In doing so he may not have allowed for the impatience such lofty goals might have instilled in an affluent and protected generation.

Spock became the first millionaire created by the Baby Boom Generation. Half a generation later, the good doctor joined his babies in the streets to protest the war in Vietnam. And this once revered man became the arch villain of a backlash against permissiveness and rebellion, as though generous feeding schedules had led to cultural revolution.

*   *   *

With a shrug and a fretful smile, parents embraced the three C's of Cold War America: containment, conformity and consumption. Television was the handmaiden of the three C's. The necessary condition for virtually everything that followed. We became the first generation in human history raised by a "third parent," an "electronic babysitter" that left many of us as close to our favorite TV stars as our parents.

DuMont Television Network

—network TV

The television age began on April 13 when the first major network established a cable connection between stations in New York and DC. DuMont even made its own television sets; manufacturers produced 6,476 this first year. The following year 178,571 more hit the market. You could buy one with a 20-inch screen for $2500 plus $45 for the antenna. By 1953 production had risen to 7 million a year. By 1967 98% of all homes had sets. Popular culture and world-wide communications were about to undergo a total transformation. When we entered the TV Age, the doors of the past closed permanently behind us. There would be no returning to slower, more communitarian times.

Television remains the fastest growing technological innovation of all time—outpacing telephones, radios, cars, VCRs, Walkmans and computers. But what made it so important to the infant generation was its formative role. TV helped create our worldview by providing standards of taste and conduct. TV gave us an impression of universality. It tied us together in ways in which no generation had been before.

Was it any wonder that kids weaned on *Howdy Doody* and acculturated by *The Mickey Mouse Club* also believed in a *Leave it to Beaver* reality? Perhaps we grew up seeking to imitate not an alien haute couture, but the predictability of pop culture. In its way just as deceiving. Little surprise that by the time we hit our late teens, some of us were beginning to ask if this was all life had to offer? Although in 1958 Dumont itself became the Portugal of TV networks when it folded after a final broadcast of the Monday Night Fights, carried by a mere five stations, television culture assumed an ever-increasing role in our lives.

*   *   *

Just hidden from the realm of the Saturdaddies and Little League summers, some clever men touched off a revolution that would eventually answer the question. Scientists at the University of Pennsylvania activated the world's first electronic, large scale, general purpose computer.

ENIAC

—Electronic Numerical Integrator And Computer

Weighing 50 tons, the first computer was 150 feet wide and ran 20 banks of flashing lights and 18,000 vacuum tubes on 174 kilowatts of power. In one second its circuits could add 5,000 numbers or multiply 14 ten-digit numbers—slightly faster than today's pocket calculator. It reduced to seconds what at the time took a human forty hours to calculate. The future was decades away, but this was the first step toward a new age of ready access to information that would enable average citizens to influence their surroundings. The dimensions of change introduced by television would be enhanced by the personal computer. It is an ironclad cinch no one at the major networks, the phone company, or even the ENIAC designers at the University of Pennsylvania, John W. Mauchly and J. Presper Eckert (the unheralded inventors of the computer), foresaw the revolution that would one day sweep Guttenberg's galaxy. Although in 1962 Eckert did predict desktop computers.

Originally a top secret WW II defense project designed to calculate firing tables used by gunners to aim artillery, ENIAC didn't quite make it into the war, but found use helping with calculations for the H-bomb until it was retired. In its eleven years it did more math than had all humanity up to 1945. Women programmed ENIAC by pulling and plugging patch cables, like telephone operators. To celebrate its 50th anniversary Penn State scientists reduced ENIAC's entire circuitry to a microchip.

Chapter 3

Faster Than You Can Say Jackie Robinson

1947. To produce a microchip, science first had to overcome heat and size. On December 16th a team at Bell Laboratories invented the transistor, a device that acts as a switch and a modulator and can be endlessly reduced in size and integrated onto an etched surface of silicon.

The Transistor

—semi-conductor

By the time production became efficient, boomers were teenagers carrying transistor radios, complete with a bulky pink plastic earplug. Man, oh man, what a revelation. Cheap and good enough to take to the beach, they swept our world, perhaps the first modern product to find its main audience among the young. For the first time it was possible to block out the parents by pumping up the volume.

* * *

Something swept the planet ahead of the transistor radio. The sort of dichotomous reality that plagued much of modern middle class life. New products may have started flooding the market, but an old one remained quite strong: war. Hoping to turn the Mediterranean into their own version of an American lake, the paranoid, imperialist Soviets began filibustering in Greece and Turkey. Frightened by George Kennan's 8,000 word "Long Telegram" describing the USSR's bellicose intentions, Secretary of State Dean Acheson proposed a response to the "global struggle between freedom and totalitarianism" that became known as the Truman Doctrine.

"It must be the policy of the United States to support free peoples who are resisting attempted subjugation by armed minorities or by outside pressure."

—Harry S Truman

Truman's March 12 address to Congress announced a policy of *containment* that included aid to Greece and Turkey and other nations fighting communist insurgency. This ambitious and sometimes reckless program became, according to Senator William Fulbright, "the guiding spirit of American foreign policy." In practical terms it meant the USA became the world's policeman sworn to protect against further communist expansion any time, anywhere, no matter how remote, no matter how indistinct the threat.

This took the CIA to Iran and Guatemala, the Congo, Chile, and GIs to Korea, Lebanon, Central America and Southeast Asia. Ultimately, containment proved successful despite the enormous cost. The Cold War brought about transformations profound and painful. Lives lost numbered in the tens of thousands, costs rose to multi-billions, distorting American culture along the way. The Cold War manufactured consent and enforced conformity.

Fear of foreign threats produced a humorous side—humor, that is, with dark circles under its eyes. Americans have always believed in conspiracies, the deeper and darker and the more it involved the government the better. In the early 19th century a political party developed based upon the widely-shared belief that Freemasonry was a conspiracy to rule the world. This century we went that hoary old tale one better.

The origins of the UFO scare had more to do with Cold War paranoia than little green men.

Unidentified Flying Objects

—national paranoia

The seminal incident took place June 14, 1947 at Roswell, New Mexico, where, according to conventional wisdom, a UFO not only landed but disgorged little aliens, some of whom the military captured. It turned out the Air Force was testing aerial monitors of Soviet nuclear tests. Their acoustical equipment was born aloft by balloons—or something to that effect. A subsequent crash contributed to the speculation that Earth had received strange visitors and the government was lying about it. The reason for the deception rested on the shaky rationale that the public couldn't handle the truth.

Elements of the government kept the test secret from the Soviets and therefore the American people. They believed they couldn't tell us without tipping their hand to the enemy. For many millions of conspiracy buffs, it was the beginning of the government's secret agenda. Despite the juvenile joy at the prospect of real live (or dead) grays, such beliefs reflected a far more dangerous problem: mistrust of the government. *This* problem was undeniably real. The only alien was created domestically and it was called the

National Security State. The conspiracy was a concerted attempt to conceal a truth about the Cold War. For a democratic government to do such a thing was threatening enough. We didn't need UFOs landing in New Mexico. Secrecy, a necessary part of any government, became central to our national survival. It led to too many secrets and too much deception. The irony of using secrecy to preserve liberty may have been lost on its architects. But the same type secrecy that spawned Roswell also spawned the Bay of Pigs fiasco, the deception behind the Gulf of Tonkin incident, Watergate and Iran-Contra. We'd been better off had it been grays all along.

The same year as Roswell, Congress created the CIA, the National Security Council, and the Air Force. These agencies were necessary, as was their need for confidentiality. But the fact remains in a democracy it's a sticky bit to allow your elected peers to lie in the name of the truth.

Democratic ideals on one hand and the fear of communism and the needs for containing it on the other led to all manner of grand conspiracies, not all of which proved as untrue as Roswell. When we discovered the ugly depth of these lies—having nothing to do with grays, but with reds and red-baiters, we were outraged.

*   *   *

Unfortunately, events are never as clear-cut as one would like. One conspiracy of silence came directly from the international blood duel concerning the military applications of aerospace.

Glamorous Glennis
Chuck Yeager's *Bell X-1*

On October 14, 1947 at Muroc Field high in the Mojave Desert, the laconic test pilot broke the sound barrier in a small orange, bullet-shaped rocket ship. Flown to 26,000 feet suspended on a chain in the bomb bay of a B-29, Yeager flew into a new era of supersonic flight that, in the X-15 in 1963, would roam as high as sixty-seven miles (unofficially), or just above the atmosphere along the edges of outer space. He celebrated by doing victory rolls during the seven minutes it took him to glide back to Earth. Not that any of us knew it. The government hid this amazing feat for national security reasons. The Air Force kept it secret for a year. The Cold War was on and we were even competing against our allies. One small, perhaps justifiable, secret heaped on another until in the government of a candid democracy secrecy had become its own precedent.

*   *   *

One conspiracy, however, did start to unravel. The same year Americans flew through Mach 1 and set up the National Security State, Jackie Robinson joined the Brooklyn Dodgers. The public campaign against racial subjugation gained national prominence when Branch Rickey took the talented black athlete away from the Negro Leagues. It marked the beginning of the end of racial segregation.

Faster than you can say Jackie Robinson

—popular saying

The American virus, white racism, has been with us since before we were a country. Our generation came of age during attempts to rectify the horrific sins of our forefathers. We were raised on the unquestioned belief in America's greatness. Realization that a tenth of the population was treated no better than Third World peasants came as a sad surprise.

Reconciling the horrors of racial oppression with the grandeur of America's promise proved too great even for the Founders. For us it crippled our idealism and planted seeds of cynicism.

Yet corrective measures were already on the way. President Truman commissioned a panel to investigate the great American divide.

To Secure These Rights

—Presidential Commission on Race Relations

The presidential panel issued findings that gave official approval to half a century of black struggle towards "the elimination of segregation based on race, color, creed, or national origin from American life." It described racial inequality as "moral dry rot which eats away at the emotional and rational bases of democratic beliefs."

For boomers growing up along the color line, the dilemma was simple and troubling. How can we be as great a nation as we say we are when so many people suffer such purposeful daily humiliation?

The question was difficult enough to ask. The answer was proving impossible. Most whites and a surprising number of blacks thought things were just as God intended. To whites life was hunky-dory. Any racial discontent was surely the work of communist subversion. Boomers came to believe that the task of killing this national virus had fallen on our shoulders. We were convinced that as we came of age and came into power, we'd give racial discrimination the lynching it deserved. How wrong we were.

    *   *   *

Racial unrest did not drive the vitriolic tenor of the times. Indeed, American Negroes were cautious in their challenge to Jim Crow. In the midst of the Red Scare, they were continually looking over their shoulder lest they blunder into league with the left. All because this question was playing on the public mind:

*"Are you now or have you ever been
a member of the communist party of the United States...?"*

—HUAC

Unseemly hearings by the House Committee on UnAmerican Activities became a cause and effect of national hysteria. You didn't have to know Marx's theories of surplus value and alienation from work to fear communism. Marxism denied God's existence, and that was all most Americans needed to know. Unfortunately, some politicians, most but by no means all in the GOP, seized upon communism for their own political advancement. Reacting to real threats from abroad, dubious threats from within and Republican attacks of being soft on communism, the Truman administration demanded oaths of loyalty from government employees and launched all sorts of scandalous intrigues at home and abroad. All carried out in the name of national security. No leader or citizen was above suspicion. The GOP won the House in 1946. Under the Republicans HUAC began investigating citizens and the organizations they worked for. From one coast to the other, they rooted through government bureaucracies and academia and didn't come up for air until they got to Hollywood. The thundering oratory, the clandestine inquiries in hotel rooms unearthed a few players, including the biggest prize, Alger Hiss, who lied about his treasonous activities during the depression-ridden 1930's.

Frank Sinatra of all people best characterized the problem created by crass and not very bright politicians. "Once they get the movies throttled, how long will it be before we're told what we can say and cannot say into a radio microphone? If you make a pitch on a nationwide radio network for a square deal for the underdog will they call you a Commie?"

Many citizens lost their livelihoods. Actors, screenwriters and directors were blacklisted. Professors were blackballed. Families split apart. Careers went down the tubes. Red Scare hysteria raised an important question that was never fully answered. Did the threat posed by the Soviets warrant denial of civil liberties? Some of the more extreme activities of both Republicans and Democrats undermined the democratic basis of society. For a while, the public rode the mad race. But when they tuned into the Army-McCarthy hearings in 1954, they got a load of Joe McCarthy turning the Senate into a demolition derby. And all that changed.

    *   *   *

HUAC's Saracen blade left the nation wondering why we weren't at war—if indeed infiltration and subversion were that widespread. The answer was—we were. "Half devils against half angels," to quote John Le Carré. And the half-devils had a devil of a weapon.

Avtomat Kalashnikova 1947

—the AK-47

Made of stamped metal, designed simply enough to be broken down by a child in Liberia, Palestine, Cambodia or East LA, yet sturdy enough to function flawlessly in the worst of conditions, the AK submachine gun became the most popular firearm in the world. Over fifty-five million have been made.

Assigned by the USSR's Central Artillery Command in 1943 to design an infantry assault weapon that would use the new 7.62 NATO round, Mikhail Timofeievich Kalashnikov spent four years perfecting the weapon that remains the weapon of choice for guerrillas, terrorists and half the world's armies. Germany produced the first assault rifle too late to have an impact on the Second World War. Its MP-44 machine pistol created a new genre: a lightweight automatic rifle that delivered high firepower at close range. The assault rifle's intermediate-sized cartridges, larger than a pistol's, smaller than a long rifle, was perfect for close combat. The US countered with the M-16 that at first had an unsettling tendency to jam.

In Vietnam GI's switched to AKs when they could. Made by the millions, they are cheap and available. Today, the price ranges from $10 in Cambodia to $13.80 in Namibia to $17 in Kurdistan to $150 in Chechnya to $500 in LA to $600 in Brooklyn. Many countries make knock-offs: China, the Czech Republic, Finland and Bulgaria. Even Israel copied its basics for its Galil assault rifle. Because they're more efficient than its temperamental American rival, the CIA bought 400,000 for the Afghani mujahideen.

Chapter 4

"No Man Who Owns His Own Home Can Be a Communist."

1948. The booms were on. Three of them: babies, bucks and belligerence. *Fortune* magazine proclaimed as much as early as 1946. "This is a dream era, this is what everyone was waiting through the blackouts for. The Great American Boom is on."

Unprecedented affluence produced a magical world of comfort and security. Even without the harsh will to conform imposed from above by red-baiting politicos and fear-mongering right-wingers, the great sprawling American masses found just what they wanted in the new suburbs with their celebratory backyard barbecues on the reliable squares of green grass. This was the true promise of American life. If it looks bland and regimented fifty years later, be wise. Back then this was utterly liberating.

The suburbs and small towns were great places to raise kids. Our parents sought out the safety of suburban cocoons. A trike on the front sidewalk, a baby pool in the backyard, and bottles sterilizing on the stove—it was an earthly paradise for the vast majority of those in or about to enter the middle class, which included most of us.

Naturally, the Cold War influenced the cookie-cutter suburbs and their conformist values. Scarcely any suburbanites cared that no blacks and few non-WASPs were allowed. Or that rules banned fences, clotheslines, unapproved paint schemes and un-cut grass. (They cut it for the slothful and sent the bill).

> *"No man who owns his own house*
> *and lot can be a communist.*
> *He has too much to do."*
>
> **—William J. Levitt**

The *burbs* provided the formative environment for the new generation of Americans. Levitt's genius was to turn suburban homes into Model T Fords. His planned communities offered modestly priced Cape Cod houses for $6,990. That came to sixty bucks a month, well within the reach of most GIs. Later he added ranch houses for $10,000. He began a boom in home construction that stimulated the economy and led to a mass migration of the white middle class from the cities to new tract houses built on surrounding farmland.

Levitt offered homes as a way for average Americans to roll up their sleeves and get to the business of containing communism by producing a society in which every family had a decent place to live. The rules were strict but the enticements were real. In addition to the famously low price, the original 4½ room Cape Cod came with a kitchen, a living room with a fireplace, and two bedrooms sitting on a 60' by 100' lot planted with fruit trees. These homes had central heating, built-in bookcases, closets, a Bendix washer and an 8" TV set that owners could pay off over thirty years. Lines formed months before the first 300 families moved in that October, with the great wave coming the following year. "Everyone is so young that sometimes it's hard to remember how to get along with older people," one Levittown housewife remarked.

They hadn't seen anything yet. Babies, babies, babies. Homes soon came with the kitchen beside the living room so mom could keep an eye on the kids crawling around in front of the TV set.

*   *   *

Dad worked while mom stayed home and minded the kids. Both had their ears cocked to the radio for news about the crisis in Berlin. It seemed a crisis was always brewing somewhere. As if the world hadn't had enough. Fifteen plus years of misery and war was enough to make conformists out of everyone. But when the Soviets closed ground access to Berlin, the Allied commander voiced concern that if the city fell to the Soviets, the dominoes would begin tumbling toward the Atlantic.

"...Western Germany will be next."

—General Lucius Clay

The general wanted to use military force to blast through the Berlin Blockade. Instead, the sly Truman used over 100 C-54s and C-47s flying upwards of 2000 tons of supplies a day into the imprisoned city. One plane dropped Hershey's chocolate to the German kids scattered in the ruined city below—the kids called it the Schokoladenflieger.

West Germany's dramatic economic recovery under the Marshall Plan, drove the Soviets to close the gates. They claimed West Berlin was a base for spying, which it was. It was also a safe haven for those fleeing totalitarian oppression in the East. The airlift continued for 321 days. Such heroism raised a symbolic torch of freedom for all the world to see. Several pilots died in crashes, but the bravery and relentless effort discredited our tyrannical adversaries and warned all the world that East-West tensions could easily flare into global conflict.

The Soviets proved themselves bullies and goons. Suffering a serious loss of prestige, they capitulated and the first significant head-to-head confrontation of the Cold War ended.

The nobility that drove much of the airlift inspired a sense of humanity throughout the world. The selflessness with which Americans embraced needy West Berliners provided a poignant reminder of the greater things for which we stood, Cold War repression notwithstanding.

"...the equal and inalienable rights of all members of the human family is the foundation of freedom, justice and peace in the world."

—Universal Declaration of Human Rights

On December 10 the United Nations General Assembly adopted this document, formulated through the hard work and prodding of Eleanor Roosevelt and many others. The "hortatory statement of aspirations" sought to replace the unspeakable horrors of the twentieth century with the nobility of compassion and brotherhood by advocating "human rights for all." At first American security concerns overrode human rights. Our leaders were so blinded by the exigencies of the Cold War they feared the human rights cause would hurt us. Conservatives especially sought to disassociate this country from the declaration. As the years passed though, we eventually saw the consistency between our aspirations and our immediate needs. Gradually the Cold War became in part a quest for human rights.

*   *   *

A war of a different kind was brewing back home in the States. At least it used to be called a war, the War between the Sexes. Looks quaint to our gender-neutralized eyes.

Sexual Behavior in the Human Male
—Dr. Alfred Kinsey

This ponderous and questionable study offered statistical analyses of a full range of male sexual experiences, right down to multiple orgasms in preadolescents and the frequency of homosexuality. Kinsey's statistical surveys claimed that 68 to 90% of men had engaged in premarital sexual intercourse. Ninety-two percent had masturbated and 50% committed adultery. A pious nation shuddered. As bad as that was, 37% admitted to at least one homosexual experience, 10% were exclusively homosexual and, God help us, 8% had had sex with animals. Accurate or not, the study became a best seller and a portent of sexual revolution. Censors sought to ban the explicit discussion of human sexuality because it ran afoul of America's deeply Puritanical outlook.

Alfred Kinsey was not the only harbinger of our Brave New World.

Chapter 5

Brave New Worlds

1949. George Orwell may have written *1984* as a warning about communism, but boomers read it as science fiction. Its bad-guy-under-the-bed themes blended Red Scare abuses with the worlds of science fiction novels.

"He loved Big Brother"

—George Orwell

The plight of Winston Smith and Julia warned us not so much of the communist menace that so preoccupied our parents but of what our own government might one day become.

War is Peace
Freedom is Slavery
Ignorance is Strength

The prospects were at once thrilling and forbidding. Newspeak slogans reminded our parents of the Nazi labor camp slogan Arbeit Macht Frei (work makes you free). Their grim irony parodied the dark potentials of our own society. We found the idea of the future as dystopia double plus good, exciting as hell.

One of the reasons so many of us took interest in a future filled with blasted landscapes came directly from the threat of nuclear annihilation we lived with.

"There is only one thing worse than one nation having the atomic bomb—that's two nations having it."

—physicist Harold C. Urey

On September 22, 1949 Harry Truman told the country and the world, "We have evidence that an atomic explosion occurred in the USSR." The second nation to build the bomb also happened to possess the world's largest army. We swallowed hard at the realization of our own vulnerability. The Redcoats were coming, again.

The invincibility we inherited from World War II disappeared in a single secret mushroom cloud. No matter how vigilant we might be, no matter how tough our defenses, with one successful test explosion the Soviets destroyed the vital sense of immunity from invasion we'd had since the War of 1812. Now we were in for it. The blast touched off an expensive and frightful nuclear arms race. This race would prove more costly than all previous races combined. And this time the cost of losing might be vaporization.

These were terrible burdens for a kid to carry into kindergarten. True, we didn't yet know about such things. But a few years of ducking and covering would teach us a lesson impossible to ignore.

"Power comes through the barrel of a gun."

—Chairman Mao

Linked in the public mind to the Soviet Union's acquisition of the A-bomb, the Fall of China, as it was called, further rattled fearful bones. The revolution on the Asian mainland ignited a war of recrimination over who lost China, as though any western nation could have long propped up the tin pot dictator Jiang Jieshi. With the world's most populous nation and a sizeable chunk of the earth now under the red star, we saw menacing red flames scorching both our coasts.

*   *   *

"We Charge Genocide."
—human rights violations in America

Something was completely out of sync. The America of our childhood was filled with both hatred of communist oppression and reluctance to consider equality for the African 10% of our population. The hypocrisy was impossible to ignore, impossible to explain away. While our leaders railed about totalitarianism abroad, blacks petitioned the United Nations to investigate human degradation at home. The impudence of the petition produced more outrage than the truth of the charges.

We were still too young to comprehend this issue—better to cower beneath our desks against the great gray mushroom clouds which were somehow more comprehensible. Early black boomers were entering the time of their lives when their doleful parents would begin slowly and carefully spelling out the bitter lessons of the color line.

*   *   *

The fifth Beetle
—the VW bug

Egalitarian dreams received a small but consequential boost with appearance of what amounted to the first world car. The Peoples' Car moved a generation. It took a while for these anti-materialistic little devils to catch on, but when they did, the Bug (and later the Microbus) became the counterculture's anti-car. They offered low gas mileage at a time when gas was cheaper than dirt. Cramped backseats at a time when cars were bedrooms on wheels. Their practicality couldn't be denied. Even considering the muscle cars of the glory years to come, the VW was the boomer automobile.

PART II

The Mythical Golden Age...

"Say kids, what time is it?"
—**Buffalo Bob**

1950-1959. Our world was the neighborhood, accessible by bicycle, always open and exciting. History was far away and hadn't penetrated our lives. The future meant what would take place on "Anything Can Happen Day." Annette defined beauty. Cubby and Karen were America's sweethearts. Rock n' roll was a cloud of dust on a very flat horizon. First it was a curiosity, then an F5 tornado sucking away tradition and leaving behind an existence exclusive of adults.

Television, the salvation of harried parents, brought us the world during these formative years for the bulk of the baby boom. (Some of us hadn't even been born yet.) *Howdy Doody, Captain Kangaroo, I Love Lucy,* Elvis Presley on *Ed Sullivan,* or cut-aways to the United Nations for deliberations over the Hungarian Revolt and other crises. By the end of the decade the crises were coming so frequently, the networks stopped interrupting regular programming to cover them. Television exposed us to the marvels and terrors of the world. It chanted the mantra of Cold War America— *containment, conformity* and *consumption.*

In the meantime, our parents were falling all over themselves keeping up with the Joneses—and staying far the hell away from anything even remotely pink. From the vantage of our new century, it may have been a Golden Age: sports, affluence, power, moral leadership, domestic tranquillity. What else could a country and a generation ask for? The 50s may also have been a hothouse for the overgrowth that followed.

Chapter 6

"I Have Here in My Hand a List."

1950. When Senator Joe McCarthy uttered this infamous lie at the McClure Hotel in downtown Wheeling, West Virginia,

"I have here in my hand a list."

—Joe McCarthy

...a frightened and gullible public believed he knew the names of...

"205—a list of names that were made known to the Secretary of State as being members of the Communist party and who nevertheless are still working and shaping policy in the State department."

He had no such list. He was a cynical opportunist and an ill-informed drunkard whose intemperance ultimately undermined his own career. The Soviets *had* infiltrated the government (although the extent remains to be seen). They *did* pose a serious external threat to our security. The FBI had been rolling up Soviet espionage networks even before McCarthy burst onto the scene with his scatter-gun accusations that included anyone who disagreed with him. Despite documented evidence of Soviet activity and fellow travelers in and out of government, for him and people of his ilk, vigilance exploded into a witch-hunt with strong class and anti-intellectual impulses. McCarthy was the wrong man to lead the anticommunist crusade, or any crusade for that matter.

This crusade was necessary. Marxist/Leninist ideology not only predicted the inevitability of conflict with capitalist systems, it was predicated upon the denial of the existence of God. For a nation as deeply religious as America, the atheistic political philosophy was anathema. The nation was so understandably alarmed at the possibility of Soviet subversion that for four furious years McCarthy got away with attacking virtually anyone.

At first most Americans countenanced his venomous paranoia. They felt he was doing more good than harm, that the threat necessitated extravagant action. In doing so the public put its trust in an Iago with the morals of a Lenin and the wit of the Three Stooges. Personal attacks, half-truths, doctored documents and outright fabrications destroyed the careers of many loyal Americans even though, as Ike's press secretary George Reedy quipped, "Joe couldn't find a Communist in Red Square. He didn't know Karl Marx from Groucho."

To its discredit the GOP backed him until he made his lunatic claim that the United States Army was riddled with communists. *McCarthyism* became synonymous not only with the era but for character assassination and demagoguery. The term itself was coined by *Washington Post* political cartoonist Herblock.

McCarthy's extremism crippled anti-communism by casting doubt on its ethics and goals. Proponents in and out of politics had to disassociate themselves from him first before going about the real business of defending the country. And even with disclaimers, their action remained suspect. Ironically, the far right, led by Joe McCarthy, did more damage to the precious dignity of freedom than the Red Menace. The tragic consequences became all too apparent when the Rosenbergs were caught in February 1950.

Right wing excesses—and remember McCarthy had just appeared on the scene—predisposed many Americans to assume their guilt.

The arrest of nuclear physicist and spy Klaus Fuchs in England revealed a spy ring that had penetrated the Manhattan Project. Which gave terrifying credibility to national anticommunist hysteria even though no credible evidence has yet surfaced of anything approaching widespread subversion. Julius and Ethel Rosenberg, two American communists, were implicated. Julius was a spy and traitor. His wife, though communist like her husband, quite possibly was neither. The information the "atomic spies" passed to the Soviets helped speed up their weapons research by at least two years and brought the hands of the atomic clock closer still to midnight.

> *"Diabolical conspiracy to destroy*
> *a God-fearing nation."*
>
> **—Judge Irving R. Kaufman**

Despite evidence casting doubt on Ethel's guilt, and illegally concealed from her defense, Kaufman sentenced both Rosenbergs to the electric chair for treason. Ike refused to commute their sentence so they might serve as an example. They were executed in Sing Sing on June 19, 1953, leaving behind two orphaned boys. After Fuchs' arrest, the freaked-out Senator Homer Capeheart cried, "How much more are we going to have to take? Fuchs and Acheson and Hiss and hydrogen bombs threatening outside and New Dealism eating away at the vitals of the nation. In the name of Heaven, is this the best America can do?"

Take a pill, Homer. Klaus Fuchs, who played a greater role in the spy ring than Julius Rosenberg, got fourteen years in the slammer. The Rosenbergs, meantime, became the first American civilians executed for espionage. Despite competing placards in front of the

White House, ample reason existed for Ike to let them die. The tide of events was behind him. It appeared as though the international communist conspiracy was marching forward unchecked.

June 25, 1950, while Truman was still in charge, the quixotic North Koreans charged across the 38th parallel separating them from pro-western South Korea.

> *"We've got to stop the sons of bitches no matter what."*
>
> **—Harry S Truman**

Our containment policy meant we would have to stop this act of aggression. Truman exclaimed, "By God, I'm going to let them have it." We almost didn't. The North Korean Army practically drove us into the Sea of Japan. The next domino appeared ready to fall until General Douglas MacArthur brilliantly outflanked them at Inchon and pressed far northward to the Yalu River border with communist China.

Then in November, the awesome Red Chinese "hordes" attacked in wave upon assault wave and we were on the defensive again. Truman fired the arrogant MacArthur for insubordination. Claiming "there is no substitute for victory," the general had sought to widen the war. General Omar Bradley brought sense to the ranting right wing who backed MacArthur and a wider war when he declared MacArthur's strategy would "involve us in the wrong war, at the wrong place, at the wrong time, with the wrong enemy." The public changed its mind, deserted MacArthur, and as the general predicted for himself, "Old soldiers never die, they just fade away."

His replacement Mathew Ridgway slogged back up the peninsula to a stalemate around the 38th parallel. Temporized at the United Nations as a "police action," the conflict produced some 33,629 dead GIs of four million total casualties, mostly Korean civilians. The *Forgotten War* produced no clear-cut results other than a cease-fire that has lasted nearly half a century. In reality the Korean Conflict was the first of a series of undeclared theater wars that characterized the Cold War. Containment, which in the end amounted to a war of attrition, came at an exceedingly high cost.

*   *   *

Containment was also the strategy in America's other Cold War, now about to go hot: racial conflict. America saw itself as lily white and Protestant. It wasn't. For that reason as the suburbs burgeoned, they drew attention to themselves. Blacks demanded access. White residents resisted. Middle class white flight from the cities had been an important ingredient in the rise of suburbia. The black middle class wanted to join them. Our most pressing domestic problem was not communist subversion.

> *"We can solve a housing problem, or we can try*
> *to solve a racial problem. But we cannot combine the two."*
>
> **—William J. Levitt**

Korea was fourteen hours and half a world away. As racial discrimination gathered more attention, Levitt came under criticism for segregating his comfortable green suburbs. All of the 82,000 people living in Levittown, Long Island were white. By the end of the decade, a full sixty million people had become suburbanites, constituting one third of the total population, a 40% growth that drove 62% of all housing construction. Levitt characterized the problem in day-to-day terms. White Americans may have been aware of inequities in the system. But they weren't about to let a little unfairness impinge on the good life behind the picket fences. America's suburbs offered better quality of life and were growing faster than any other segment of society. And they were twenty to one white over black. White parents' misguided attempts to orchestrate reality were heroic in the extreme...

Chapter 7

"What Are You Rebelling Against?"

1951.... Yet unsuccessful.

Popular culture penetrated even the safest neighborhoods. No fences were high or solid enough to ward off the real world. One way or another life slipped in. Science fiction movies were modern day fairy tales—carrying the message to us that the world was neither green nor safe and that evil was lurking just behind Dad's new red brick barbecue. From giant ants in *Them!* (1954) to zombies in *Invasion of the Body Snatchers* (1956), they warned of losing one's soul to things foreign.

> *"I bring you a warning—to every one of you listening to the sound of my voice. Tell the world, tell this to everyone wherever they are: watch the skies, watch everywhere, keep looking—watch the skies!"*
>
> **—The Thing**

Science fiction movies played upon anticommunist hysteria with their message of evil in the night sky. Movies such as *Invaders from Mars* (1953), which featured lobotomized humans doing alien bidding, and *This Island Earth* (1955), in which aliens posed as scientists bent on capturing our minds, urged parents to maintain vigilance against unseen, unheeded subversion that could turn loyal Americans into automatons. For kids these movies offered a neat way to spend a Saturday afternoon. We went home hoping they were true. The sense of adventure stirred the youthful soul far more than any vague threats of subversion. Besides, it beat cutting the grass and raking leaves.

Another alien threatened the peaceable suburban kingdoms (and everywhere else). An early warning came to the Saturday morning Rialto in the form of real alien speak:

"Gort! Klaatu barada nikto!"
—The Day the Earth Stood Still

These words, spoken to the robot Gort, told him to cart Michael Rennie's body back to the spaceship and throw it into the born-again machine. Which, being dutifully programmed in Issac Asimov's Three Laws of Robotics, Gort promptly did. Their saucer had flown at the unheard of speed of 4,000 miles an hour and landed on the Mall in Washington, DC. Six years later Sputnik would circle the planet at more than four times that speed. Fortunately it burned up in the atmosphere before it landed anywhere.

As Klaatu, Michael Rennie delivered an ultimatum about atomic recklessness lest we incur the wrath of forces beyond the solar system. "Your choice is simple. Join us and live in peace or pursue your present course and face obliteration. We shall be waiting for your answer. The decision rests with you." The Japanese had already made their decision. They had been turning out dozens of low-budgets horror flicks using gigantic monsters as metaphors for the A-bomb's capacity for total destruction. The most famous—*Gojira (1954)*—hit America two years later as *Godzilla, King of the Monsters*, with scenes of Raymond Burr awkwardly spliced into the original footage and most of the anti-nuclear sentiment removed. The dubbed English was flat stupid, but it didn't matter. Mutated from an American nuclear detonation, Godzilla became the baby boomers' biggest boomer.

Meanwhile, Earth's response to Klaatu was to try to blow his ass away as he stood in the doorway of his flying saucer still parked within shouting distance of the White House. He could have suffered worse at the hands of DC's parking meter Gestapo. Who'd this effete snob think he was dealing with anyway? This wasn't the real world. In the real world he would have offered to help us destroy the Red Army.

*   *   *

Until that blessed event, we got our first dose of "reality television" at a time when about one and a half percent of American homes had a TV. That figure represented a sharp rise in viewership. Television was still so immature there wasn't yet enough programming to fill either days or nights. "Prime time" was years away. On March 12 congressional hearings being held in New York City were broadcast over a primitive network as much to fill open slots as expose Mob activities to the viewing public.

> ### *"Mr. Costello doesn't care to submit himself as a spectacle."*
> #### —the Kefauver Hearings

Thus, we began to learn about the power of the media. Freshman senator Estes Kefauver's televised crime hearings made him the first politician to rise to prominence because of the tube. Hoping to prove his respectability, perhaps sensing even then the unblinking eye would reveal hidden truths, the crime boss Frank Costello didn't want his face shown. Instead, the cameras trained on another part of his anatomy. The images of his twisting, fumbling, sweating, clenched hands, clawing at his handkerchief and ripping up pieces of paper, convinced the viewing public of his dishonesty. People were glued to their TV screens as a real spectacle unfolded before them, live, in grainy black and white. The countrified, inarticulate Kefauver earned the Democratic vice presidential nod in 1956 largely on the strength of this exposure. Costello's telegenic hands changed history.

*   *   *

Terror from beyond, crime from within plucked threads from the social fabric. The fraying was slight but allowed alienation to peek through. A reclusive writer gave us our man for all seasons before we were old enough to appreciate him. Baby boomers, meet 17 year old Holden Caulfield.

"That's all I'd do all day. I'd just be the catcher in the rye and all. I know it's crazy, but that's the only thing I'd really like to be."
—The Catcher in the Rye by J. D. Salinger

The story was about his adventures in New York City after he was expelled from prep school. Poor Holden was alienated from everything and everybody, especially middle class pretensions, except perhaps the abandoned little kids running through the field of rye toward the cliff. How like a baby boomer to be at odds with himself and his surroundings and yet at the same time defining himself in terms of saving others. He was us not yet realized.

Holden Caulfield's rebellious other, older self appeared the same year on celluloid in the leader of a motorcycle gang. Based on a true incident involving ex-GI bikers who raised drunken hell in a Northern California town, this movie set an early tone for youthful contempt for the button down, gray flannel world of our parents. It also foreshadowed the defiant revelry that would come to mark or plague (take your pick) our generation.

> *"What are you rebelling against?"*
> *"Whaddaya got?"*
>
> **—Marlon Brando in *The Wild One***

For the time being though, Brando's arrogant response was emblematic of the juvenile delinquency that was causing such stir during the Golden Age. Smart-aleck youth dressed in workingman's dungarees and sporting a D.A., sideburns and a bad attitude resounded through society. It had to be the work of the communists.

The seeds of the sixties had already sprouted in the precocious springtime of the fifties.

Chapter 8

Duck and Cover

1952. War hero and model for the household detergent, Mr. Clean, Dwight Eisenhower provided the country with just the sort of wise leadership it needed at a time when the economy was booming. Brando and Caulfield aside, the sky was not exactly cloudy with rebellion. Hideous years of the Red Scare and McCarthy's depredations stilled dissent. Americans seemed frightened of their legendary individualism. More important though was the anti-intellectualism of the period. Republican attack dogs like McCarthy and Richard Nixon ridiculed Ike's Democratic opponent, Adlai Stevenson, as a pointy-headed intellectual. McCarthy liked to "slip" and call Adlai Alger, as in Hiss. Tail Gunner Joe was such a sweet man.

I Like Ike

—Republican campaign slogan

America comprised just six percent of the world's population. Yet we were producing and consuming over a third of the world's goods and services. At the same time we held righteous fear for our collective safety. Here, by the way, lay the newest seeds of American ambivalence toward the world: a consuming need for acceptance tempered by an attitude of disdain. For now, if anyone could keep both the craven politicos and the communists at bay it was Ike. The country thought the cadet from Kansas much more capable than the liberal "egghead" Adlai Stevenson. Through his confident bearing, Ike reassured our parents they still held a VIP pass to the good life. Everything was going to be just fine. Once in office he surprised a lot of people by maintaining the New Deal at home and counseling firmness and caution abroad. Everyone liked Ike.

Caution was one thing, faint-heartedness in the face of aggression was another.

"I will go to Korea."

—Ike

Renowned foreign-policy expert Joe McCarthy insisted the Democrats were to blame for "American boys dead in the mud...their faces shot away by Communist machine guns." Ike campaigned for president with a pledge that he would put his wise old head to the effort of establishing a just truce to the bloody stalemate with the Red Chinese. He bluffed the use of atomic weapons while offering concessions. Joseph Stalin's timely death brought slightly more moderate leadership to power in the Soviet Union, and we were able to negotiate a truce with the eccentric "Great President" Kim Il Sung. Government by personality cult made a formal peace treaty subject to the personal whims of Kim and much later his "Dear Leader" son. So we never got one. Even the most dimwitted, obfuscating bureaucrat in Washington could operate with greater wisdom and efficiency than the North Korean government.

    *   *   *

Although leaders rejected the nuclear option in Korea, atomic weapons proliferated. Many, if not most Americans took comfort in our nuclear shield. We made it clear to the Soviets and anyone else that we'd nuke 'em if need be. We'd done it once and we'd do it again. The public found the bold strategy reassuring, which from the vantage of half a century, appears to have worked. It's hard to tell what the Soviets would have done had they not been threatened by Ghengis Khan, Napolean Bonaparte and Adolf Hitler in the form of a tidal wave of nuclear tipped ballistic missiles. The Soviets were never quite willing to call the bluff. Good thing, too. It wasn't a bluff.

Such a bold strategy had inevitable consequences. Nuclear paranoia—nuclear mania—took hold of the middle class in the form of fallout shelters, built into the basement or in the backyard. After all, our nuclear strategy involved a nightmare scenario known as MAD—Mutually Assured Destruction. If the Soviet Union or its allies attacked us or our allies, we would respond with a Massive Retaliation, involving the nuclear option, thereby guaranteeing a dramatic alteration of human life, at minimum. We were preparing for the maximum. At school that year air raid drills joined fire drills. Good kids that we were, we dutifully hid beneath our desks from the pretend radioactive fallout. If we happened to be riding our Schwinns through the streets of our own particular Levittown and saw a blinding flash in the sky, we were told to dump the bike immediately and…

Duck and Cover

—Civil Defense drill

Preferably against a curb. So said Burt the Turtle, the Cold War version of Barney. The simple solution to nuclear vaporization. We were too young and callow to ask the obvious question, "Then what?" The idea was we'd survive an atomic attack and tune to Conelrad, 640 or 1240 AM for further instructions, like how to rebuild society. Or possibly restarting human life. In 1959 *Life* magazine featured a couple planning to spend their two-week honeymoon in their backyard fallout shelter, saying, "Fallout can be fun." So can Russian Roulette.

*　　　　　　　*　　　　　　　*

At least somebody posed a proper question. Even if it was the first boomer *Idoru*. "Conform," said our parents. "Consume," said the TV. "Hate communism," said our leadership. Alfred E. Neuman had the perfect answer for them all.

"What—Me Worry?"
—Alfred E. Neuman in *Mad* magazine

In August of '52, the first issue of *Mad* hit the stands. At first a comic book featuring "Tales Calculated to Drive you MAD: Humor in a Jugular Vein," it changed to a tamer format several years later after being attacked for spreading juvenile delinquency. Still, it offered broad though often juvenile parodies, which they called satires, of middle class foibles and the full-gated insanity of Mutually Assured Destruction. Alfred E. Neuman didn't appear until 1956, when he offered himself as a write-in candidate for president. Although the magazine would one day cast a jaundiced eye upon the counterculture, for the 50s its irreverent motto was the perfect anodyne for the irrationality of Cold War times. It hit big among boomers, spawning several copycats. Its strongest progeny was the iconoclastic *Rolling Stone* magazine that appeared a decade and a half later.

More universal in appeal by light years but still offering a certain take on the frivolities of middle class life, *I Love Lucy* first aired in 1951.

> *"Loociee, you got some splainin' to do!"*
>
> **—Ricki Ricardo**

When Lucille Ball became pregnant with her own little boomer, Desi Arnaz, Jr., it was written into the show. Forty-four million people watched the 1953 episode in which Little Ricky was born. The sensitivities of the day were such that the show's producers felt it propitious to insert the word *expecting* for *pregnant* into the dialogue. *I Love Lucy* defined the sitcom in innocuous, inoffensive and slapstick terms that had no equals, only imitators. By 1954, 50 million people were watching. Hollywood execs went the extra mile to protect Lucille Ball from the great Constitution-whomping black ball of Red Scare Hollywood purges. By then America's favorite redhead had become an icon, winning her zany way into the hearts even of young boomers. Meanwhile, her bastard half-brother and kindred spirit Alfred E. Neuman lurked blithely, like Kilroy, just beyond the high wall of respectability, even though their spoofs of life's outer absurdities were strikingly similar.

Chapter 9

The Dawn of the Sexual Revolution

1953. I Love Lucy was decidedly non-sexual. She wasn't even allowed to share the same bed with her real-life husband and co-star. But this wall of make-believe had a shaky foundation. Relentlessly curious human nature meant it was only a matter of time before this first great sequel of our era appeared. (No, not *Return to Peyton Place*.)

Sexual Behavior in the Human Female

—Dr. Alfred Kinsey

A companion to the 1948 study of men, the twin best seller sounded the tocsin of the sexual revolution. *Father Knows Best* asexuality could slow but not stop it. This compilation of six thousand case studies purported to show that women had healthy sexual appetites and weren't as homebound and faithful to their husbands as outwardly conformist America wanted to believe.

Kinsey concluded that half of American women had had premarital intercourse, 62% had masturbated and 13% sex with another female. Perhaps most worrisome, 26% committed adultery during the period of the study. Such findings released in the Fall seemed modest, even for *I Love Lucy*, and scholars supported them—at first.

Accompanied by such works as Grace Metalious's scandalous 1956 novel about life in a small New England town *Peyton Place*, Kinsey's studies revealed long-concealed truths about adult behavior. Critics claimed these studies "paved the way for communism." To others it was evidence of the descent of American morals into lust and filth. "It is impossible to estimate the damage this book will do to the already deteriorating morals of America," wailed Billy Graham. An angry Dean Rusk pulled Kinsey's Rockefeller Foundation's sponsorship.

The reaction was so strong legislators put "In God We Trust" on our money and added "under God" to the Pledge of Allegiance. Ever wary Hollywood studios began turning out Biblical epics. And with a deep sigh of relief, *Time* commented, the "Christian faith is back in the center of things." It was never far away from the center to begin with.

Kinsey's critics wept over our declining morals when in fact America remained as strait-laced as ever. Faith and morals have always kept uneasy company with sexuality, as though sexual pleasure was the devil's own. In the 1950's as the country became more cosmopolitan, the tenor of that company began to change. Urbanization, materialism and our rise to globalism kicked at the white picket fence, even as Madison Avenue was busily reinforcing the image. Alterations in what we once upon a time called "civilized sexual morality" (which even forbade public discussion of sex) occurred as our mighty, expansive economy forced us to drop our isolationist knickers. It was a real double whammy. Our free market economy produced mass culture and its kissing cousin conspicuous consumption, both of which revolutionized the sexual market place. Americans may have nodded at the tedious stipulations of anticommunist conformity and paid lip service to those moral leaders who claimed sexual activity outside wedlock played into the hands of the commissars in the Kremlin. But it was with a wink and a nod. Americans yearned for a little latitude.

And, by Hef, they got it. As though to confirm the tide of sexual change, in December a new publication appeared that celebrated hedonism and materialism as though the two were utterly indistinguishable. Started for a mere $10,000, this magazine staged a full frontal assault against anti-pink American Calvinism. The sexual revolution was underway.

Playmate of the Month
—Hugh Hefner's *Playboy Magazine*

Hefner's daring magazine—instantly popular—dressed up naked girls in bourgeois attitudes. A star named Marilyn Monroe was the first Playmate. She became the very definition of the middle class male dream—beautiful, voluptuous and willing, yet vulnerable. She exhibited a surprisingly uninhibited attitude in those repressed times. Of the photo shoot, she remarked, "I had nothing on but the radio." The American male was entranced. Hedonism had come to the market place linking sexual pleasure with material possessions and upward mobility. Sex, especially recreational sex, was about to become big business. And Hugh Hefner, far from being a fellow traveler, became king of the bourgeois.

*   *   *

America reached the zenith of its economic and military strength relative to the rest of the world this decade. At first leap, it might seem rather odd her citizens displayed such a heartfelt reliance upon a vigilante impervious to bullets and calumny. But vigilantism is as fundamental a part of our heritage as our work ethic.

Only now TV allowed us to sublimate such vigilante dreams by watching them on the tube.

"Up in the air. It's a bird, it's a plane. It's Superman!"

—a super hero

Well, *some*body had to defend flagging virtue. Maybe it had become a job for the super-hero. The comic book character appeared before World War II, but it was his elevation to television that made him an icon. The exemplar of right and rectitude fought petty villains in defense of Truth, Justice and the American Way. His appeal crossed generational and political lines. The Man of Steel was chaste in his pursuit of Lois Lane and stayed within the law when making his weekly round of citizen's arrests. Invariably, America's preeminent vigilante did the right thing. The man from Krypton was so completely American surely his home planet was located somewhere in the heartland.

*   *   *

Viewers by the millions spent their evenings watching the "Caped Crusader" and dozens of other prime-time shows. Inevitably, given all the other labor-saving innovations of the era, pre-prepared frozen meals would hit the market to facilitate viewing.

TV Dinner

—a labor-saving device

They came as a great relief for housewives "burdened with baby-boom offspring." Dinnertime became pleasure time. All mom had to do was pop a couple of delectable Salisbury Steak dinners into the oven and her family could enjoy moments of culinary ecstasy without missing a single moment of what was on. Yankee ingenuity followed up with TV-tray tables. Families could now forgo the centuries-old dinnertime torture of talking to one another over home-cooked meals. It was a barbaric ritual anyway. Industrial progress let them huddle like cave men staring at the fire over their aluminum-flavored, chewable grub while John Cameron Swayze brought home the "Camel News Cavalcade" followed by hours of Golden Age programming. Progress was obviously our most important product.

Chapter 10

"Separate is Inherently Unequal."

1954. May 17, 1954 was as important a date in our lives as November 22, 1963 and August 7, 1964. In many respects the events of this day put the American Dream on trial. We boomers would test inter-racialism. If we could manage to live, work and play together, then the Dream had legs. If not—we couldn't live separately and *equal*.

This pleasant spring day in a sunny capital, the Supreme Court ended the Constitutional validation for racial segregation.

> *"Separate is inherently unequal."*
>
> *—Oliver O. Brown versus the Board*
> *of Education of Topeka, Kansas et al*

Had Chief Justice Earl Warren not included that idea in the unanimous decision in *Brown vs. Board of Education*, the decision might not have carried such significance. In writing the decision, he sought to gut the 1896 *Plessy vs. Ferguson* decision that sanctioned racial subordination. As important—and still overlooked—he also addressed the issue of *equal* separate facilities.

"Does segregation of children in public schools solely on the basis of race, even though the physical facilities and other "tangible" factors may be equal, deprive the children of the minority group of equal education opportunities? We believe that it does."

Powerful words. A lesson for our times. The Warren court held that the two great American races could not exist apart under any circumstances. The decision held out the promise of unlimited access to the subjugated. It should have inspired everyone. It could have inspired most everyone had Ike not opposed it. Executive support was painfully slow in coming. The law changed, life did not. Appearing so decisive at its inception, *Brown* turned out to be merely a tentative first step. A furious Ike opposed even that, as he had the integration of the military. When asked what he thought of his appointment of Earl Warren, California governor and vice-presidential candidate, he erupted, "The biggest damfool mistake I ever made."

*   *   *

What a complex society that could craft legends around frontier individualism and righteousness while simultaneously beating down any black American who dared practice them. Morality had two meanings, even then.

> *Be sure you're right and then go ahead.*
> *It's up to you to do what Davy Crockett said.*
>
> **—Walt Disney's *Davy Crockett***

Beginning in December, the "King of the Wild Frontier," as embodied in the uber-WASP image of 29 year old Fess Parker, brought to TV an attractive view of right and wrong, self-assuredness with a little history about western expansion before the Civil War thrown in. The real Davy Crockett was cooked up as a rustic rival to Andrew Jackson. The real David Crockett actually said, "Know you're right, *than* go ahead."

Forty million Americans tuned in to *Disneyland* on ABC that first Wednesday night *Davy Crockett* aired. Disney had the insight to film the three-part episode in color for eventual release in theaters. Although ninety million viewers watched on TV, the movie version (three episodes spliced together and bridged thematically by the "Ballad of Davy Crockett"), brought in $2.5 million. In 1958 *Disneyland* became *Walt Disney Presents* and in '61 *Walt Disney's Wonderful World of Color*. The show itself had been on since late October.

The coonskin cap came to represent America's moral authority, even to Euro-boomers who loved the wholesome TV shows and movies every bit as much as we did. The lesson in simplistic righteousness was for all the world to see. Manufacturers caught on, too. By springtime boomers were running their neighborhood wearing coonskin caps, fighting fabled rough and tumble riverboat pirate Mike Fink, giving their lives defending the Alamo from Santa Ana. The shows overlooked the fact that the Mexican general was trying to enforce the ban on slave importation while holding onto the northern third of his country. But never mind.

Companies such as Sears and Roebuck were sure they were right about one thing. Lots of money was there to be made in Davy Crockett wear. Our parents shelled out $10 million for coonskin caps alone before the craze ended. It came to $100 million in all, including buckskins, chaps, powder horns, sheets, blankets, toothbrushes, lunchboxes, plastic versions of Old Betsy, and the record, the "Ballad of Davy Crockett," which was translated into twenty-six languages and sold four million 45s. Three thousand different items all told. This first boomer craze drove up the wholesale cost of raccoon from 25 cents a pound to $8. Manufacturers had to switch to squirrel and rabbit when they ran out of raccoon.

The Coonskin Congressman was truly king. We'd been playing Cowboys and Indians for years. There'd been Hopalong Cassidy, Gene Autry, Roy Rogers, Wyatt Earp ("None could deny it, the legend of Wyatt, forever would live on the trail"), the Cisco Kid, and last but not least The Lone Ranger, who started as a radio western in 1933. One after another we followed them right through the decade, blazing away.

*   *   *

Billions Served!

—McDonald's Famous Hamburgers, Buy 'Em By the Bag

Had there been fast food on the wild frontier, Davy Crockett would no doubt have endorsed it. In an ironic way his activities are connected to fast food. Along with frontiersmen such as Lewis and Clark, Daniel Boone and Zebulon Pike, Crockett opened up thousands of acres of land suitable for grazing beef cattle, thus transforming the American diet to red meat. But it was Ray Kroc and his peers who brought affordable red meat to the huddled masses. Before World War II, Americans ate mostly pork. The fast food industry changed all that. Prosperity enabled baby boomers and their parents to make the once disreputable hamburger (it was considered slightly better than garbage) America's favorite food. Convenient and inexpensive, its hand-held format made it perfect for kids. Besides that, working class families finally had a place they could afford to eat outside the home. In the honk of a car horn, America became a red meat-eating country, our new diet protein-rich and fat-laden.

In Southern California in 1948 the McDonald brothers invented fast food based on menus reduced to hamburgers, french fries and milkshakes, which cut waiting time from twenty minutes to seconds. In 1954 Ray Kroc, their former milkshake mixer salesman, became their franchising agent, stressing cleanliness and Cold War regimentation. "We have found out," he claimed, "that we cannot trust some people who are nonconformists. We will make conformists out of them in a hurry." In 1961 the McDonalds sold the entire business to him for $2.7 million.

Although intended as a place where working class families could take their kids to dinner, McDonald's succeeded because of boomer attraction to fast food joints, where we could assemble and eat while sitting on the hoods of our cars, arrayed in the parking lot like a laager of covered wagons. Our car culture owes a lot to Dick and Mac McDonald and Ray Kroc—and Davy Crockett, too. We couldn't cruise for burgers if there weren't any burger joints to be cruised. The marriage of convenience between entrepreneurial capitalism and the emerging youth market re-directed the American diet and youthful social activity. By 1970 Americans were spending about $6 billion on fast food, bulging out to $100 billion by 1997. These days we spend more on fast food than higher education, PCs and new cars combined. The price we've paid for the convenience of the "McDonaldsization of America" was high, stretching well beyond numbing uniformity. We became a nation of lard butts.

*   *   *

As fascinated by the wonders of the new-fangled tube as we were, our parents were forced to confront the dark possibilities that lurked like sandworms beneath the surface of planet America. With the specter of a South Vietnamese village named Bien Tre yet a ghost in the white noise, our parents finally came to grips with the fact that the junior senator from Wisconsin was doing more damage to the political fabric than pinkos, fellow travelers or outright communists, not to mention a parking lot full of juvenile delinquents.

In what can only be explained as the insanity of self-promotion, this runaway train accused the United States military of being riddled with these traitorous types. After an extensive "investigation," McCarthy came away with one "trophy," an army dentist at Fort Monmouth, New Jersey, with a leftist past. The victory came at the expense of his career. The televised Army-McCarthy hearings showed this abusive liar to be unworthy of his Senate seat. When Army Counsel Welch chastised him for his gutter-sniping, ad hominem attacks, damn few people watching at home disagreed. Even the timid (in those days) press corps broke into applause.

> *"Until this moment, Senator, I think I never really gauged your cruelty or your recklessness...If it were in my power to forgive you for your reckless cruelty, I would do so. I like to think I am a gentle man, but your forgiveness will have to come from someone other than me...sir, at long last, have you no sense of decency?"*

—Joseph Welch during the Army-McCarthy hearings

An abashed McCarthy shrugged as if to say, "What did I do?" Through his own Nixonian musings about his life, he gave new meaning to the question Ike posed about him, "How stupid can you get?"

While it was true he was not responsible for the Red Scare, this egregious fool of a man, who accused the Democratic Party of "twenty years of treason," distorted and cheapened the political process. His legacy, which his supporters must inevitably share, was hate, divisiveness and demagoguery disguised as "Awl shucks" populism.

The Senate censured him in December and he died a broken, disgraced alcoholic three years later.

Chapter 11

M-I-C-K-E-Y M-O-U-S-E

1955. They weren't describing McCarthy's intellect. Perhaps had the show appeared a year or two earlier and had the senator been aware of Uncle Walt's father, he might have turned from investigating communism in the military to ferreting out the subversive elements of *The Mickey Mouse Club*.

M-I-C K-E-Y M-O-U-S-E

—the Mousketeers

The show appeared on television the same year Disneyland opened in California. Disney's enterprises included feature-length animated movies such as *Pinocchio, Snow White and the Seven Dwarfs* and the trippie *Fantasia*. Despite having been an American institution since the 30s, Walt Disney Studios didn't generate the profits needed to sustain either Disney himself or the enterprise. Disney needed the amusement park to save his business. Making deals and borrowing heavily, he created a self-sustained fantasy world in Anaheim, off the freeway purposely shielded from the outside world. "I don't want the public to see the world they live in while they're in the park," he said. "I want them to feel they are in another world." A world that transmitted "educational and patriotic values." The separate theme worlds of Fantasyland, Adventureland, Frontierland and Tomorrowland were even shielded from each other.

Disneyland opened on July 17. With a price tag of eleven million dollars and twenty-four live cameras, sixty-three technicians, three months of rehearsals, and Bob Cummings, Art Linkletter and Ronald Reagan hosting—just about everything went wrong, including a malfunctioning sprinkler system that dowsed Fess Parker as he entered in full Davy Crockett regalia. No matter, Disneyland was a smash. In ten years it made $273 million and put Disney Enterprises on the Fortune 500. Disneyland became the world's Fantasyland. With its power cables and telephone lines buried, Main Street had the feel of an old European city—minus the brand name shops and stores and inhabited by talking animals that walked upright. Although Walt Disney died on December 12, 1966, his empire survived and grew into a major media conglomerate.

For most boomers, it wasn't the movies or the theme park that held our interest. It was the Mickey Mouse Club. Every weekday afternoon, the Mouseketeers with Annette Funicello, Cubby and Karen came into our homes with songs and skits that had us all wishing upon a star. The show was part of the agreement Disney had made to raise money for his amusement park. We just wanted to be on it with all those other talented kids, maybe get to be Annette's boyfriend.

Commercial television may still have been a young medium, willing to try anything once. But *The Mickey Mouse Club* and *Howdy Doody* reflected the demographics of the viewership. Kids, lots of kids, demanded lots and lots of kid stuff. Our numbers created new industries and invigorated others, from di-dee services to toy manufacturers. We saw much of this in the form of advertisements on kid shows, which we'd been watching since age two. By age six 500 hours; by eighteen we'd spent 24,000 hours glued to the television. By the time we hit our twenty-first birthday, we'd seen 300,000 commercials. That was a quarter of our lives: more time than we'd spent in school or doing anything else except sleeping. When you get right down to it, watching TV was *our* national pastime. The family room had morphed into the TV room and we spent far less time with our parents as a consequence. How many of us look fondly back on our childhood in terms of the TV shows we watched and loved? The indelible men and women of childhood fiction came not from literature or movies but from television. Which means these heroes were less complex and more universally appealing. And not a few of them were pure fantasy.

Captain Kangaroo

—Bob Keeshan

He was twenty-eight years old when he first appeared on morning television as a pleasant grandfather bumbling around his Treasure House. Along with Mr. Green Jeans and puppets like Mr. Moose, who dropped ping pong balls on him, and Bunny Rabbit, who stole carrots from his pockets, he taught us games and learning fun, while extracting wondrous toys and baubles from his pockets that were way deeper and far more enchanting than our parents' meager pockets. Captain Kangaroo had the perfect pockets for our bottomless demands. The venerable captain piloted his ship of the young on a cruise into the brave new world of affluent America: stuff, lots of stuff. He'd been Clarabell on *Howdy Doody*, and, as the chubby, gray-haired Captain, originated a children's program whose only concern was the welfare of its viewers. He stayed on the air until 1992—9600 shows, the longest running children's show and longest running character in TV history.

Our poor parents got the bills for all our whims, fads and fantasies. No doubt they still clung to a few fantasies of their own. For instance, how to get their chance on a television stage in New York City. From there in those materialistic times the sky was the limit. TV quiz shows were awarding life-transforming amounts of money. Money enough for dream houses, vacations, debt-avoidance and maybe even early retirement. And what's more, it all seemed so easily within reach, a low-hanging branch of the tree of opportunity. After all, those people up there were remarkably average, were they not? That was the point. That's why we all watched. It could be you!

The $64,000 Question

—television quiz show

Every evening the family assembled in front of the great wooden cabinet that was our television set to watch game shows galore. To a nation with a major shopping-jones, winning a fortune by answering tricky questions was the quickest route to riches. Easier even than Jack Bailey's *Queen for a Day* on daytime television. Winners on the benchmark *$64,000 Question* and *Twenty-One* became national celebrities. By century's end, the grand prize on the *64,000 Question* would be worth $373,116.45. Their struggles to win fortunes made them famous—until October 1959 when the public found out the quiz shows were rigged. *Twenty-One* champion Charles Van Doren, who won $129,000 in fourteen weeks, shocked a public that believed in its institutions and took seriously what it saw on TV when he admitted he'd gotten the answers in advance. The quiz show scandals were an early component of the creeping doubt in our institutions that would in ten years erupt into a national malady. Ike called the rigged games, "a terrible thing to do to the American people."

    *   *   *

So much of what proved formative about the fifties makes little sense unless viewed through the prism of tumult that followed. The Civil Rights Movement, the Long Hot Summers, the Beatles, the counterculture, the War, the assassinations and the rebellion—the whole nine yards—no one foresaw upheaval on such a scale. It proved to be risky business giving young people such high expectations.

Rebel Without a Cause

—James Dean

James Dean died before he grew old. The icon for all seasons was gone before he destroyed himself through self-indulgence or was deconstructed by the media. Through his languid eyes shone frustration, estrangement and a heartbreaking lack of fulfillment. His persona represented one of a few barely noticed signs of dissatisfaction.

Though most boomers didn't know who he was when he crashed his Porsche Spyder 350 near Cholame, California, on September 30, we would soon be imitating his angst if not his flame-out.

    *   *   *

We weren't aware of Miss Rosa either.

In those days white domination was so complete a black person could not safely or legally say no to a white person. Rosa Parks did. "Look, woman," the bus driver said to her, "I told you I wanted the seat. Are you going to stand up?"

No.
—Rosa Parks

The law said she had to. When she refused to give up her seat to a white man on a Montgomery, Alabama, public bus, she kindled a protest movement that changed our country in a highly dramatic way. Her action also gave us the great moral leader of our era, the Reverend Dr. Martin Luther King, Jr. As Eldridge Cleaver later wrote, "Somewhere in the universe a gear in the machinery had shifted."

Although several more years passed before the gears engaged, Rosa Parks' simple heroism set the standard for future protest. Her beau geste couldn't have came at a more necessary moment.

Why? Because little de-segregation took place following the *Brown* decision, and virtually no integration. In fact, the most significant response was the rise of Massive Resistance. Southern states created pupil placement laws that allowed school boards to decide if students were psychologically suited for particular schools. White Citizens Councils formed to resist integration. Southerners called them the middle class Klan. Mississippi created the State Sovereignty Commission which spied upon and harassed thousands of its citizens. Prince Edward County, Virginia, even shut down its entire school system rather than admit black children. Arguably what slight progress had been made since World War II was wiped away in the reaction to *Brown*. The NAACP went back to the Supreme Court to ask the justices to enforce their decision. Instead, justices issued a compromise decree that amounted to the emptiest of all empty gestures. The South, the court admonished, must de-segregate...

"With all deliberate speed."

—the Warren Court

Warren had been forced to compromise on enforcement to obtain a unanimous vote in the original case. The phrase itself was coined by Felix Frankfurter, who borrowed it from Oliver Wendell Holmes. Yet even this massive cop-out was not good enough for the white South for whom "prompt and reasonable start" rang like the second fire bell in the night. Many more would ring before Jim Crow was reduced to ashes. Not until 1969 did the Supreme Court replace Warren's deliberate accommodation with "at once."

*   *   *

Unfortunately, no medication or inoculation could ever completely eradicate a disease that produced lynch mobs, massive resistance and an impenetrable veil of genteel discrimination. Most of us didn't know a racial problem even existed, so used were we to living in a world in which everyone was the same, right down to their Fruit of the Looms. Black boomers found out otherwise at a much younger age. The norm was separate and vastly even, and it was so ingrained it seemed part of God's inscrutable plan.

Until the 50s that plan included a horrible disease that stole youth away from the young. For us kids it was far worse than racism. Would that there had been a Jonas Salk for racism. At least Jim Crow didn't keep us from going out to play. For kids condemned to life in an iron lung or a wheel chair and leg braces, he was an avenging angel. Dr. Salk developed a vaccine that had an immediate, dramatic effect.

"One of the greatest events in the history of medicine."

—chairman of the AMA

Polio was the most dreaded disease of early boomer years, crippling many, killing a few. It haunted the Dream. Though when you think about it, as terrible as it was, we had it worlds better than previous generations who were regularly decimated by diphtheria, tetanus, measles, mumps, and whooping cough. We were the last generation to grow up threatened with these diseases. Had we been aware of this, those eerie lines at school where we waited to get our polio shots might not have been quite so terrifying. The government spent millions eliminating this childhood blight. Overnight, images of kids with braces on their legs faded. Over six and a half million boomers got polio shots in school. And the March of Dimes had to look for a new disease.

*   *   *

As happy as their Golden Age kids were, parents were wandering a middle-aged world beset with divorce, depression and anxiety—the middle class, mid-life blues. Angst hit suburbia just as the Red Scare picked up and left.

The Man in the Gray Flannel Suit

—by Sloan Wilson

Upwardly mobile and chronically in debt, Tom and Betsy Rath symbolized the problem that had a name—and everyone knew it: "Keeping up with the Joneses." Although successful, with three kids and a house on Greentree Street in Westport, Connecticut, they were dreadfully unhappy. Their plight was discontentment, in a pretty place. They wanted more and felt cheated they couldn't have it. More money, more room, more cars, more respect, and a more civilized life without television and hamburgers.

Rath made $7,000 working in Manhattan (that's about $41K these days). He and his wife fought over money and prayed a new job might bring their ship in. It did, that and an inheritance. (Convenient deus ex machina, that.) To boomer kids who suffered the spectacle of their half-trashed parents tearing each other apart at cocktail parties, the Raths represented everything sour about growing up amid plenty. The harsh mistrals of dissatisfaction and envy swept through the dogwoods while everyone pretended it was the wind in the willows.

Chapter 12

"The Best Minds of My Generation"

1956. What was it about *Howdy Doody Time* that made it more popular than *Kukla, Fran and Ollie,* or *Romper Room*? Is it possible that Howdy Doody supervised a crew every bit as motley as *Seinfeld's* head cases living in a neurotic Doodyville, USA, replete with weird characters and zany antics? Was Howdy Doody Seinfeld for young kids with the fifteen inch Howdy as the young Jerry, Chief ThunderThud as his sidekick George, Princess Summerfallwinterspring as Elaine and Clarabell as proto-Kramer?

> *"Say, kids, what time is it?"*
>
> **—Buffalo Bob**

> *"Howdy Doody Time!"*
>
> **—the Peanut Gallery**

The number one children's show had been on since December 1947. This year it switched to Saturday mornings from its 5:30 PM daily time slot. Featuring wooden puppets interacting with human actors, and the show's creator Buffalo Bob Smith enjoining noise from the studio audience with, "No comments from the Peanut

Gallery," it presented weekly skits and dramas generally cooked up by Newman's predecessor, Doodyville's mayor Phineas T. Bluster.

For 2500 shows Clarabell never spoke a word until the final show on September 24, 1960, when he said, "Goodbye, kids." Goodbye but never forgotten.

While it provided comfort to the majority, consumer culture acquired a few acid critics. On the West Coast, a small but influential group of writers and artists gazed upon America in its Age of Affluence and concluded that crass materialism was gnawing away at the national soul. Buffalo Bob had probably once thrown them out of the Peanut Gallery for using bad words.

> *"I saw the best minds of my generation destroyed by madness, starving hysterical naked, dragging themselves through the negro streets looking for an angry fix."*
>
> **—Allen Ginsberg, *Howl***

San Francisco police charged Ginsberg with obscenity for his poem, published by Lawrence Ferlinghetti's City Lights Bookstore. Heavily influenced by mind-altering substances and free-form jazz-style writing best exemplified by Jack Kerouac, Ginsberg's screaming poem graphically expressed the Beat Generation's dissatisfaction with Cold War conformity. They claimed America was too vast, too exciting, too promising to be so confining.

You could see how Beat discomfort with a country they clearly loved produced such a nightmare of ambivalence. All this grand space, all this opportunity, all these cookie cutter people. Yet the problem wasn't so simple as busting out. We weren't alone in the world. We had responsibilities stretching beyond the next mad high. We had enemies and they often behaved like barbarians. Even if literary criticism bore some disturbing nuggets of truth about our "Air Conditioned Nightmare," as Henry Miller described suburban culture, beneath the hipster condescension, life was not always a matter of dark shades and cool jazz. The Soviets were offering a somewhat more acerbic critique.

"Whether you like it or not, history is on our side. We will bury you."
—Nikita Khrushchev

This drunken little Cossack was impossible to ignore. Whether uttering this gem to a group of diplomats, or pounding his shoe on his desk at the U.N. General Assembly as Secretary General Dag Hammarskjöld spoke, or bragging that his missiles could hit a fly in outer space, or standing on his hotel balcony in New York City with his shirt sleeves rolled up jovially insisting he was trying to be like an American, his antics were as menacing as they were comic. When Soviet troops crushed the Hungarian revolt with a ruthlessness reminiscent of the Nazis, it only emphasized the Soviet threat to the world. Bomb-throwing, southern rednecks we could deal with. Violent, trash-talking Reds were another matter. It doesn't take much perspective to see, at this point anyway, much of what the Beats were saying was more than a little self-indulgent.

"This is Radio Budapest signing off."
—the Hungarian Revolt

In hushed voices, laced with anxiety, our parents warned us there might be a war, and this time our country would not be spared. The revolt of the Hungarian freedom fighters that began on October 23 prompted a renewed wave of fallout shelter construction. This was the first case of Soviet repression any boomers were old enough to be aware of. Families who could afford it prepared for life after a nuclear holocaust. And a conservative Congress passed a major new public works project proposed by a rather conservative president because it assisted in the national defense. On June 29 legislation came up from the Ike's White House that underscored the presence of both the Beats and the Reds. The bill recognized both the demands of a mobile and expanding population and pressing dangers from abroad.

> *"In case of atomic attack on our key cities, the road net must permit quick evacuation of target areas."*
> **—the Defense Interstate Highways Act**

Think where we'd be today without the Interstates lacing our country together. The fifty billion dollar highway construction program, ninety percent of it funded by the federal government, was justified as ensuring *rapid* evacuation of the cities in the event of nuclear attack. So long as the Soviets didn't surprise us during rush hour, when it rained or snowed or on Saturdays we'd be just fine. Supporters also sold it as an efficient way to move troops and equipment from place to place to defend against invasion. All of which showed that no matter how luxurious your car, how frosty the AC, how effortless the driving, the Cold War was never far from your daily comings and goings.

With the coming of the Interstates, the federal government got into the business of building roads, once the province of state and local governments. An efficient transportation network was needed to ship goods from one metropolitan complex to another. Although this network of macadam, steel and concrete makes up just one percent of the total highways, it carries half of the traffic. The Interstate System acknowledged the spread of mass, mobile society while contributing mightily to its growth.

That's because automobiles and suburbia had become cultural and ideological soul mates. The flirtation with the automobile that began at the turn of the century and blossomed into love during the 1920s resulted in marriage in the 1950s. The car culture moved into the neighborhood and bought a big house.

> **"See the U.S.A., in your Chevrolet."**
>
> **—Dinah Shore**

That culture spawned shopping centers, drive-in movies, fast food restaurants and motels. America, Nat King Cole sang, was getting its kicks on Route 66. Threats from abroad be dammed. Detroit was turning out seven to eight million cars a year. It was the era of tail fins, push button drive and automatic transmissions.

And right out there celebrating were the Beats. Who could resist?

Chapter 13

"You Ain't Nuthin' But a Hound Dog."

1957. None of them better represented the spirit of freedom and openness than Jack Kerouac. His book was a long tone poem to spontaneity, experimentation and sensuality.

> *"...rows of well-to-do houses with lawns and television sets*
> *in each living room with everybody looking*
> *at the same thing and thinking the same thing at the same time."*
>
> **—Jack Kerouac in *On the Road***

Whether pursued in a big Chevy or a tiny Nash, this was about finding the Yellow Brick Road to spiritual renewal. It promised to liberate your psyche from tract houses in converted cow pastures. Beatniks weren't giving up on America, they were seeking new approaches to it, fresher ways to celebrate individualism. Their optimism, tinged more with melancholy than anger, was infectious.

> *"...the only people for me are the mad ones, the ones who are mad to live, mad to talk, mad to be saved, desirous of everything at the same time, the ones who never yawn or say a commonplace thing, but burn, burn, burn like fabulous yellow roman candles exploding like spiders*

*across the stars and in the middle you see the blue
centerlight pop and everybody goes 'Awww!'"*

Of equal interest was their sensibility of life lived on the edge. It
gave rise to a cult of hipness that Norman Mailer would immortal-
ize in 1957, for good or ill, as "The White Negro."

*"...the American existentialist—the hipster, the man who
knows that if our collective condition is to live with instant
death by atomic war...or with a slow death by conformity
with every creative and rebellious instinct stifled...why
then the only life-giving answer is to...divorce oneself from
society, to exist without roots, to set out on that uncharted
journey into the rebellious imperatives of the self.... So it is
no accident that the source of Hip is the Negro for he has
been living on the margin between totalitarianism and
democracy for two centuries."*

The Beats were sexual polymorphs, and just as free with drugs.
Their embrace of Eastern mysticism, their unwitting condescension to blacks, whose jazz culture they idealized, diminished the
cogency of their ideas.

*   *   *

Meanwhile back on planet earth, those role models for hipsters
were getting their heads beaten trying to integrate the all-white
Little Rock, Arkansas, high school.

"Two, four, six, eight, we don't want to integrate"
—whites protesting at Central High

Nine brave high schoolers were the first well-known integrators.
Their victory wasn't easy. They arrived at Central High that first
morning in September to face a mob demanding the lynching of at

least one of the kids before it would disperse. In a televised speech in which he said he couldn't guarantee the safety of the students, the pusillanimous state governor, Orval Faubus, whipped up lynch fever to insure his own re-election. There had been no indication of violence. To the contrary, most whites appeared willing to go along with this token gesture. But Faubus sought political gain by playing the race card. This most reprehensible of Americans called out law enforcement officers not to protect the Little Rock Nine but to keep them from going to school. The state had been preparing to integrate since the *Brown* decision three years previously. So much for "all deliberate speed." A furious Ike sent the 101st Airborne to enforce national authority over the cynical racist governor and the mob rule he'd fomented.

For the rest of the school year, GIs escorted the students to classes. Not since Reconstruction had federal troops been used to enforce the civil rights of black Americans. Ike, of all people, had broken the ice. Kennedy, then Johnson could justify their use of troops by his actions. The other lesson was not lost on southern whites either. The race card still worked. Faubus easily won re-election.

*   *   *

While "the Little Rock Crisis" raged into October, on the 4th the Soviet Union launched mankind's first artificial earth-orbiting satellite.

Sputnik

—Soviet satellite

The good news was that "Little Companion" helped many of us get to college. The bad news was it heightened the hysteria. When the Soviets launched this 184-pound missive to America, our parents went into a frenzy. The "artificial moon' circled the earth once every hour and thirty-five minutes, 560 miles up, at the unheard of speed of 18,000 miles per hour, emitting a wailing beep (hearable by short wave radio) that mimicked the fearful howl of air raid sirens. How, they demanded, could an atheistic, communist nation run by a gang of cut-throats beat God-fearing Americans into space? If our society was so superior to theirs, how—why— had they gotten there first? Was this a test from God? Were we slipping? Questions not easily answered. Spies? Traitors? Shock became chagrin, then embarrassment.

Our attempts to match them resulted in a succession of humiliating, nationally televised fiascos at Cape Canaveral. One failure followed another as rocket after rocket exploded on the launch pad or was quickly snuffed as it strayed wretchedly off course. When the Navy finally put Explorer I into orbit on the last day of January, the Soviets dismissed it as a grapefruit in space, even though ours was technologically more advanced. It discovered the Van Allen radiation belt. We half-expected Sputnik to drop an atomic bomb on us. In actuality, it dropped money. The following year Congress passed the National Defense Education Act offering low interest college loans to just about anyone who asked, all for the price of swearing one's loyalty to America.

Enough students were coming along that a few short years down the road a NDEA loan would become a prime vehicle for college. Sputnik played a major role in getting thousands of boomers a college education. And the truth was, we weren't behind the Soviets at all. We just weren't ahead yet.

```
***************************
*  THE BABY BOOM PEAKS  *
*        (4,308,000 births)        *
***************************
```

We were everywhere, though not quite ready for ivy-covered walls. Single story buildings with a large playground was more our speed. Out in the suburbs, thousands of new junior high schools rose like miniature Levittowns. As we were funneled from elementary into the sixth, seventh and eighth grades, our class sizes swelled like Clarabell's balloons. We entered a world we dominated. Our great bubbling herd moved along bright new corridors into rooms smelling faintly of paint, concrete and mortar. As we got to high school, freshmen, sophomore, junior, senior classes of over a thousand became commonplace. Protected in school, comforted by sheer numerical strength, we began to see the world through our own collective generational lens. The world responded by tilting in our direction. There was money to be made—youth to be served.

And by God, they were going to be the cleanest, healthiest, brightest, most presentable kids in history.

"Look, Mom—no cavities"

—Crest ad

Maybe the cult of American hygiene didn't begin with this TV ad, but concern about moss-mouth and cavities sure sold toothpaste. We grew up worrying like no generation before us about offensive body odors. What other generation would fall for the necessity of vaginal sprays? Perhaps one fixated on perfectibility, or sex? Or both?

Then the Pied Piper of teenage rebellion happened along with his unclean image and outlandish behavior. Suddenly cavities were the least of our parents' worries.

"You ain't nuthin' but a Hound Dog."

—Elvis Presley

Before he was the King, he was Elvis the Pelvis. He burst into the national consciousness with two appearances on the *Ed Sullivan Show*, the first time gyrating his hips and bumping and grinding to *race music*. He caused a national sensation, complete with predictions about rising crime and declining morals. We thought he was real cool. And it sure beat "How much is that doggie in the window?" All that energy and enthusiasm, all that brooding; the defiant sensuality; the slicked back hair—and those sideburns! The second time he appeared, they shot him from the waist up so as not to offend parental sensibilities. Too late, the damage was done. Elvis and a few other rockers like Chuck Berry, Sam Cook, Bill Haley and the Comets, Buddy Holly and the Crickets had already announced the arrival of a new and separate age group between childhood and adulthood with its own music and values. "Teen-age," the word itself didn't even appear until 1950. And it carried an identity and set of problems all its own.

The music was the thing. Rock 'n' roll defined the youth culture. Explicit in its themes and rhythms, it made holy causes of disaffection and rebellion. All you had to do was listen to Elvis to know something strange, forbidding and wonderful was in the air. Seeing Elvis perform the music was believing.

Inevitably some clever soul would capitalize. Perhaps also temper and homogenize. Though he featured black Doo Wop groups, this was about bringing new music to a new and eager white audience.

> *"It's got a good beat and you can dance to it."*
>
> *—American Bandstand*

On August 8, 1957 Dick Clark's Philadelphia show went nation-wide on ABC. The first song played was enough to rattle every adult bone in the country: Jerry Lee Lewis' "Whole Lotta Shakin' Goin' On." Clark was the first entrepreneur to make a successful career catering to teen culture. All those afternoons we spent playing Rate the Record, watching the bands lip sync their hits, trying to pick up the latest dance step, we were taking part in a vast shared experience. We were connected to each other through the tube. No longer was it kids' games and dreams of Disneyland. *American Bandstand* was about growing up and growing away from our parents. Dick Clark wore thin before the sixties (Somehow the moniker "America's oldest teenager" fit Rufus Thomas much better. Clark should have walked his own dog sooner rather than later.), but his show kept us parked on our elbows in front of the tube after school and out of trouble.

For those disinclined to get into trouble between the 3:30 bell and dinner time, there were other problems.

"Awl, gee, Wally."

—Beaver Cleaver

Existential crises behind the white picket fences. Poor Beaver was the Holden Caulfield of the suburbs trying to make sense of his world. The Beaver handled the obnoxious Eddie Haskell, "clunky girls," and his insipid older brother with shuffling dignity. He got through the day, just. He was our EveryBoy, our alter ego, our neighborhood Christ come to save us from life's calumnies in the form of bullies and bad news. If Beaver could navigate the shoals of confusion, so could we.

Life for Beaver was a tough chore. In the *Father Knows Best* world of sitcom America, conflict stemmed from household foibles. It was a world of comfort, a world not at all undesirable. The problem, we later saw, wasn't so much that these shows unintentionally parodied lily white, middle class America, but that they shielded off other dimensions of life. For good or ill, we were the first TV generation. We might not have completely believed everything we watched. But one day soon we would be outraged to discover the surreal depths of its unreality. We were as misled by the sitcoms as any adult who idealized Charles Van Doren.

*   *   *

Flat Flip Flies Straight. Experiment!

—the Frisbee

Odd that the Frisbee actually preceded the Hula-Hoop. The little plastic disks became such an essential part of beach/campus culture. We did flip them flat, and many other ways as well, thank you. But not for another decade. For now, we were too busy swiveling our hips.

Chapter 14

"Don't Leave Home Without It."

1958. Fads bounced across the country with the whimsy of pogo sticks. Since 1952 college men had been celebrating spring by staging panty raids on women's dormitories, demanding various delicacies and tokens of co-ed esteem. But that was nothing compared to a slender plastic hoop known as…

the Hula-Hoop

—Wham-O, Inc.

This first real boomer fad chased the coonskin cap from state to state until it overwhelmed the nation. More obsession than fad, it was more entertaining than Silly Putty, more fun than a Slinky, and a whole lot more palatable than swallowing goldfish or stuffing nineteen MIT math majors into a telephone booth. The idea came from the Land Down Under, one of the few other countries with a baby boom of its own,* where gym teachers had been using a three-foot bamboo hoop for physical training. Once the bamboo ring showed up on Art Linketter, the craze was on. Wham-O sold

---

*   The others were Canada and New Zealand. The European baby boom faded in the early 1950s.

twenty-five million polyethylene toys in four months at $1.98 per. Production cost was fifty cents. At the peak of the craze, Wham-O and its competitors were churning out some 20,000 a day, triggering Hula-Hoop contests to see who could hula with the most hoops, or hula the longest. Not a few parents found the suggestive gesture inappropriate for their young daughters. What the hell. If it was good enough for Elvis, it was good enough for Peggy Sue. They hadn't seen anything yet. Two years later when sweet little sixteen next gyrated in hula-hoop fashion, she did it with her boyfriend in a new dance called the Twist.

Hula-Hoops were really nothing compared to the barnyard that thrived in most boomer homes. Animals, we wanted animals! The more the better. We sparked a boom that had our parents doing the financial hula. Dogs (up 25% since the boom started), cats, parakeets (up 900%), canaries (12%), hamsters, white rats and mice, guinea pigs, ducks, rabbits, pee-pees, and the leader: tropical fish (120 million in 20 million homes). Our desires were insatiable, the products aimed at us as infinite as a hula's hoop. Then in 1959 along came Barbie.

    *   *   *

And you could buy it all on our Easy-Payment-Plan! Ah credit, where would we be without it?

Don't leave home without it
—American Express Card

The catchy phrase didn't come along until later. But with the appearance of this credit card in 1958, buying things became worlds easier. For an annual fee the American Express Card provided instant credit for airfares, hotels and rent-a-cars, and soon, that holy of holies, merchandise. The little magic wand sure beat Lay-Away. While the Diners Club card was actually the first to appear (1950) and the Bank of America's BankAmericard (now VISA) introduced buying on time (for a usurious annual interest), with American Express consumerism took a "Great Leap Forward." New worlds of purchasing power opened up to average Americans, further stimulating the great wave of materialism that dwarfed the laughable economic experiment in Red China. Chairman Mao would have served his people better had he paid attention to American marketing techniques. He struggled with empty rhetoric and mass murder, while the running dogs of capitalism came up with a simple piece of stamped plastic that actually did transform the standard of living for the average Joe.

*   *   *

Easy credit meant greater revenues and greater demand. It meant the market value of just about everything was about to change. Even baseball.

For us, the national pastime would never be the same after the fifties. Baseball has gloried through several heydays. This was ours. Mickey Mantle, Willie Mays, Ted Williams, Stan "the Man" Musial, Yogi Berra—heroes to several generations. Larger than life, greater than great. Baseball was the New York Yankees, with their tradition of excellence dating from Ruth and Gehrig through Dimaggio, the last gentleman sports star, on to the latter day heroes. The Bronx Bombers' string of victories and their record of excellence made them the sports dynasty of all time. But the team of teams was to be found across town in the borough of Brooklyn.

Symbolic of the frustrations of big time athletics, so affectionate and loyal were their fans, they were the team to follow (even if they were in the National League). When they took the series from the Yanks in '55, the love of their fans was confirmed. They'd gone from the Bums to the Best. At long last, it wasn't the close of yet another dismal season:

Wait til next year!

—The Brooklyn Dodgers

Unfortunately, next year would be in Los Angeles. Big time sports had entered the big time marketplace. The Brooklyn Dodgers left the Big Apple for LA for money. The New York Giants followed with a move to San Francisco. Forsaking the loyalty of their fans, which in the case of the Brooklyn Dodgers was deep and emotional, team owners began moving their franchises for greed, and nothing more. The trend that these teams started became commonplace. Integrity and tradition in sports died the day the Bums split for the Coast.

*   *   *

It didn't matter so much to us then. Now, of course it's a different story. Tradition has gotten to be a dirty word. Integrity is no longer associated with those in high places. Mr. Clean himself set the proper standard when, as a candidate, he'd disparaged the corruption during the Truman years. Now, he had his own to face.

"Elected officials must be above even the appearance of wrong-doing."

—Ike

On September 22 Presidential assistant Sherman Adams was accused of accepting a freezer, a vicuna coat and other things in return for influencing an SEC investigation of industrialist Bernard Goldfine. Ike set a high standard of conduct to which few of his successors were able to rise when he dismissed Adams in the

name of credible government. We paid just about as much attention to his sage advice as we did his warnings about the anti-
democratic alliance between the military and the defense industry.
This was a lesson never learned. What the hell, many of us were
still playing with dolls.

Chapter 15

Carpenter, Cooper, Glenn, Grissom, Schirra, Shepard, Slayton

1959. The Princess Di of Toyland was designed after a real baby boomer named Barbie Barton. With her impossible waist, gravity-defying breasts and her marvelously pliant personality, Barbie became the world's first artificial beauty whore. Great role model, a reflection of idealized real life blondes from Jean Harlow to Marilyn Monroe, Michelle Pfeiffer to Diana.

"You can tell it's Mattel, it's swell."

—the Barbie Doll

First a teenage fashion model and ballerina, later an astronaut and surgeon, aerobics instructor, rock star and UNICEF ambassador, and lately a WWC soccer player and working gal dressed in gray, this shapely blonde doll for all seasons still rules. And she can accessorize better than anyone living with well over 1000 outfits and a world-wide fan club of millions. When Barbie turned twenty-one in 1980, there were 100 million of her in circulation. Plus two million more of her boyfriend Ken, sister Skipper and cousin Francie. Not to forget Gay Bruce. She hit forty in 1999 after experiencing her first year of declining sales. Barbie honey, enjoy yourself, it's later than you think.

Adults needed toys too. Ones that shouted excess from the rooftops of Ford's Detroit headquarters. Even Barbie, no stranger to gaudiness, would have avoided this trinket.

"It even looks like a lemon."

—the Edsel

Even geniuses have bad days. Except that this was probably not an act of or by geniuses. With Ford Motor Company's Edsel, Ford had a bad three years. No amount of advance hype, no amount of advertising could convince the car crazy public that this white elephant named after Henry Ford's son looked like anything other than a man sucking a lemon. It was as cumbersome as Daddy and Granddaddy Ford's egos combined. Ford sold 11,000 before withdrawing it. The Edsel lugged along from 1957 to 1959, providing an unwitting commentary on the ascendance of form over function. The marketplace had few values, but credit-happy consumers weren't complete fools. Besides, money not spent on a tawdry, meretricious, poorly designed, uncomfortable automobile could be better spent on more playthings for us kids.

Even the country needed toys, especially when the Soviets had bigger ones. Critics dismissed these gigantic model toys as unnecessary. The left argued America had too many problems at home to be embarking on such expensive endeavors. Conservatives dismissed it as just another government boondoggle. They got it wrong, decidedly wrong. Exploration and discovery define a great nation's greatness. There was the imperative of competition from the Soviets who'd beaten us into space. But the larger point was simply that our dreams and our destiny pointed towards outer space.

Scott Carpenter, Gordon Cooper, John Glenn, Gus Grissom,
Wally Schirra, Alan Shepard, Deke Slayton

—Mercury Astronauts

Unified under NASA, which was formed October 1, 1958 in response to Sputnik, our space program introduced America's first cosmic voyagers on April 9, 1959. Manufactured, Disneyesque characters or not, these test pilots became national heroes for their phlegmatic good humor and laconic bravado. Competitive as athletes, they provided a showcase for our formidable engineering prowess, vying behind the scenes for the honor of being the first American into space. We witnessed their bonhomie, their mutual respect, their "Right Stuff" and were dazzled. Even if *Life* magazine did deify them as space-age Davy Crocketts, they became our champions in the quest against the Soviet Dark Knight.

More important, the Mercury astronauts, later the Gemini, Apollo and Space Shuttle astronauts (along with the Soviet Cosmonauts), played as critical a role in human history as Columbus or Magellan or Lewis and Clark. Fitting that they should appear on the cusp a new decade that would thrust aside many old values and shop-worn traditions for a future of new ideas, new technologies and new challenges. Through their strength of character and steadfast competence, the Mercury astronauts helped the country navigate the unexplored and often barely navigable passages that lay dead ahead.

*   *   *

When we asked the grand old man of mid-century America to characterize the fifties, he came up with his own rarefied affirmation of American distinctiveness.

"Things are more like they are now than they ever were before."

—Ike

This classic bit of Ike-speak captured the essence of the blithe spirit of America's Golden Age. A time, we now believe, of stability, tranquility, prosperity and optimism, girded by an edgy vigilance. Such was not the case. In fact, the period was the staging ground for the revolutionary overthrow of the great (and illusory) American Status Quo. In fact, our country is significant for its blitzkrieg of changes, for its *lack* of status quo. Beneath the placid surface, the forces of industry and commerce were about to transform a social order only recently reformed by the horrors of depression and war. Power brought prosperity unimaginable to previous generations. By 1960 one fourth of all housing had been built during the past ten years. So many consumer goods, such an urge to possess them that a crab grass of false virtue spread through the burbs stressing materialism and sameness as the ultimate form of patriotism. Individualism was bad for business.

Things were not going to be like they ever were for much longer. They never were anyway. By the time Nixon and Kennedy were debating our future on national television, it was already too late. The Edsel aside, the future favored form over content, and form was too easily manipulated.

    *   *   *

"The Day the Music Died."

—dead rock 'n' rollers

February 3, 1959, Buddy Holly, Richie Valens and the Big Bopper died in a plane crash in Iowa. These deaths marked the end of rock's formative era, relegated now to specialty shops, collectible sales and moldy basements. Rock 'n' roll wasn't going to be more like it is now than it ever was before for much longer. Holly was twenty-two and had something like ten hits, including Rave-On and Peggy Sue. He was the first white rocker who performed his own material rather than covering songs by black artists such as Little Richard and Chuck Berry. The Crickets took the bus.

PART III

Where were you when…?

"Talkin' 'bout my g-g-generation"
—The Who

1960–1969. Baby boomers will forever identify with and be identified by the Sixties. It began with high idealism and expectation and ended in bitter alienation and rejection. As an era, it actually stretched into the 70s, marking the chaotic period from the first sit-in on February 1, 1960 through the resignation of Richard Nixon on August 9, 1974. As one of the century's distinctive epochs, it defined us and became the reference point of our lives.

We set about joyously re-wiring the culture towards greater social conscience, more personal liberty, individual expression and creativity. We wanted to stimulate a greater sense of inclusion and a more vibrant sense of community while re-igniting the fires of American individualism. Heady emotions, idealistic intent, all earnestly pursued. Regardless of the year we were born, as individuals or as a cohort, or how much our conservative majority condemned it, we will forever be linked one way or another to that tumultuous time.

The Sixties heaped one wild event upon another, put our country to tests most nations could not have survived, and changed it irrevocably. We ended up with higher standards of government, greater concern about the personal well-being of all people, a holistic attitude toward the world in which we live, pronounced concern for individual and social responsibility, and temperance for the consequences of too much unchecked power. The excesses of those clamorous years were more a result of exuberant ambition than wrong-headedness.

We entered our adolescence with misty-eyed belief in our great good nation, inspired by the heroes of the Civil Rights Movement, the peerless leadership of Martin Luther King, Jr. and the elan of John F. Kennedy. We entertained self-centered illusions about ending hypocritical traditions. We would challenge convention and create a better world. We believed it was our destiny to change the world.

Then one assassination after another, one cataclysmic lesson after another taught us the hard truth about re-making the world. The harder we pushed history, the harder history pushed us back. We believed we'd been denied our birthright. Worse, we ended up seduced by the will-o'-the-wisp of sex, drugs, rock 'n' roll and bogus notions of "alternative lifestyles." Idealism faded into despair. Despair gave birth to rejection. Before this generation that had never been told no in its collective life had time to take stock, its revolution of hope had become a rebellion of hopelessness. If it was indeed true that the Sixties raised too many questions that no one could answer, the period also rekindled the expectation that America would at last fulfill its promise.

Chapter 16

The American Dream

1960. This brave notion lies at the heart of what it means to be American. More than sentiment and less than reality, it's the elusive burden of perfection. It's the promise of liberty and opportunity this grand land makes to all its people.

It's also big houses, fast cars, and an open line of credit. It's material possessions, lots of material possessions. It's a place to live, as Garrison Keillor might say, "where all the women are strong, the men are good-looking and the children are above average." It's a good education. It's secure health. It's a holiday. It's a second home. It's wealth. It's power. It's recognition. It's fifteen minutes of fame. It's the lump in the throat when the flag passes on the Fourth of July. It's...

The American Dream

—Archibald MacLeish

The American Dream is the chance to accomplish any of these. The American Dream is self-fulfillment. It's liberty. It's the promise that "all men are created equal, that they are endowed by their Creator with certain unalienable rights, that among these are life, liberty and the pursuit of happiness."

Such promises become a tremendous burden when they become exclusionary. This bedrock of American values holds that anyone without regard to race, ethnicity, gender, or social, economic and political circumstance can aspire to a high standard of living, home ownership, the presidency—or the Chicago Bulls.

How surprising that the term didn't appear until 1960. Although the concept might be traced back to "the Patriot's Dream" from Kathryn Lee Bates' *America the Beautiful* in 1893, and to Carl Sandburg writing in 1920.

"The republic is dream
Nothing happens unless first a dream."

After MacLeish coined the expression, Norman Mailer and Edward Albee picked up on it. Since then we've taken for granted the inevitable triumph of good over evil.

*   *   *

We entered with the conviction that God would ensure our future, that the Sixties were the time the dream would be delivered. Although our faith in Him was explicit and strong, Marxist/Leninism threatened that certainty to depths that monarchies, strong-armed dictatorships and Nazism did not. Our panic over communism wasn't as much about military defeat, although that was surely important, as it was about its challenge to a way of life predicated upon strong Christian traditions. Hence, we grew up hearing the curious notion that it was better to surrender life than to go on under the communists.

Better Dead Than Red

—the communist menace

So much for the spirit of Valley Forge. We had better sense than our elders. The widely held belief that life after a communist take-over wouldn't be worth living was extraordinarily misguided. As though such a thing were even remotely possible. Life is always worth living, especially when you haven't lived much of it yet. Such verities seemed bleak for a generation that had just won the greatest war in human history. The outlook made little sense to our generation spoon-fed on optimism.

Still, there it was in all its pessimistic glory. Questioning it meant questioning not only your parents but your country. Tall order for kids still using Stridex. Especially because its defeatism—Too late! The reds are already under the bed—contradicted the newer generation's ringing calls to arms. The 60's were about to happen. The place: Greensboro, North Carolina. The date: February 1.

"It's time that we take some action now."

—the first sit-in

Four college freshman entering their second semester at North Carolina A&T set the world on fire. A dorm room bull session led to a modest plan. They were tired of waiting for equality. They'd take matters into their own hands by violating an immoral law. "Let's go down and just ask for service." Which is what they did. The next day after class these four inseparable friends, Franklin McCain, Ezell Blair, David Richmond and Joseph MacNeil, went to the Woolworth's in downtown Greensboro, purchased some items and stopped at the lunch counter for a bite to eat. Rather than standing at the end of the counter for carry-out, as the law stipulated, they sat down and ordered coffee, a hamburger, orange juice.

They were told what every black person in America heard all too often. "We don't serve your kind here." Showing their purchases, they politely demurred, and stayed there until the place closed. The next day even more students showed up and the arrests began.

Students took the place of those arrested at the "Greensboro Coffee Party," as it was first called. This act of civil disobedience ignited a wild fire of activism that to this day has not completely burned out. A few white ladies offered words of encouragement that such action was long overdue. The fact was, though, once whites got over their shock, mobs of them began dumping salt and mustard and putting their cigarettes out on the nonviolent protesters. Over the days and weeks to come, as the sit-ins spread, gangs of punks beat and kicked the demonstrators, who were then charged with trespass and other crimes.

The audacious idea that young people could re-shape their world was as revolutionary as the idea that American blacks ought to have every right accorded American whites. This was the American Dream all right. This was possibility coming to call on promise, and youthful heroes were delivering the message. Justice was about to roll down like the waters. Freedom was about to ring. The sit-ins started a grassroots uprising that became known as the Civil Rights Movement. Its impact on our country and most especially on us would be profound.

*   *   *

The contradictions in the world sometimes bordered on parody. Sputnik and the quiz show scandals plucked at our trust. But no one was prepared for the first great debacle of the Cold War. Not even the reporters who covered the story could believe that the president would deceive them and the nation. Yet he did, and his deception planted seeds of doubt that future government duplicity would fertilize.

In May Ike was concluding a successful international goodwill tour that would culminate in a summit conference with Nikita Khrushchev in Paris. From there he would travel to Moscow. His farewell gesture to the people of America and the world, he hoped, would be a lasting peace. Alas, it was not to be.

U-2

—American spy plane

On May 5, Khrushchev announced the Soviets had shot down an American spy plane over their territory. The State Department fired off an outraged denial, labeling it more of the Big Red Lie. When the Soviets produced the wreckage, Ike's people claimed it was a weather plane astray over Turkey. "Oh, yeah?" cried the Soviets, and produced the pilot, one Francis Gary Powers, who confessed in a Moscow show trial.

Ike was trapped in a big fat lie. The American people were stunned. Mr. Clean had intentionally misled us. Worse, America had been caught fibbing about something few of us thought we'd ever do: spy on other countries. We were so naïve in those days the majority of the population found it difficult to swallow the necessity of God's chosen people doing such an immoral thing.

But there it was. The real world was intruding on the Golden Age. Against his better judgment, Ike had authorized one last flight over Soviet territory to ensure he had up to date information when he got to Paris. The supposedly invulnerable U-2, with its super sensitive camera developed by Edwin Land of Polaroid fame, was shot down by a near miss. Although by this time U-2 flights had calmed fears of Soviet military strength (not that they bothered to convey this information to the quaking public), our military didn't think they had missiles capable of flying so high or so accurately.

Even the Washington press corps—not yet hated—was stunned. "...Many of the leading lights of Washington Journalism," reflected *Washington Post* reporter Don Oberdorfer in 1993:

were indignant and almost incredulous that a spokesman of their own government would deliberately lie to them.... That was 1960, and...I see that as the first big blow to the relationship between the government and the press. The news today would be greeted with a shrug...there was shock when we learned that State Department spokesman Lincoln White had been instructed to describe as a 'weather research plane' that unaccountably had drifted off course was, actually, Gary Powers' U-2 spy plane, shot down on a pre-planned mission over the Soviet Union.

That monitoring our enemies was an utter necessity mattered little to Americans wrapped in their Levittown cocoons. Soon we came to realize the need. But the initial impact was devastating. If Ike would lie to us, so would any of our leaders, Red Menace or no Red Menace.

Speaking of which, one of the foremost anti-Communists of the day wanted to be president. He represented much of what was duplicitous and unwholesome about the 50s, while his opponent came to represent hope for the future. Both images were misleading.

Would you buy a used car from this man?

—Democratic campaign slogan

Richard Nixon rose to public awareness as a member of HUAC where he worked with manic urgency to flush out Alger Hiss. His efforts won him election to the Senate and elevation to the vice presidency as Ike's red-baiter. Unfortunately, Nixon brought his flawed character with him. Some surmount their own weaknesses or turn them into strengths. Nixon was never able to escape his. In public he mimicked Herblock's famous caricature of a sleazy "Tricky Dick," a character assassin with a five o-clock shadow and sweaty upper lip. Voters could not quite bring themselves to put this awkward, shifty-eyed politician in the White House. Despite his intellectual and experiential superiority to the handsome, well-bred and shallow JFK, Nixon invited scorn. Sometimes he seemed almost to welcome it. Tricky Dick lost his 1960 presidential bid by fewer than 100,000 votes. He blamed his loss on Joe Kennedy's money. He had a point. Though, in retrospect, it appears he was so deceitful, so undeserving of high office that the unfair sobriquet that attached itself to him—"the man you love to hate"—seemed more than deserved. For such a loathsome man, he didn't have nearly the number of committed enemies that Bill Clinton would acquire.

Elements within his own party, and despite the many resentments he harbored throughout his life, found his career far too wed to the East Coast elite and his policies far too statist. The conservative wing of the GOP did not believe Nixon was one of them. In truth, he wasn't.

"Grow up, conservatives."

—Barry Goldwater

Whether or not he was the "first potent dissenter of the decade of dissent," as George Will seems to think, Goldwater issued this challenge at the Republican nominating convention. It was essentially a call to arms against the moderate/liberal wing of the Republican Party led by Ike, who conservatives deeply resented. They considered the former general an interloper and his presidency a continuation of FDR's New Deal. Goldwater's speech signaled the beginning of a conservative counter-revolution against the New Deal inspired welfare state. Never mind our welfare state was negligible compared to Western Europe. To conservatives any federal social program, including Social Security and especially civil rights was anathema. Conservatives would eventually seize control of the GOP, vanquish liberalism, and spread their anti-federal government, anti-welfare state ideology throughout America. But they would have to wait until 1980 for their champion. Meanwhile:

> *Let's grow up, conservatives. We want to take*
> *this party back, and I think some day we can.*
> *Let's get to work.*

More reactionary than visionary and more libertarian than most conservatives realized, Goldwater's philosophy of government was by no means devoid of merit. His emergence began the struggle of wills over efforts to make America live up to the promise of the Declaration of Independence. For now, however, the conservative view of that promise—low taxes and a limited government that allows individual self-reliance—found itself at odds with the reality of America's incomplete journey towards greatness.

No greater example of that conflict existed than in race relations, where conservatives clung to "the metaphysical subtleties" of ideology, to borrow from Jefferson. Not all conservatives were racists by any means (not all liberals were free from it), but far too many were. Barry Goldwater's refusal to vote for the Civil Rights Act of 1964 provided the clearest indication of the merit of liberalism's solution to the problem of the color line, that the government could and should act to improve the quality of life for the American people. Conservatives held otherwise and had no answer to America's racial dilemma.

> *"What's the use of integrating lunch counters when*
> *Negroes can't afford to sit down to buy a hamburger?"*
>
> **—Ella Baker**

Although in her forties, Ella Baker played a central role in organizing the Student Nonviolent Coordinating Committee (SNCC). In her speech at its April founding, which became known as "More Than a Hamburger," she argued for basic economic reforms to lift blacks out of a poverty bred of centuries of slavery and subordination. At the time leaders such as Martin Luther King were touting integration as the means to that end. Baker stressed the racial imbalance in accumulated wealth.

Her insight that the real spirit of the Civil Rights Movement emanated from the idealistic, energetic college-aged activists staging wildfire sit-ins across the South was key. She counseled them against affiliating with Dr. King's SCLC, urging SNCC to go its own way. Which it did, providing grass roots leadership and a more militant agenda.

*   *   *

Revolution was in the spring air. On May 10, 1960 the FDA approved "the pill" for general use. For the first time in history women had a simple and effective means of preventing pregnancy. The result was even more revolutionary than the sit-ins.

Enovid

—birth control pill

So complete has the revolution been that yesterday's common-place is today's unimaginable. Prior to the pill, sex was largely at the mercy of conception with women shouldering the bulk of the responsibility. Each act of intercourse threatened to bring a new baby. The result was often unanticipated pregnancy and early and unwanted marriage. Beyond that, the pill allowed women to enjoy sex as they never had before. For countless women, and, you'd have to assume, a few of their men, the quality of sex improved. Sex got less inhibited. But it was about a great deal more than free sex. "Modern woman," wrote Clare Boothe Luce, "is at last free as a man is free, to dispose of her own body, to earn a living, to pursue the improvement of her mind, to try a successful career."

More dream than naked reality—social stigma played a significant role in inhibiting sex—her remark nevertheless reflected the amazing fact that for centuries the inability to avoid pregnancy had seriously restricted the activities of most women. Becoming sexually aggressive was an important first step in liberation. The pill helped women forget about the stigma, the baby, and get on with it.

Chapter 17

"Ask Not What Your Country Can Do For You..."

1961. The "sexual revolution" became an instant cliché, no less true for its popular usage. Another cliché entered public awareness on January 17, 1961 as Ike's presidency wound down. During his farewell address to the nation, he warned the country about the dangers of excessive militarism, especially in Southeast Asia. "An immense military establishment and a large arms industry" threatened to dominate the economy and undermine our basic freedoms. According to historian James Patterson, it might "poison the wells of international relations and...dominate domestic policy."

> *"In the councils of Government, we must guard against the acquisition of unwarranted influence, whether sought or unsought, by the military-industrial complex."*
>
> **—Ike**

Although embarrassed before the public over the U-2 incident, Ike nevertheless left office in high esteem. His warning about the anti-democratic hazards of arms industry pressure took on greater significance half a decade later when we became ensnared in Vietnam. His sage advice has been oft-quoted and too little appreciated.

Perhaps Ike's message received only superficial attention because three days later his successor introduced a new era of idealism.

> ### *"Ask not what your country can do for you, but what you can do for your country."*
>
> **—JFK**

These words created an era. Blending Civil Rights Movement idealism and liberal optimism, JFK stirred the national soul. His ringing eloquence reminded us what our great nation stood for. No other president since FDR or Lincoln soared to such rhetoric heights.

> *Let every nation know, whether it wishes us well or ill, that we shall pay any price, bear any burden, meet any hardship, support any friend, oppose any foe to insure the survival and the success of liberty. This much we pledge and more.*

These days such utterances would be political suicide. What politician would dare challenge us to serve America? For a generation coming of age, the young president gave patriotism a meaning as clear and compelling as a Sunday school lesson. Kennedy's youth symbolized the arrival of the boomer generation that would ride the wild idealistic surf for years to come. After all, it was up to all Americans to prove their country's greatness. It was up to the young to carry the torch. This much we tried and more.

These were bold times. The challenges formidable. The competition stiff. The stakes more so. Just as national rivalries produced the opening of the Western Hemisphere 500 years before and enabled America to be born, the Cold War pushed man into space.

On May 25, JFK issued a challenge with a flourish.

*"I believe that this nation should commit itself to achieving
the goal, before this decade is out, of landing a man
on the moon and returning him safely to Earth."*

A-OK

—Mercury control

Issued after Soviet Cosmonaut Yuri Gagarin became the first human to orbit the Earth, JFK launched humankind's greatest gambit. First the Mercury orbital flights. Alan Shepard's May 5 morale-boosting 15-minute sub-orbital flight made him the first American in space ("Why don't you fix your little problem and light this candle?" he grumbled, sitting atop the Redstone rocket.) Then the Gemini preparatory flights, followed by the Apollo lunar voyages. We got there first for the wrong reason—to beat the Soviets—but we got there. The space program was Kennedy's most momentous achievement.

*   *   *

Earthly struggles continued relentlessly. In fact, they got worse. American and Soviet successes in outer space did nothing to ameliorate the hostilities that more than once brought the world to the verge of nuclear holocaust.

Die Mauer

—the Berlin Wall

On August 13, the East German border guards began erecting barriers and barricades to block egress to West Berlin. Berlin had become the weakest link in the Iron Curtain, a point where East Germans and thousands of other oppressed people could escape to freedom. Considering East Berlin was the Mecca of the communist world, the contrast between its empty gray streets and the bright lights of the prosperous Kufürstandam shopping district on this side of the wall was profound. Soviets claimed the wall was necessary to keep out Western spies. West Berlin may have been a base for American intelligence activity, but the real problem had little to do with spies. People were streaming out of the Iron Curtain countries for the fresh air of freedom in the West. The brain drain was significant. Fifty people died during the Wall's first year trying to make it across. For boomers old enough to be aware, the wall was a surreal re-creation of the dirt walls we regularly built and destroyed in our own backyard war games. Except we didn't have tanks lined up facing each other at fifty yards.

Maybe it was the nightmare of nuclear oblivion. Maybe it was the grim countdown to war reported on TV. Our lack of sophistication denied us access to the subtleties of geopolitics and nuclear blackmail. Yet even considering the gruesome news footage of bodies hung up in the barbed wire, the notion of destroying the Earth to deny another power its domination produced a deep ambivalence.

"That's some catch that Catch-22."

—Catch-22 **by Joseph Heller**

The indelible anti-war novel spoke of futility and said more about the times we were entering than the World War II era we'd left behind. *Catch-22* sounded like our leaders dragging the country from Germany's Folda Gap to the rice paddies of Vietnam.

There was only one catch and that was Catch-22, which specified that a concern for one's own safety in the face of dangers that were real and immediate was the process of a rational mind. Orr was crazy and could be grounded. All he

had to do was ask; and as soon as he did, he would no
longer be crazy and would have to fly more missions.

*   *   *

Sports is war by yet another means. When it comes to international competition, most of us got our first taste of it here.

The thrill of victory, the agony of defeat
—ABC's Wide World of Sports

Every Saturday afternoon this ever-graceful show taught us there was more to sports than baseball and football. We probably learned more geography and international relations from this show than in school. We also learned about the heroism in sport from Vinko Bogataj, the hapless Yugoslav ski jumper who hurtled sideways off the ski jump in Obersdorf, Germany. He became synonymous with the agony of defeat, the Sunday duffer as icon.

That comically gruesome scene was akin to the live remote radio coverage of the Hindenburg crash. The spectacle of elbows and kneecaps off a ski ramp created a demand for more cameras to capture even more thrills and spills. It whetted the viewing public's taste for a little disaster to spice its diet of sports, sports and more sports. Reality television and vulgar talk shows were decades away but the possibility of witnessing a tragedy turned the young medium into a less than perfect centerpiece of popular culture.

A few observers caught on early.

"A Vast Wasteland"
—Newton Minow

The chairman of the FCC shocked the television industry with his cogent indictment of its pandering effort to maximize profits through the lowest common denominator. The "Golden Age of Television" had passed by the time Minow issued his encyclical. More and more critics saw the medium as a cultural and intellectual tube of redundancy.

That, however, was an opinion not shared by millions for whom TV played a much welcomed man who came to dinner. For despite all its critics—and their numbers grew with the viewership—TV was a wasteland only if popular culture was a wasteland.

*   *   *

Another aspect of the technological revolution went awry first. Late in the year, the fifteen-minute nightly news broadcasts carried reports about inadequate testing of one of the many wonder drugs being cranked out during the revolution in pharmacology. To a country still undergoing a transcendental birthing spree, pictures in national magazines of boomer babies with fingers squiggling out of their shoulder sockets struck more fear than Strontium 90 in milk and called into question our blind faith in science and technology.

Thalidomide babies
—birth defects from a tranquilizer

The mere sight of legless babies with flippers for arms ended belief in the perfectibility of progress. The prescription pill taken in Europe for asthma, nausea and sleeplessness, produced two dozen misshapen babies in America, nearly two hundred in Canada, before the FDA stood up to industry pressure and banned the drug.

The Thalidomide scandal gained immediacy when "Miss Sherrie" of *Romper Room*, thirty year old Sherrie Finkbine, became pregnant with her fifth child. Miss Sherrie had taken the Thalidomide pills her husband picked up in England. She petitioned her home state of Arizona for a legal abortion. In August, after the court predictably turned her down, she flew to Sweden to remove the deformed fetus. This first public abortion caused a national scandal. Even though legal, her action aroused far more indignation than the heedlessness of Thalidomide's manufacturer.

Chapter 18

The Other America

1962. Science and technology kept right on churning out wonders. On February 20, America experienced its greatest space age achievement thus far.

"Go with God, John Glenn."

—the first American into Earth orbit

John Glenn's four hour and fifty-five minute three-orbit flight aboard Friendship 7 made him a national hero. He was the third Mercury Astronaut to go into space. "Boy, what a ride!" exclaimed the ever-enthusiastic Glenn, who returned to a John Glenn Day in DC and ticker-tape parade in the Big Apple attended by four million jaded New Yorkers.

Speaking before a Congressional committee seven days after the flight, Glenn promised that America would beat the Soviets to the moon, even though at the time we lacked a booster powerful enough to pull it off. "There will be failures," he warned. "There will be sacrifices." He was right on all counts. After a successful career in the Senate, a 76 year old Glenn returned to space aboard the space shuttle Challenger.

*   *   *

JFK was smart enough to learn from the debacle at the Bay of Pigs not to trust his military advisors completely. He learned the lesson well.

> *"We're eyeball to eyeball and I think the other fellow just blinked."*
>
> **—Dean Rusk**

Otherwise this dicey situation would have ignited a nuclear war. In October U-2 flights revealed Soviet medium range missiles capable of putting a nuclear warhead in every major American city except Seattle with a only few minutes warning. The intimations we'd had with Sputnik and the Berlin Wall cascaded into insignificance before this monolith of terror. War seemed inevitable. Kennedy's grave, almost ashen face on TV the night of October 22, a week after the sites had been discovered, shocked the world sober. We faced Armageddon.

The crisis was a whole lot worse than we knew. Many of his advisors, older and wiser men, clearly more experienced, proved themselves damned fools. They urged either an air strike or an invasion. The U-2s missed some of the missile sites and had not spotted 42,000 Soviet troops. Had we attacked, we would have faced a second Bay of Pigs and a retaliation that may have come in Berlin or on our own cities—or both—and would surely have gone nuclear. Hiroshima + Nagasaki = Washington + New York. Not a pretty thought. Mistakes as potentially costly as these are not always avoided. This time we got lucky.

Thanks in large part to Kennedy's decisive leadership involving a blockade and a secret agreement to withdraw our missiles from Turkey, we managed to slip past disaster. The president's cool and collected men maneuvered the shaky Soviet leadership into face-saving concessions that defused a near calamity. The Cuban Missile Crisis was the closest the world has ever come to nuclear cataclysm.

*   *   *

As Kennedy triumphed, Nixon stumbled and fell. Less than a month after JFK avoided catastrophe, Nixon ran smack into one in sunny California where voters turned down his comeback attempt.

> ### *"You won't have Dick Nixon to kick around anymore."*
>
> **—Dick Nixon**

After losing the gubernatorial race, Tricky Dick, the "used-car salesman" with the five o'clock shadow, bade a bitter farewell to the press and public. Haunted by eight years of humiliation under a contemptuous Ike and overwhelmed with self-pity for his two electoral defeats, he said goodbye to politics forever. His graceless exhibition of sour grapes should have marked his permanent exit from the American political scene. Unfortunately for his country, he never really retired. He was gone for less than six years. A master at self-rehabilitation, he repaired political bridges, built new ones, and watched from the sidelines as America entered one of the most tumultuous periods in its history. All of which gave him the chance to re-emerge as the national savior.

*   *   *

The need for leadership was already critical. New problems erupted, older ones festered. In the space of a year, three books came out detailing these problems. They became the most influential books of the Sixties. Two were published in 1962. The third, by Betty Friedan, the following year.

Silent Spring

—Rachel Carson

She wrote of toxic chemicals raining "indiscriminately from the skies." Her book spawned the renascence of environmentalism. Not since the days of Teddy Roosevelt had we been so concerned for our natural environment. An experienced marine biologist, Rachel Carson warned that DDT and other chemicals were murdering the earth's fragile ecology. The wide use of synthetic pesticides (another aspect of the technological revolution), which she called "biocides" for their indiscriminate poisonings, had increased 400 percent since the end of World War II.

Attacking agri-business for its recklessness, she faced rancorous criticism from the pesticide industry that dismissed her as "emotional and ignorant." Her path-breaking work showed just who was ignorant. Although often overlooked, Rachel Carson gets the lion's share of the credit for changing public attitudes about the environment. She found an audience of true believers among those who had the longest to live, especially boomers. And the ecology movement was born.

*   *   *

The affluence of the fifties fooled us into believing poverty had been eliminated. Leaders were talking about improving the quality of life for everyone. Trouble was destitution happened to be rife. Along with Rachel Carson, Michael Harrington had enormous influence on the era for his *re-discovery* of so many poor among so much plenty.

The Other America

—Michael Harrington

This slender book revealed the sad truth that one-fifth of the population, roughly 25 million Americans, was living in poverty. The elderly, farmers, urban blacks and Hispanics, migrant farmworkers, Indians, and people in Appalachia all dwelt in abhorrent conditions. Whites made up eighty percent of these forgotten and shunned Americans; the rest were minorities. The poorest were old people in rural areas.

Edward R. Murrow's disturbing documentary *Harvest of Shame* put visual images to Harrington's claims about migrant workers. Murrow showed us the unfortunate fruit pickers who followed the cross-country circuit for extraordinarily low wages, returning each year without any money in their pockets. Their kids never made it out of grade school. National concern about this new problem induced the Kennedy administration to initiate what would eventually become a "war on poverty."

     *   *   *

Grassroots uprisings appear spontaneously and carry relentless energy. Often they trample their own goals. Two boomer-led grassroots movements, the New Left of the 60s and the New Right of the 90s, share these strengths and weaknesses. The New Left came first and made its cause a defining element of the era.

> *"We are the people of this generation, bred in at least modest comfort, housed now in universities, looking uncomfortably to the world we inherit."*
>
> **—The Port Huron Statement**

The first reaction to life in the mass, technological societies of the atomic age came from college students, many of them heavily influenced by the Civil Rights Movement. Espousing what today are solidly conservative notions of local government, participatory democracy and self-sufficient individualism, Students for a Democratic Society (SDS) sought to salvage individual identity in a world racked with racism, poverty and the nuclear nightmare of Mutual Assured Destruction. Laced with humanism that put the emphasis—and burden—on the individual, this "Agenda for a Generation" created a political movement critical of big government as dehumanizing and anti-democratic.

Written largely by Tom Hayden and owing as much to Benjamin Spock as to 19th century utopianism, the statement argued for sweeping social changes. Young people were seeking emotional wholeness through "self cultivation, self direction, self understanding and creativity." New Left ideology linked inner fulfillment with a more perfect world. It was a striking attempt to overcome the sterility created by mass advertising and the leveling effects of popular culture. In a few years, individualism would be a political statement, as would smoking a joint, long hair and free sex.

Herbert Marcuse and C. Wright Mills were the New Left's true mentors. Marcuse argued in *Eros and Civilization* (1954) and *One-Dimensional Man* (1964) that "benign" social control, which he called "nonterroristic totalitarianism," gave people the illusion of happiness while diverting sensual pleasure to the needs of consumer capitalism. He argued that conformity had taken away our ability to express opposition, to exercise our right of dissent. Consumer culture was so pervasive it neutralized even the working class. Marcuse's pleas for the end of sexual repression struck a chord, as might be expected, from boomers just coming into sexual bloom and about to face restrictive *in loco parentis* rules on college campuses. For the fledgling student movement the essential goal was to make all things...

Relevant

—the student movement

That meant black studies courses, lacking from just about every major university. Later women's studies and ethnic studies. Student activists began to demand their courses relate to their lives and to social problems. No area of study, they felt, was adequate on its own merits unless it confronted and dealt with the issues. They wanted more control over their course of study, and many institutions obliged by dropping the general education requirements, which often took up to half a student's four-year course load.

C. Wright Mills' anti-authoritarian *Power Elite* (1956) condemned not only the emerging military-industrial complex but also the alienation of the managerial class from its employees. Reflecting his Texas background, Mills mourned the loss of our once strong sense of community and rugged individualism to an increasingly stratified society. He castigated white collar America—our parents—for *selling out.* Simplistic though such analyses may have been—he overlooked the many vestiges of pluralism—his views resonated.

Hayden wrote, "We would replace power rooted in possession, privilege or circumstances, with power rooted in love, reflectiveness, reason and creativity." The SDS began with sixty members and grew to some 100,000 by 1968.

Chapter 19

"I Have a Dream."

1963. This proved to be one of the two critical years of the decade. (The other was 1968.) What started with a racist call to arms ended with a presidential assassination that left the country radically transformed. Virtually all aspects of what it meant to be an American were about to be altered.

> *"Segregation now...segregation tomorrow... segregation forever."*
>
> **—George Wallace**

Yet another in a long line of race-baiting southern politicians, the newly elected Alabama governor went to the well of white supremacy in his January inaugural. Most of his speech was written by the white supremacist Asa Carter, who eventually decided he was an American Indian. Wallace lost the '58 race to an even worse racist, if that can be believed. "Well, boys," he said as he prepared to address his followers that year, "no other son-of-bitch will ever out-nigger me again."

By June, after authorizing the repressive violence in Bull Connor's Birmingham, this half-pint redneck, whose eventual mother-in-law said stood "only tittie high," was standing in an Alabama schoolhouse door to prevent integration. The image of this strutting American Mussolini, the governor of a sovereign state, blocking the doorway of the University of Alabama at Tuscaloosa to prevent the admission of two black students pushed toleration for bigotry to its very tolerant limit. Although he later claimed his racism was more politics than ideology, he sure championed it body and soul.

The previous month, a national television audience had stared in disbelief at the Birmingham police turning police dogs and fire hoses on peaceful black demonstrators marching for the citizenship rights everyone else took for granted. Most white Americans and a few lucky blacks had never seen such vicious racism before Bull Connor gave the country a history lesson it would never forget.

The good white folks in Birmingham, "the most segregated city in America," refused to back down. In a dramatic test of wills, King finally goaded Bull Connor into turning bark-peeling fire hoses and clothes-ripping German shepherds on the protesters. Eugene T. "Bull" Connor, who couldn't have been a better caricature of southern law enforcement had he come straight out of central casting, believed he was upholding law and tradition. That right was on his side. And he reveled in his duties. He gave the Klan fifteen minutes to beat up Freedom Riders and joked that he wanted to see local civil rights leader, Reverend Fred Shuttlesworth, carried away in a hearse. If his boys got out of hand, well, the protesters were disrupting the tranquility of local society.

In the face of this—his greatness emerging with each passing day—Dr. King assumed direct leadership of the month-long confrontation. Jailed, put in solitary confinement for demonstrating without a permit, he answered with sublime eloquence a plea published in the *Birmingham News* by moderate white ministers who were finally moved to endorse his goals while urging him to go slow. His response to them became one of the great documents in our history.

Letter from a Birmingham Jail
—Rev. Dr. Martin Luther King, Jr.

As you read this, imagine George Wallace using his own body to block the education of black children and Bull Connor bragging about the violence he had visited upon the demonstrators, all of whom were American citizens.

> *"We have waited for more than 340 years for our constitutional rights...*
>
> *Perhaps it is easy to say 'Wait'. But when you have seen vicious mobs lynch your mothers and fathers at will and drown your sisters and brothers at whim; when you have seen hate-filled policemen curse, kick and even kill your black brothers and sisters; when you see the vast majority of your twenty million Negro brothers smothering in an airtight cage of poverty in the midst of an affluent society...when your first name becomes 'nigger' and your middle name becomes 'boy' (however old you are) and your last name becomes 'John,' and your wife and mother are never given the respected title 'Mrs.'...then you will understand why we find it difficult to wait."*

These are the profoundly moving words of America's greatest moral leader. King's impact on the generation of blacks and whites coming of age was considerable even though some black leaders took strong exception to his tactics. Rev. J. H. Jackson, for example, the powerful head of the National (Black) Baptist

Convention, ran King out of the organization and denounced both him and SCLC for their confrontational style. But that struggle was walled off from the rest of the country by the very segregation King was fighting. Nationally, though, it took more than King's torrents of sublime eloquence to move the country off dead center.

Like everyone else, the Kennedy brothers watched the officially sanctioned mayhem on television. JFK claimed he was physically sickened by what he saw. Such vile acts were unworthy of a great nation, especially when compared to the heroism of the victims.

The Civil Rights Movement had been pushing hard for legislative action. At 8:00 PM on June 11, the day Wallace stood in the schoolhouse door, Kennedy made a dramatic speech to the nation about the racial dilemma. "We are confronted primarily with a moral issue," he said. "It is—

As old as the scriptures and as clear as the American Constitution."

—John F. Kennedy

"The heart of the question is whether all Americans are to be afforded equal rights and equal opportunities...." With these words, JFK became the first president in history to state publicly and unequivocally that blacks should be fully equal to whites. While it is true that JFK was dragged kicking and screaming to this position, once there, he took a singular stand. The historic speech has long been overlooked. That a man so devoid of personal morals as JFK could come out with it makes it even more remarkable. A week later he sent corrective legislation to Congress that would eventually become the Civil Rights Act of 1964.

"I Have a Dream"

—MLK, Jr.

Contrast Wallace's wretched misanthropy with Martin Luther King's transcendent visions. We saw both for what they represented. King's peroration reached to the heart of what it meant to be an American.

"I have a dream that my four little children will one day live in a nation where they will be not be judged by the color of their skin but by the content of their character. I have a dream today."

Like JFK, the man was personally flawed. But his message was clear and unflawed. His speech before 230,000 people at the August 28 March on Washington for Jobs and Freedom provided the spiritual wellspring for our generation.

When the architects of the republic wrote the magnificent words of the Constitution and the Declaration of Independence, they were signing a promissory note to which every American was to fall heir...the promise that all men, yes, black men as well as white men, would be guaranteed the unalienable rights of life, liberty, and the pursuit of happiness."

*   *   *

A week after submitting the powerful civil rights act, Kennedy was off to Europe. In Berlin two and a half million people, shouting "Ken-na-dee, Ken-na-dee" turned out to see him. Standing in the shadow of the Berlin Wall, he declared, "As a free man I take pride in the words...

"Ich bin ein Berliner."

—JFK

Kennedy continued the pledge he made in his inaugural to maintain an active posture against aggression. Since the late forties Berlin had been the locus of East-West tension, heightened all the more by the infamous wall. The Kennedy mystique that spread across the Atlantic with his visit to France, where in June 1961 he'd quipped, "I am the man who accompanied Jacqueline Kennedy to Paris," grew still sharper in Berlin as he declared himself in sympathy with those living in the shadow of communism.

With his powerful civil rights legislation, his campaign against poverty, and his skillful brinksmanship in the Cuban Missile Crisis, Kennedy was beginning to emerge as more than a media star. How good a president he would have become cannot be supposed. He was so immoral it undoubtedly would have caught up with him. His affair with Judith Campbell Exner, who also "dated" Mafia figure Sam Giancana, his nude frolics in the White House swimming pool with secretaries "Fiddle and Faddle," his use of the Secret Service as pimps and lookouts, his bragging that if he didn't "get it" everyday he got a headache, these sorts of things revealed a man lacking a moral center. It also manifested itself in hits against foreign leaders and illegal covert operations not equaled again until the Reagan Era.

Scandal over at least one of his multitudinous sexual improprieties (with an East German spy named Ellen Rometsch) was about to break on Capitol Hill. At the very least, it would have disastrously damaged his reputation. More likely it would have led to his impeachment. When warned by J. Edgar Hoover that his recklessness was endangering his presidency, that the public would not forgive him if it found out, Kennedy replied off-handedly (and prophetically), "By the time the public finds out I won't be president."

Standing above this secret, loosely held by a press corps that chased after JFK like orphaned puppies, lay the glaring fact that his administration, his family life, soon to be called Camelot, was a façade. The Kennedy mystique was one long photo opportunity created for public consumption. JFK was the first president who sold himself like a Hollywood actor with a manufactured persona.

The charade went undetected while he lived, which is not to say he didn't have problems. Some Americans believed JFK was a communist sympathizer for his loss of nerve at the Bay of Pigs. His stand on civil rights had crippled his re-election chances. Thus, the trip to Dallas to shore up flagging political support. As far as boomer memories of him are concerned, Kennedy's presidency began with his assassination in Dallas at 12:33 PM on Friday, November 22, 1963.

An estimated 180 million viewers witnessed the indelible three-day nightmare: Walter Cronkite's tearful announcement, the tragic funeral and John-John's callow salute—capped by television's first live murder. The police officer cuffed to Lee Harvey Oswald as he exited the basement of the Dallas courthouse saw a local Mafia figure coming at him, pointing his snub-nosed pistol. All he could do was swear in surprise.

"Jack, you sonofabitch."

—Jim Leavelle

Jack Ruby, the man who killed the man who killed Kennedy ("You killed my president, you rat!"), was a nightclub owner whose place Oswald had visited on more than one occasion. Oswald had connections to the CIA and FBI, something these agencies concealed for thirty years. He'd defected to the Soviet Union and been re-admitted to this country without a hitch.

The Single Bullet Theory that became essential to proving Oswald the lone gunman strained credulity. Its extravagance lent credibility to pervasive rumors of conspiracies involving the right wing, Castro, the Mafia, even the CIA and FBI. Yet for all its flaws, the Warren Commission's conclusion was essentially correct. Lee Harvey Oswald, acting alone and for reasons unknown, killed John F. Kennedy. Today a majority of Americans still disbelieve the conclusion.

It would take his death, the elevation to power of an arm-twisting master legislator, and anger in the streets to drive Kennedy's legislative initiatives into law. Even so, Kennedy's image changed history. Had Nixon won in 1960, or LBJ for that matter, and been assassinated, the impact would have been closer to the murder of James Garfield. Instead, John F. Kennedy became an icon whose death headlined a disturbing phenomenon. Before that day in Dallas, eighty percent of the people believed their leaders and felt they always acted in the best interests of their constituents. By decade's end, the numbers had reversed.

    *   *   *

In October JFK's Presidential Commission on the Status of Women concluded a 22-month study by recommending equal pay for equal work, paid maternity leave and child care. In response Kennedy appointed a cabinet level panel to consider corrective legislation.

Like civil rights, our leaders would soon be playing catch up.

"The problem that has no name."

—The Feminine Mystique

"Is this all?" asked left-wing author Betty Friedan. Was the idealized life of the suburban housewife all there should be? If so, why did so many women feel such emptiness in their lives? Why did they lack a sense of accomplishment? According to Friedan, they found the role of homemaking, child-rearing helpmate unfulfilling. To overcome it, women needed "goals that will permit them to find their own identity." Goals such as careers and new lines of work—as well as equality before the law. In articulating this vague feeling of dissatisfaction shared by many middle class white women, her book laid the groundwork for the Women's Liberation Movement.

*   *   *

Harbinger of the rights revolutions to come, the Civil Rights Movement led to protests by many and varied groups from senior citizens to environmentalists to homosexuals. A lot of people, it turned out, felt they had something to overcome. Many did. A newer version of a 1901 religious folk song/Baptist hymn titled "I'll Overcome Some Day," copyrighted by a white school teacher captured the peaceful, idealistic spirit of the times.

We Shall Overcome

—the protest song

Music was vital to the Civil Rights Movement. This lilting song became its anthem, voicing all the soulful optimism and earnest determination of the thousands of young blacks and the few hundred whites who joined in the struggle to overcome and elimi-nate racial injustice.

Music became the perfect anodyne for the dissonance of the day. Every new pop tune that came out reinforced the growing emphasis on being young and having fun. One man's music is the bane of another's existence, which was part of the fun. Here was the anthem that provided the most oft-repeated three-chord progression in the history of Western Civilization.

Louie Louie

—the Kingsmen

This song was the very heart of rock 'n' roll, important for both its "tune" and the urban legends surrounding its lyrics. Here are two that ought to be true, even if it they aren't. The FBI spent considerable time trying to decipher the lyrics to determine the extent of their obscenity. They finally gave up, concluding that the words were too slurred to have any meaning. One of the reasons the lyrics were so indecipherable owed to the Kingsmen's lead singer (a marginal band at best) singing through his braces while stretching up to a microphone that was suspended too far above his head.

According to composer Richard Berry, "Louie, Louie" is a sea ditty about a sailor pining to a bartender named Louie about his far away love.

> *Louie Louie, me gotta go. Louie Louie, me gotta go.*
> *A fine girl, she wait for me.*
> *Me catch the ship across the sea.*
> *I sailed the ship all alone.*
> *I never think I'll make it home.*
> *Louie Louie, me gotta go.*
> *Three nights and days we sailed the sea.*
> *Me think of girl constantly.*

Louie Louie, me gotta go.
Me see Jamaican moon above.
It won't be long me see me love.
Me take her in my arms and then
I tell her I never leave again.
Louie Louie.

Now for a little harmonizing...

Chapter 20

"I Wanna Hold Your Hand."

1964. It appeared on our shores in the form of four mop-topped limeys with more talent than a dozen symphony orchestras and a thousand Montavanis. They performed on *Ed Sullivan* before a mere 67 million people.

> ***"I wanna hold your hand."***
>
> **—the Beatles**

February 9, 1964, just three months after JFK was assassinated, the youth culture became page one news with the arrival of "the Fab Four." Beatlemania swept the nation with a jubilation that deposed the King himself. With their cheeky manners, mod suits and bright music, the Beatles occupied the vital center of the youth culture. Their clever tunes defined what it meant to be young in those days. Through the genius of their music, John, Paul, George and Ringo made rock acceptable and the Beatles founding members of what would soon be known as the Counterculture.

First, we needed wheels.

"Tack it up, tack it up. Baby, gonna shut you down." For ten sweet years Detroit made muscle cars. Stripped down light, with huge, thirsty, gut powerful engines, these babies hauled serious ass.

GTO

—Muscle Car

Pontiac's John Delorean designed the GTO (named for Ferrari's Gran Turismo Omologato) by dropping a V-8 into a light Tempest body. What followed made drag racing a national craze: triple deuces, twin four barrel carbs, fuel injection, four on the floor, tuned duel exhaust, mag wheels, 327s, 389s, 409s—and 4 miles to the gallon. In 1966 Chrysler came up with 426-cubic-inch, hemi-head engine that produced 425 horsepower. You could drive it out of the showroom to the drag strip and blow the doors off any A-Gas competitor. The Arab Oil Embargo in 1973 shut that down. But that was a decade away. Meanwhile, there was a lot of cruisin' and boozin' to do.

> *"Little GTO, you're really lookin' fine.*
> *Three deuces and a four speed and 389.*
> *Listen to her tackin' up now,*
> *Listen to her why—ee—eye—ine.*
> *C'mon and turn it, wind it up, blow it out, GTO."*

—Ronnie and the Daytonas

If speed wasn't your thing, try a little sportiness. British racing green TR3s made for a lot of sport. So did '55, '56 and '57 Chevies. But the sportiest car of them all was a Ford product.

The Mustang

—a car for baby boomers

Introduced on April 17th, it had a style that made it just right for the car craze. Taken from design to show room in just 18 months,

the Mustang was invented for America's young and affluent generation—the first generation to grow up with (and in) automobiles.
The Mustang still holds the record for first year sales, a cool
million. Sporty though affordable, underneath it was really a
clunky Comet.

*   *   *

This man was no clunky Comet. He was a mouthy twenty-two
year old when he defeated the formidable Sonny Liston to win the
heavyweight championship of the world, a feat almost no one
thought possible.

"I am the greatest!"

—Muhammad Ali

A true champion and possibly the greatest boxer ever, he was
cheekier than the Beatles and at least as talented. He made up
rhymes predicting the rounds in which his opponents would fall
("They all must fall in the round I call.") and delivered. He waved
his blackness in white America's alternately amused and outraged
face. The young were much more tolerant than their parents. Then
Ali announced his conversion to the Nation of Islam and changed
his name from Cassius Clay. He had his heavyweight crown taken
from him for refusing the draft. At the height of career he was the
best known man in the world.

*   *   *

License to Kill

—007

The Beatles weren't the only British import that changed our
perception of the world. Except this soon to become best known

fictional character in the world was cheekier than the lads from Liverpool. JFK once made an off-handed remark that he liked to read James Bond novels. In a heartbeat Ian Fleming's fanciful tales of British secret agent James Bond, who was authorized by the British government to kill people, became best sellers. Bond was a world-class womanizer, an expert with weapons and nasty with his fists, and in film would employ all manner of hi-tech gizmos against *SPECTRE.*

Always ready with a quip or a bullet, Bond was the updated version of the lone gunslinger of the past, who hated violence so much it made him plum violent. The first movie, *Dr. No*, came out in '62, followed by *From Russia with Love.* But Bond (and Sean Connery, the man who first played him) didn't hit the big time until the release of *Goldfinger.* With that movie, 007 became the "shaken not stirred" personification of Cold War sophistication. The filmed versions knocked the rough edges off him and turned him into a fantasy role model for adolescents, and many who weren't. Eventually, the films lapsed into intentional self-parody. Neither that nor the frequently changing leading men diminished 007's popularity.

        *   *   *

In May thousands of college students, some of whom surely went to James Bond movies, followed Ali's rising star and owned or wanted to own a Mustang, trained with SNCC to spend their summer in the Deep South registering black voters.

Chaney, Schwerner, Goodman
—the Civil Rights Murders

When these three young civil rights workers, James Chaney, a local, Mickey Schwerner and Andrew Goodman, were killed at the beginning of the Mississippi Freedom Summer, the country, indeed the world, began to understand the true depth of white racism. Bull Connor was bad enough. But Mississippi was America's South Africa. No measure was too extreme for this state. The legislature had created the State Sovereignty Commission to block integration. It operated like a secret police, spying on thousands of citizens while working closely with the Citizens Councils to harass civil rights advocates and intimidate white moderates. Violence was tolerated, winked at, or in some cases advocated. In this case, the perpetrators were local law enforcement officers and their buddies.

This was pure terrorism. And more commonplace that we wanted to believe. Our skepticism grew as it took a reluctant FBI two months to solve the case (with a $30,000 bribe). Agents finally located the bodies in an earthen dam in Bogue Chitto Swamp in Meridian County. Andrew Goodman had been in the state one day. True to tradition, the local sheriff, his deputy, and their accomplices were acquitted in local court. Eventually they were convicted on federal charges and given light sentences. We believed that our generation would end racism. If we had our way events such as this and people like Sheriff Lawrence Rainey and Deputy Cecil Price would never darken our world again. Time would prove us dead wrong.

White America was stunned that two of its own could be murdered—and by police. The sympathetic mood created by police mayhem in Bull Connor's Birmingham grew stronger with these killings. The nation rallied behind corrective civil rights legislation as America entered a period of liberal reform.

"This is an idea whose time has come.
It will not be stayed. It will not be denied."

—Senator Everett Dirksen (R, IL) commenting on
the Civil Rights Act of 1964

If the Cold War was a deadly cloud hanging over us, white racism was its tainted ground water. Signed by LBJ on July 2, the Civil Rights Act of 1964 was the single most important law passed during our young lives. The sweeping legislation ended formal segregation in America by overriding thousands of discriminatory state and local laws. The process of granting full citizenship to one of the oldest segments of the population took a giant stride forward. Under law at least, blacks now had full equality. This giant stride would eventually encompass fuller civil rights for women and minorities.

One of the persistent ironies of the Civil Rights Act was that JFK's death made it possible. Had he lived and had he managed to get his version of this bill through the conservative Congress, it wouldn't have been nearly so powerful. National grief over his loss and LBJ's bullying, strong-arm legislative tactics were critical to the bill's passage. Conservative southern Democrats and their supporters in the GOP filibustered for 534 hours. In the end, however, Senate minority leader Dirksen rose to the challenge. His endorsement made the critical difference. The bill passed because of GOP support. A greater percentage of Republicans voted favorably than Democrats (80%—60%). All the southern Democrats voted nay.

*   *   *

LBJ may have triumphed in civil rights, but he was unable to stifle rumors of an assassination conspiracy. They had an air of inevitability to them.

Single Bullet Theory
—the Warren Commission

The bedrock of the Commission's September 1964 report was that a lone assassin killed JFK. Intended to quell rumors, the findings only heightened belief in a cabal and a subsequent government cover-up. As unlikely as it was that Oswald's second shot hit both Kennedy and John Connally and survived intact on Connally's stretcher, it was...conceivable. The round was steel-jacketed and capable of holding its shape. Besides, as any urban emergency room attendant can tell you, bullets follow unpredictable routes through human flesh.

We would have been better off had the Warren Commission claimed in its sloppy 888-page report that there *might* have been a conspiracy. But not one shred of concrete evidence could be found to support such a conclusion. This remains so to this day. Unfortunately, the rushed, incompetent report engendered passionate doubts rather than calming our worst fears. The irony is that despite its shoddy workmanship, the Warren Commission got it right. Regardless, public distrust of government deepened inexorably.

*   *   *

Then this scintillating bit of right wing wisdom.

> *"Extremism in the defense of liberty is no vice!*
> *Moderation in the pursuit of justice is no virtue!"*
>
> **—Barry Goldwater**

And we thought right wing radicalism died with Joe McCarthy. In those days, most Americans considered this sort of right wing rhetoric extreme if not vaguely unAmerican. In November, Goldwater ("In Your Heart You Know He's Right") lost to LBJ in the only Democratic landslide in our lives. LBJ received over 61% of the popular vote, more even than FDR in 1936, his best year.

In reality and even though the '64 election ushered in the heyday of liberalism, the Goldwater campaign was merely the conservative counter-revolution's opening volley. Throughout the Sixties it acquired adherents as fast as the Great Society could generate social programs, Black Nationalists mouth inflammatory rhetoric, and the New Left churn out the position papers. Although Goldwater's ideas were shunned then, they have since become the touchstone of a powerful and angry political movement.

Appearing on ABC's "Issues and Answers," Goldwater proposed using low-yield nuclear weapons to settle the little problem in South Vietnam once and for all. What a field day for the Democrats. LBJ ran as the peace candidate!

The Daisy Commercial

—the first attack ad

LBJ's presidential campaign created a TV spot that featured a young girl picking petals off a daisy as the voice-over counted down to a nuclear detonation. Once the blast occurred, the ad cut to a picture of Barry Goldwater laughing. Although the ad ran only one time, it created a sensation. Widely condemned and even apologized for by the Johnson campaign, it broke the ice for what has become the mainstay of politics—the attack ad. As much as politicians claimed to abhor them and as much as they further debased the national eye-gouging matches, they worked. Those wanting to know where "the politics of personal assassination" began need look no farther than the Daisy Commercial.

*   *   *

With images like this on the tube, it should come as no surprise that by the fall semester with the first wave of baby boomers entering college the nation's young people were restive. By 1960 there were already 24.6 million kids between the ages fifteen and twenty-four. The teenage population itself amounted to about 21 million. We were becoming, as historian Paul Boyer said, "a nation within a nation." Three million boomers reached college age in 1964, with three million more following like Mongol hordes in madras prints. By the end of the decade eight million boomers were in college.

And we didn't like what we saw there. Universities now characterized themselves as "multiversities," "knowledge factories," or "service stations." We felt lost in the campus crowd. We were processed, housed and graded according to our social security number. At most universities registering for classes took two days or more. Classes of several hundred students were commonplace. Many of us got lost in these overcrowded chicken coups. We'd been jerked out of secure suburban or small town enclaves and thrust willy nilly into a place where we were mere numbers.

It was a rude way to find out that the world did not exactly consist of sainted neighborhoods of plenty. We were the first kids to confront America's new mass society, and we resented being treated like those ubiquitous IBM punch cards.

I am a Human Being—Don't fold, spindle or mutilate.

—button slogan

But that was just the start. *In loco parentis* policies left over from the conformist Fifties affronted our determination to wade through the impersonal multiversities with our identities intact. The ludicrous "three-foot rule" required three feet to be on the floor at all times during a co-educational dorm room visit. The door could be closed no more than the width of a textbook. Although one can easily imagine the inspired search for slender texts, this was arbitrary and insulting to people who'd risked their lives during the Mississippi Freedom Summer, for example, or soon would be in Southeast Asia.

Frivolous though in loco parentis guidelines now appear, these sorts of rules fomented demands for free speech and increased student autonomy. So, they served our purposes. Students began insisting society needed reforming from the university outward, arguing they alone possessed the insight, the wisdom and the lack of venality to make America live up to its promise. That was exactly what the early protests were about: college students, both black and white, reacting to the arbitrary and impersonal regimentation of their lives by capricious bureaucracies.

One student returning from the Mississippi Freedom Summer captured the explosive mixture of youthful arrogance and idealistic anger. Since elementary school we'd been taught America was all but perfect. Now, we were finding out such was not the case.

> ### *"Don't trust anyone over thirty."*
> ### —Jack Weinberg

At UC Berkeley, the administration sought to control the nature of political discourse by banning the tables set up in front of Sproul Hall to distribute literature from CORE (manned by Weinberg, a math grad student) and other civil rights groups. Because dissemination of political literature had long been the rule, students were outraged at such an arbitrary attempt to block open and free discussion. They rioted. They overturned a police car and eventually seized the administration building.

The Berkeley Free Speech Movement was born in a heady atmosphere of intellectual fervor and high-minded reform. The phrase, which spoke so directly to growing generational mistrust of adults, was actually directed toward older communists, for whom

Weinberg and indeed the FSM held deep suspicions. The FSM was non-communist and sought to disassociate itself from it. Nevertheless, the phrase resonated. Why?

Motivated by racial turmoil, white students returned to their northern campuses in the Fall, bringing with them, as sociologist Todd Gitlin has said, "a respect for the power of civil disobedience, a fierce moralism, a lived love for racial equality, a distaste for bureaucratic highhandedness and euphemism, a taste for relentless talk at intense mass meetings...."

Another grad student also returning from the Mississippi Freedom Summer named Mario Savio became the leader of the FSM, our first skirmish with

The Establishment

—the world of our fathers

"After a long period of apathy during the fifties, students have begun...to act.... There is a time when the operation of the machine becomes so odious...that...you've got to put your bodies upon the gears and upon the wheels, upon the levers, upon all the apparatus, and you've got to make it stop."

That machine, the establishment, another way of saying the Power Elite, was comprised of people from a generation or more before the baby boom. The term became shorthand everything the young considered flawed about the world of our parents and grandparents. But there was a great deal more to it than age. Had it been merely generational, the troubles—not to say the changes—may never have amounted to much.

White Anglo-Saxon Protestant

—E. Digby Baltzell

Sociologist Baltzell originated the acronym to describe the leaders of Boston society. But this four-letter word quickly came to represent the entirety of the ruling class. In fact, during the 60s the two notions became indistinguishable. WASP, establishment—was there a difference? Obviously. But, America defined itself in terms of its English heritage, through customs, morals, and manners. The WASP paradigm was supreme, to the exclusion of others. For this reason WASPs, especially WASP males, became the bad guys and were condemned for the nation's, if not the world's, ills: racial and sexual discrimination, the class structure, despoliation of the environment, corruption and war.

These assumptions were as sweeping as they were unreasoned. Critics failed to acknowledge the great gifts a handful of WASP men had given humanity through documents such as the Declaration of Independence and the United States Constitution and its Bill of Rights. Both will withstand the test of time far better than their critics. The prosperity enjoyed by individuals and families, not to mention communities and states, was a direct result of the Protestant Work Ethic. The WASP paradigm also gave us an invaluable emphasis on individualism, while linking it to social responsibility and religious faith.

Until the avarice of the Reagan Era, these men and women acted more or less selflessly. They placed national interest over the special interests of class, region and industry, and public service over private gain by mediating among special interests rather than siding with one against another. WASPs defined the ideal of public service.

Not bad for such villainous infamy.

The Sixties began the replacement of the WASP ruling class, an irreversible process that, for good or ill, is still underway. It would be healthier for the nation if someday something other than absolute evil were ascribed to white, Anglo-Saxon Protestant America.

Still, the world of our fathers was *far* from perfect. And it was alien to us even when it appeared friendly and admirable. By the mid-60s America's young had changed the nature of what it meant to be young. Gone forever was the centuries-old notion that children were miniature adults. We were not adults and we wanted all the world to know it. If anything we were *anti-adults*, glorifying youth by specifically rejecting the vestiges of adulthood in action, manners and attitude. Contempt for things WASP and establishmentarian, rebellion, drugs, music, dress all represented a youth culture that was asserting its right to determine its own manners and morals.

And such manners and morals they were! On the West Coast the wild, experimental and just plain off-the-wall Merry Pranksters that formed around writer Ken Kesey, author of *One Flew Over the Cuckoo's Nest*, set out on a journey to New York in a 1939 Harvester school bus painted up in lurid Day-Glo, its destination "Furthur."

"You're either on the bus or off the bus."

—Ken Kesey

With painted faces, loud music, madman Neal Casady at the wheel, and a copious supply of LSD, marijuana and other drugs, the Pranksters set out for the New York World's Fair hoping to arrive in time for the publication of Kesey's next novel, *Sometimes a Great Notion*. Well, sorta. They made a 40-hour film of their adventure that documented the early stirrings of the counterculture. Kesey had discovered LSD in a 1960 VA hospital experiment and was anxious to meet the Man. They stopped in Milbrook, New York, at Timothy Leary's League of Spiritual Discovery so Kesey could pay homage to the already legendary LSD guru. It didn't exactly work out. The self-important Leary was tripping at the time and couldn't be disturbed.

A sign on the back of the bus read, "Caution: Weird Load."

*   *   *

As the final month of that last carefree summer of '64 began, the country took a first fateful step into the quagmire that would undo the era. Off the coast of North Vietnam, North Vietnamese torpedo boats fired on an American electronic eavesdropping ship. Joined by planes from a nearby carrier, the USS Maddox returned fire.

> *"The other side got a sting out of this.*
> *If they do it again, they'll get another sting."*
> **—Secretary of State Dean Rusk**

Two days later, in heavy seas, the US mistook a second attack. America got its dander up. Despite highly dubious evidence of an attack, we launched retaliatory air strikes. LBJ took this opportunity to secure Congressional authorization...

> *"to take all necessary measures to repel any armed attack*
> *against the forces of the United States and to prevent*
> *further aggression."*
> **The Gulf of Tonkin Resolution**

Congress accepted administration's portrayal of the incidents as "deliberate attacks" and "open aggression on the high seas." LBJ concealed the covert raids the ships had been supporting. On August 7, 1964, the resolution passed the House unanimously and the Senate with two dissenting votes. One dissenter, Ernest Gruening, (D-Alaska) called the resolution a "predated declaration of war." LBJ promised, "We seek no wider war." And at first he didn't. His main concern was his broad domestic agenda. Ultimately, a wider war was what we got. The sting Rusk gloated about turned out to be self-inflicted.

*   *   *

The load carried on B-52s was infinitely weirder than the load on Kesey's bus. A warning about obsessive anti-communism and Mutual Assured Destruction hit these shores just ten days before the Beatles.

> *"Well boys, I reckon this is it, noo-cleer combat, toe-to-toe with the Rooskies."*
> *—Dr. Strangelove or:*
> *How I Learned to Stop Worrying and Love the Bomb*

Directed by Stanley Kubrick, an ex-patriot American living in England, and starring Peter Sellars in three roles, this atomic age black comedy almost literally sneaked in under the national radar. The plot involved a psychotic Air Force General named Jack D. Ripper who launched a sneak attack on the Soviet Union in retaliation for attempts by the International Communist Conspiracy to "sap and impurify all of our precious bodily fluids."

Unfortunately, the Soviets had installed a "Doomsday Device" set to go off if they were ever attacked. The result wasn't exactly war, as the bomb-bucking, nuclear cowpoke Slim Pickens proclaimed. The result was Armageddon.

> *"Mein Fuehrer, I can walk!"*

*   *   *

Speaking of mortal danger, the government issued a finding that directly and immediately affected more Americans than the bothersome threat of nuclear war, toe-to-toe or otherwise. This report set off decades of trench warfare over sot-weed, a golden gem of a plant that had for hundreds of years made fortunes and destroyed lives. To this day tobacco remains a bigger killer than drugs, alcohol and nuclear fallout combined.

"Cigarette Smoking May be Hazardous to Your Health."

—Surgeon General's Report

Dr. Luther Terry's 300-plus page finding made official what was already well known. A strong causal connection existed between cigarette smoking and lung cancer, emphysema, and heart disease. Cigarettes also induced nicotine addiction, which was at least as hard to kick as heroin or alcohol. Two years later Congress forced tobacco companies to put cautionary advice on their cigarette packs. In the short term, smoking fell off. In the years to come, as we became more concerned about our health, it declined permanently. In 1964, though, no one foresaw the lawsuits against the tobacco companies or the "non-smokers' rights" campaign that turned cigarette smoking into an absurdist form of oppression.

*   *   *

By the end of the year, few Americans with their heads above the dunes disagreed that something unusual was blowing in the national wind. What it was wasn't exactly clear. Revolution, disaster? The master barometer of our times said it best.

"The times, they are a-changin'."

—Bob Dylan

The changes had just begun. By the time we were finished, society would be unrecognizable.

> *Come mothers and fathers throughout the land*
> *And don't criticize what you can't understand*
> *Your sons and daughters are beyond your command.*
> *There's a battle outside and it's ragin'*
> *It'll soon shake your windows and rattle your walls...*
> *For the times they are a-changin'!*

The War was not yet an issue. Hip-shooting, war-mongering politicians weren't quite yet the focus of all things youthful. It wasn't entirely about in loco parentis, either. Nor Cold War conformity. We'd been raised to expect the best from ourselves and from the world in which we lived, and that's what he hoped for. Strange, though, how the confluence of change fell onto the national head all at once.

Chapter 21

Hippie

1965. Where Martin Luther King spoke of civil rights, Malcolm X spoke of human rights. Rescued from a life of crime and self-destruction by the Nation of Islam while in prison, Malcolm became its national spokesman only to break with the black nationalist organization in 1964 and form the Organization of Afro-American Unity.

> *"By any means necessary"*
>
> **—Malcolm X**

Of all black leaders, Malcolm most clearly understood white racism's effects on the black population. His message hit home especially for black boomers. He claimed that blacks first needed to acquire a stronger sense of identity, pride and dignity before they could even consider anything else. This was essential to survival as a colonized minority in a hostile country. While advocating a liberation struggle, he never urged blacks to pick up weapons to attack whites. He favored self-defense against racist violence and police brutality. Rejecting the cooperative, pacifist spirit of King's "Beloved Community," Malcolm X placed primary emphasis on self-help, solidarity and a separate existence from white America where possible.

Though King and Malcolm X met just once, cordially, on March 26, 1964 in the halls of the Capitol Building, of all places, during the Senate filibuster against the Civil Rights Bill, they remained antagonists. Malcolm X ridiculed King as a "traitor" to his race, a "chump," and a "fool." King considered the Black Muslim a "hot-headed radical with a dangerous emotional appeal." Neither man ever voiced a remotely accurate assessment of the other. Had they survived possibilities for cooperation would have stayed remote, at least in the short run. They were just too different in background and outlook. In the cruelest of all fates, the very people that saved Malcolm X from self-destruction assassinated him in Harlem's Audubon Ballroom on February 28, 1965.

Before he died Malcolm X shared the podium with Coretta Scott King and other Civil Rights leaders in Selma, Alabama. By then Malcolm was offering to support any cause that might improve the lives of black people. That might even include working with white people. The Hajj to Mecca had worked changes on him, although we should never assume the ultimate direction of those changes. The same holds true for King's radicalization at the end of his life.

Malcolm's metamorphosis was a bellwether for transformations among the politically active at mid-decade. The Civil Rights Revolution brought forth a surge of hope among blacks. When those hopes were not immediately fulfilled, many embraced Malcolm's more radical, less compromising stance. In a larger sense, civil rights inspired hope for re-inventing America. We didn't know how exactly it would be done, or where it would end up. But we were confident that wherever it led would be a better place. Change within change was in the air.

*   *   *

> **"You don't need a weatherman to know
> which way the wind blows."**
>
> **—Bob Dylan**

How strong or fair a wind remained to be seen. Even this age of high aspirations kicked up a few squalls, blowing the dust off its share of jokers, knaves and charlatans.

> **"Turn on, Tune in, Drop out."**
>
> **—Timothy Leary**

As a Harvard psychology professor, he achieved notoriety giving LSD to his students. Thrown out in '63, he holed up in a mansion in up-state New York, dignified as a sort of a hip ashram, to continue his "experiments" with LSD and psilocybin, ultimately fashioning himself into the Pied Piper of half-witted social rebellion. He preached we could live fuller and more useful lives by taking psychedelic drugs. Sort of a counterculture get-rich-quick scheme. As though people in their teens and early twenties had anything close to the equanimity necessary to process such information. To our eternal discredit, plenty of us embraced Leary's foolish ideas. We were young and immersed in our dreams. Drugs taken to expand our minds ended up ruining lives and diminishing our generational promise. They destroyed the very counterculture they were supposed to liberate. Leary turned out to be nothing more than a self-serving bounder, selling snake oil as insidious as anything advocated by the Hemlock Society. Social commentator Theodore Roszak termed his drugged-out maunderings, "impenetrably occult narcissism."

Needless to say, next to no one reached nirvana by dropping acid. Although a whole lot of well-intentioned people tried awfully hard. And more than a few thought they had.

Truth be told, heads older and wiser than ours were taken in by LSD. First synthesized in 1938, for a brief time it was thought to improve creativity and offer a genuine path to enlightenment. No less a light than Aldous Huxley actually advocated psychedelics for this purpose. Even *Life* magazine bought into this nonsense with its ludicrous cover story on "LSD Art." And let us not forget Sigmund Freud's infatuation with cocaine. In the end, it does us well to admit that these drugs were illegal for good reason.

The king of the underground chemists began manufacturing acid in enough quantities to make it cheap and available to the masses, though not one whit less treacherous.

Orange Sunshine

—Augustus Owsley Stanley III

This "renowned acid chemist," as Todd Gitlin called him, cooked up the highest quality psychedelic drugs. There was so much from which to chose. In addition to Owsley's generational martini, the underground offered a Day-Glo pharmacopoeia.

Psychedelic

—mind manifesting (allegedly)

Blue Meanies, Chocolate Chewies, Purple Microdots, Blotter acid, Flesh acid, plus the sugar cube. In California on October 6, 1966 possession of LSD became a misdemeanor.

Conjuring such wild images of fluorescent people and weird tribal doings, the word...

Hippie

—Michael Fallon

...was coined by Fallon in a September 1965 article for the San Francisco *Examiner* by contracting Norman Mailer's hipster, much as Herbert Caen had added the diminutive to Beat to coin *beatnik*. Fallon described the strange communal happenings in the Haight-Ashbury section of San Francisco, particularly activities at the Blue Unicorn coffeehouse. Beat, he wrote, was alive and well and dressed in vivid finery purchased at the Salvation Army.

Why? As Mailer explained:

> *the authority had operated on their brain with commercials, and washed their brain with packaged education, packaged politics. The authority had presented itself as honorable, and it was corrupt as payola on television, and scandals concerning the leasing of aviation contracts—the real scandal as everyone was beginning to sense was more intimate and could be found in all the products in all the suburban homes which did not work so well as they should have worked, broke down too soon for mysterious reasons. The shoddiness was buried deep...*

The owner of the Blue Unicorn described the youth revolution as "a revolution of individuality and diversity that can only be private. Upon becoming a group movement, such a revolution ends up with imitators rather than participants." That was precisely what would happen once the consumer culture grabbed hold of it.

For now, hippies were pretty much located in the Haight and were more or less imitating Beat art with generational artifice. Soon an East Coast version would appear in Greenwich Village. By the early 70s, there were maybe three million "hairy-headed hippies" (to quote Kris Kristofferson) out and about. True hippies were actually dropouts from mainstream society living on communes. By then so many young people were slouching around in long hair and "bell bottom blues" (to quote Eric Clapton), the meaning of what it meant to be a hippie had become so loose you could easily make the case for upwards of sixteen million flower children by the time of Nixon's re-election.

Were hippies actually "hip"? Ultimately hipness became the standard by which they judged themselves. Despite the intimate connection, hippies would have evolved without LSD. In the early years they were all about survival. Sounds foolish to jaded ears, but a sense of anomie and loss of control drove many boomers to seek out alternative ways of navigating life. When they dipped their toes in, many found it impassable. So they looked for new ways.

Being a hippie meant leading a simpler, more open and honest life. It meant rejecting materialism and competitiveness. It didn't take long for these ideas to become benchmarks against which anyone under 30 (and all too many over) were measured. When hippies became hip, the counterculture they hoped to establish, this kinder, gentler Woodstock Nation, ceased countering the things that led to its creation and became just another aspect of American mass culture, defined only by age (young) and attitude (defiant). And it was every bit as exclusive as any country club. Cocktail parties with all their backbiting and false pledges moved to the fields and communes and substituted blacklights for barbecues. When marijuana and hashish became the generational alternative to alcohol, the counterculture, for all the good it might have brought, set off on a speedy voyage to its own demise.

Detractors such as California's governor Reagan had a slightly different interpretation. A hippie, he once quipped, is someone who "dresses like Tarzan, has hair like Jane, and smells like Cheetah."

Typical Reagan: great sense of humor that missed the point entirely. Tarzan (he must have forgotten) was intended as a humanizing commentary on the hypocrisy and materialism of the Victorian world.

Peace and Love

—Flower Power

The smelly long-hairs of the counterculture offered a gentler outlook on the hectic, madding pace of life. Displaying the two-fingered peace sign or a flag, decal, amulet or patch bearing the peace symbol implied rejection of the "straight" world. For a while "freaks" embraced notions of no alcohol, no harshness, nothing plastic, everything real and up-front and genuine.

Such things might seem childish and frivolous, but there was a time when these Tarzans, Janes and Cheetahs provided a breath of fresh air to an obsessed, compulsive and tranquilized society. Was it wrong to view the world in vivid Peter Max colors and designs? Hippies offered a different viewpoint that was not nearly as threatening as it was taken. Just because the counterculture failed shouldn't mean all its ideas were wrong. One had only to observe the world of the establishment to know the counterculture had a lot to counter. Longhairs were about a great deal more than the War. Hippies appeared before most of us knew about Vietnam. Southeast Asia didn't even start to become a major issue until March. Even then it nibbled at the periphery.

*   *   *

In its early years, before drugs and politics distorted it, the exotic world of the counterculture conjured images of a separate, escapist existence filled with gentleness and harmony. An ethereal world mixing fantasy and reality. Perhaps that was why J.R.R. Tolkien's trippie saga of the rich and complex lands of Middle Earth during the Third Age took hold as it did. Good triumphed over evil, although at the price of great sacrifice. The exploits of Frodo the Hobbit, his compatriots ("an unobtrusive but very ancient people, [who] love peace and quiet and good tilled earth [and were] shy of the 'Big Folks'") and Gandalf the Grey on their quest to Mordor as they encountered assorted elves, fairies, ents, humans attracted a "cult following" in the millions.

Treebeard is an Ent
—The Lord of the Rings

Released in paperback in 1965, the 3-volume fantasy went through more than two dozen printings by the end of the decade. Tolkien started with *The Hobbit* in 1937 because he thought C.S. Lewis' *The Chronicles of Narnia* lacked detail. Interrupted—and obviously influenced—by World War II, Tolkien followed the well received story of Bilbo Baggins with the five books that eventually comprised *The Lord of the Rings* trilogy that was first published in 1955.

*   *   *

In August of 1965 a folk-rock song, sung by gravel-voiced Barry McGuire, about cataclysm and despair reached number one. Five weeks after its release, and despite being banned on many radio stations, it was the fastest rising rock record ever.

The Eastern world, it is explodin'
Violence flarin', bullets loadin'
You're old enough to kill but not for votin'
You don't believe in war but what that's gun you're totin'
And even the Jordan River had bodies floatin'
Tell me over and over and over again, my friend,
You don't believe we're on the...

Eve of Destruction

—P.F. Sloan

Hobbits aside, this pop tune expressed the contempt we were beginning to feel for the world. The notion that our parents had somehow made a mess of things became pervasive. The message was vociferous and carried a certain element of prophecy. Here was our hellfire and damnation sermon to our parents:

Look at all the hate there is in Red China
Then take a look around to Selma, Alabama...

We'd just about reached full-tilt generational arrogance.

"Talkin' 'bout my generation"

—the Who

We'd begun st-st-st-strutting our stuff to the point of tr-tr-trashing our instruments on our g-g-g-generational stage. "Hope I die before I get old...."

Well, maybe after splitting for the Coast first. The attraction was genetic. Americans had been heading west since Jamestown. Sooner or later almost all boomers felt the tidal forces pulling them across the continent where something strange and wonderful was happening.

All of it was distinctly American. Though not all of it was about defiance and rebellion. Some of it was just plain f-u-n.

"Wish they all could be California Girls."

—the Beach Boys

The *surfing sound,* begun by guitarist Dick Dale and raised to new heights by the Beach Boys, Jan and Dean and others, meant fast cars, blondes in bikinis and wild weekends at the beach. At a time when the war in Vietnam was escalating, the cities burning, and the country entering a period of uncertainty, there was still time to have fun, fun, fun. T-Bird or no T-Bird. For the moment, twin pillars of the youth culture, surfers and hippies, existed side by side in an easy symbiosis. The War would change that. In a few years even surfers took sides.

But for the time being, these were the sunny days of youth, as we might wish them always to be. Before the counterculture came to define what it meant to be young, our world was divided between the...

Mods and Rockers
or
Surfers and Greasers

Mods were the Edwardian influenced, pre-preppies from England. The Rockers were pre-punks. The American version was less divided along class lines. But it pitted those who peroxided their hair, wore madras, and hung out at the beach or wanted to against their slicked-haired, side-burned counterparts, who hadn't quite gotten past Elvis.

Sun, surf and sand were luxuries that not everyone could afford. Historical travails did not roll over for the coming of the Age of Aquarius. Not by a long shot.

*   *   *

Escalation

—The War

Using the Gulf of Tonkin Resolution as his license, a desperate and despairing LBJ sent combat forces to South Vietnam. The situation there was deteriorating. The government we backed lacked popular support. Buddhist monks were dumping gasoline on themselves in the streets of Saigon and striking a match in protest of the government's lack of concern for the Buddhist masses. The bloodthirsty Vietcong had so destabilized the country the ARVN (South Vietnamese Army) was incapable of holding it together.

Our concern about the spread of monolithic communism, our misunderstanding of the nature of the conflict, LBJ's determination not to be the first American president to lose a war, all spelled trouble. By God, trouble is exactly what we got. Trouble of the ass-ripping variety. March 8 two Marine battalions waded ashore at Danang air base to protect it from NVA (North Vietnamese Army) retaliation for our bombing campaign on the North, known as Operation Rolling Thunder. One hundred eighty-four thousand more men were scheduled to be in country by the end of the year.

Public support for the Gulf of Tonkin Resolution had been broad. Public opposition to escalation was surprisingly strong. The earliest vestiges of anti-war sentiment appeared at some of the nation's finest schools. A few weeks later, moved by the success of the sit-ins, several dozen professors at the University of Michigan held an all night…

Teach-in

—the Anti-War Movement

…during which 3,000 students and faculty debated the expansion of the war. Other colleges and universities followed suit, including Harvard, Columbia, and Berkeley. The anti-war movement staged its first demonstration on April 17, 1965 when 16,000 people marched in DC to protest the presence of those 25,000 combat troops. The demonstrators were far more reformist than radical. They carried signs saying…

"No More War"
or
"We Want Peace Now"

Many of them wore suits and only four were arrested. A far cry from what would happen two years later as the war—and opposition to it—continued escalating. A few Democratic Senators urged LBJ to negotiate a settlement with the North. He refused. *The New York Times* warned of "lives lost, blood spilt and treasure wasted on fighting a war in a jungle 7,000 miles from the coast of California."

At first it was easy to discern the difference between "hippies of the psychedelic movement" and "peace activists." Those distinctions—appearance, thought and attitude—merged over the years as the forces of history took over.

*   *   *

"The real hero of this struggle is the American Negro."
—LBJ on the Voting Rights Act of 1965

America got more violent after Congress passed the Civil Rights Act of 1964. Murders and police violence surrounding Bloody Sunday in Selma, Alabama, convinced Congress to pass additional legislation. Proposing the act LBJ said,

> *"There is no constitutional issue here. There is no moral issue...There is only the struggle for human rights...Every American citizen must have an equal right to vote...This cause must be our cause. It is not just Negroes, but all of us, who must overcome the crippling legacy of bigotry and injustice. And we shall overcome."*

The Voting Rights Act reinforced the previous year's ban on literacy and understanding tests for voting and sent federal examiners into various regions of the South to register black voters. This strong act led to an explosion in the number of black elected officials that by the 1990s had septupled.

*   *   *

To everyone's surprise, black and white leaders alike, trouble lay dead ahead. Five days after LBJ signed the Voting Rights Act, Watts erupted.

Burn, Baby, Burn
—the Long Hot Summers

Although the Long Hot Summers actually began with the Harlem riot of the previous year, the destructive riot in LA set off a wave of urban upheavals that extended through the next several summers. The worst riot came in Detroit in 1967 where thirty-three blacks and ten whites died and over a thousand were wounded during the six-day uprising. Just prior to this blacks rioted in Newark, resulting in over twenty-five deaths. That had been expected considering Newark's high unemployment, crime, maternal mortality and tuberculosis, presided over by a callous all white city administration. But Detroit came as a real shock. Home to a thriving auto industry, the city showcased the country's most prosperous black community.

Outrage and police brutality had pushed urban black America to a state of insurrection. Over 90 people were killed in the '67 riots alone. All told, in over 400 riots from 1964 to 1968, counting the April '68 riots after King's assassination, half a million people had participated with 8,000 casualties and 50,000 arrests.

Traditionally, whites rioted against blacks. The Long Hot Summers established a new norm—black revolt against white intransigence. Trapped in pitiless ghettos, poor urban blacks rioted to gain access to the mainstream that had all but shut them out. Feeling left behind by the Civil Rights Movement, rioters underwent a *revolution of rising expectations*. In the face of persistent police brutality and public indifference, they rejected King's pacifism in favor of Malcolm X's violent self-defense. In the inner cities police attitudes, de facto segregation, bad housing and no jobs—problems not touched by the movement—brought forth the fires of anger and desperation. "As I see it," LBJ remarked, "I have moved the Negro from D+ to C-. He's still nowhere. He knows it. And that's why he's out in the streets. Hell, I'd be there too."

Rather than sensitize white America to the abject conditions among urban blacks, the riots produced two negative consequences. One, they spurred a backlash that left some blighted urban areas unreconstructed for decades. Two, they gave whites a convenient excuse to disown the race problem. As the rioting spread, they declared society had done enough and turned their backs.

The Long Hot Summers showed anyone who cared to notice that ending legal discrimination did not automatically produce equal opportunity. LBJ attempted to guarantee it through his Great Society programs, which included Affirmative Action, a program designed to assist qualified blacks.

> *Government should "act affirmatively to recruit workers on a non-discriminatory basis."*
>
> **—LBJ, executive order no. 11246**

Later expanded to include gender, sexual preference and the handicapped, Affirmative Action mandated equal treatment of all Americans before the law. Although its fundamentals didn't involve quotas or reverse discrimination, it eventually produced both as minorities and women sometimes received preference over better qualified white men. In 1972 Nixon expanded Affirmative Action with the "Philadelphia Plan" that set numerical "goals" for hiring minorities for companies with federal contracts. Statistically and despite legitimate complaints, however, white men as a whole did not suffer from this now moribund set of guidelines. As LBJ explained it:

> *"You do not wipe away the scars of centuries by saying, now you are free to go where you want, do as you please and chose the leaders you please. You do not take a person who, for years, has been hobbled by chains and liberate him, bring him up to the starting line of a race and the say, 'You are free to compete with all the others'...It is not enough just to open the gates of opportunity. All our citizens must have the ability to walk through those gates."*

Compelling though LBJ's logic may have been, white America greeted Affirmative Action with skepticism that turned into resentment. Older boomers, especially, confronted these policies in school and the job market. Reverse discrimination or not, the fact remains Affirmative Action played an indispensable role in the creation of the black middle class.

*   *   *

That fall cities in the Northeast experienced a different kind of black power. Considerably more benign than the one rumbling through the inner cities.

The Great Northeast Black Out

—power failure

What started on November 9 as a power surge through a regional grid eventually spread into an amoebae of darkness encompassing New York, Connecticut, Massachusetts, Vermont, New Hampshire and Maine that left some 30 million people in the dark. Quite understandably this led to a mini-baby boom nine months later. After all, people had to do something during the down time. Since they couldn't go to the movies, they resorted to humankind's first indoor sport. The event even spawned a movie, *Where Were You When the Lights Went Out?*

*   *   *

Doubtful those procreating in the dark needed any advice from a glossy magazine. Just in case they did, one had recently become available.

Cosmo Girl

—Helen Gurley Brown

"I just think that when you stop having sex, that's when you stop being a woman." There's the Cosmo philosophy. Sounds like it was ghost written by Hugh Hefner. Beginning with her 1962 book *Sex and the Single Girl,* which detailed her sex life in what was then shocking detail, continuing three years later with her editorship of *Cosmopolitan* magazine, Brown made household conversation out of transforming oneself from a "mouseburger" into a sex object that enjoyed generous sexual activity, flirting and, when necessary, affairs. Her magazine became an American institution. Her Cosmo Girls had cleavage rivaling any Playmate's.

*   *   *

Unsafe at Any Speed

—Ralph Nader

Modern consumerism began with this exposé of the cynical carelessness with which the American automobile industry built its cars. Nader, a Harvard law school graduate, claimed that the desire for profits drove car makers to mock social responsibility. Incensed over his deconstruction of the Corvair, General Motors gave Nader added credibility by hiring a private eye to check out his sex life (good luck, he read neither *Playboy* nor *Cosmo.*). Nader sued and used the $425,000 settlement to found public interest groups staffed by the bright and earnest Nader's Raiders. A congressional committee investigated the Corvair and found Nader wrong or inexact on almost every count. The Corvair turned out to be safer that the VW Beetle.

Despite its weaknesses, Nader's book was one of the most influential books published during the Sixties and made many of us aware of the possibilities for citizen-driven reform.

Chapter 22

Man of the Year: Twenty-Five and Under

1966. "Untold adventure awaits him," *Time* magazine enthused.

"Well educated, affluent, rebellious, responsible, pragmatic, idealistic, brave, 'alienated' and hopeful...He is the man who will land on the moon, cure cancer and the common cold, lay out blight-proof, smog-free cities, enrich the underdeveloped world and, no doubt, write finis to poverty and war."

Man of the Year: Twenty-Five and Under

—*Time* magazine

Far out, man.

"With his skeptical yet humanistic outlook, his disdain for fanaticism and his scorn for the spurious, the 1966 Man of the Year suggests that he will infuse the future with a new sense of morality, a transcendent and contemporary ethic that could infinitely enrich the 'empty society'."

The trouble was we believed ourselves not only capable of such God-like feats—but destined to accomplish them before we hit the Big Three-oh. Despite the ludicrous hyperbole, the collective sense of destiny was real.

       *   *   *

In January a three-day festival featuring music, dancing and a light show simulating "an LSD experience without LSD" took place in San Francisco's Longshoreman's Hall, except that there was plenty of acid to be had for cheap.

The Trips Festival

—Stewart Brand

Ken Kesey and the Merry Pranksters showed up ready to hold an Acid Test. Kesey was dressed in a silver space suit. Tom Wolfe called it a "huge wild carnival" that grew out of the Pranksters' delirious and controversial Acid Tests (LSD was still legal), which he described as "manic screaming orgies in public places." The Pranksters had been holding Acid Tests since '65. Hundreds attended these mini-Fantasias every weekend. Organized by Brand, the Trips Festival led Bill Graham to begin staging concerts in the Fillmore Auditorium.

Whether it was in San Francisco or along LA's Sunset Strip, the ferment was everywhere. *Time* described this new generation as a "minisociety" governed by its "own lights and rights."

Feed your head

—Grace Slick

Which was exactly what was happening. The drug ethic was widening. "Enlightenment by any means necessary," as Todd Gitlin said of the Merry Pranksters. (And whether you needed it or not!) Jefferson Airplane was one of the early psychedelic bands from San Francisco promoting alternative lifestyles. Their music was clever and innovative. Grace Slick was about as winsome a hippie chick as a groovy dude could ever hope to get into.

Feeling Groovy
—Simon and Garfunkel

If the East Coast had a counterpart to psychedelic music, Simon and Garfunkel was it. More cerebral and less orgiastic (after all, this was the uptight East), their melancholy harmonies and Paul Simon's existential lyrics spoke directly to longings shared by so many middle class young. A little marijuana and new way to look at the world—bingo we're into a bright new day. (The duo's popularity endured strongly enough to culminate in a reunion concert on September 19, 1981 in Central Park that attracted half a million now middle aged fans.)

The music never stopped. Although rhythm and blues had been crossing over since the 50s, it hit its stride with Berry Gordy's Detroit-based Motown Records.

I cream in my jeans when I hear the Supremes.
—the Motown sound

Talk about endless talent. The Supremes, Smokey Robinson and the Miracles, the Temptations, Martha and the Vandellas, Marvin Gaye. When you add Otis Redding and Phil Spector's wall-of-sound girl groups, man, you've got the dominant music of the day.

Urban black America may have been in deep trouble, but this music was a celebration of life. Everywhere you went, "There was music, sweet music...."

*   *   *

The Civil Rights Revolution lasted until the 1978 *Bakke* case. For the Civil Rights *Movement*, however, the end was at hand. The fragile coalition of SCLC, SNCC and CORE reached its zenith during the Selma campaign and died thereafter. Inter-racial cooperation never again attained the strength of those few weeks early in 1965. Dr. King remarked that Selma put a giant 'X' on the country. He meant that coming from differing places, the two races, black and white, joined in an outpouring of brotherhood—then went their separate ways.

After Selma the nonviolence and Christian brotherly love that characterized the movement stepped aside for the new kid on the block.

"What do you want?
Black Power!
Say it again
Black Power!"

—Stokely Carmichael

When Stokely Carmichael (later Kwame Touré) stood on the trailer in Greenwood, Mississippi, during the June Meredith March against Fear and proclaimed Black Power (with King standing haplessly nearby), the proof was there for all to see. The movement was on its last legs. His militant call for Black Power all but capped the coalition. The rise of Black Nationalism marked the decline of King's influence and signaled a momentous shift in racial protest. Self-consciously pro-black rather than integrationist, Black Power dismissed the white power structure as hopelessly racist. It advocated voluntary racial separatism and an emphasis on things black, from African culture to community politics. Although they alarmed whites, militant Black Powerists merely reflected what whites had been practicing for centuries.

The times and the rhetoric were taking an unfortunate turn. People who should have known better got so caught up in the reductio ad absurdum of radical cant they lost their way. The descent into radicalism among young whites and blacks felt inevitable. Not only was the establishment refusing to budge, it was seeking to clamp down on protest. In the face of this, radicals argued themselves into a corner by shifting to destructive rather than constructive alternatives that betrayed the democratic impulse underlying the protest movements.

Power to the People

—Black Power

Inflammatory rhetoric aside, though, the heart of Black Power expressed a desire to instill self-awareness and pride in a people who lacked it. Since W.E.B. Du Bois wrote about it at the turn of the century, little progress had been made toward establishing a sense of heritage. As Malcolm X, the spiritual father of Black Power, used to say, "You can't tell where you're going until you know where you've been." Black Power was necessary to end the notion that white meant good, black meant bad.

"Say it loud—I'm black and I'm proud."

—James Brown

Awl, shit, James, you old sex machine. The godfather of soul, the grandmaster himself put the black nationalist message of racial and cultural pride into a tune that asked its black listeners, "How you gonna respect if you ain't cut your process yet?" A far cry from "We Shall Overcome."

The new message rang loud and strong.

Black is Beautiful

—Cultural Nationalism

Huge Afros and African dashikis. Later, orange patterned Kente cloth appeared on everything from hats and scarves to cummerbunds and book bags. It also meant more substantial things such as celebrating Kwanza, converting to Islam, adopting African surnames. Despite centuries of psychological, political, economic and social backwardness, a positive identification with Africa began to emerge. Ties with one's ancestry are so fundamental they get taken for granted. For millions of black Americans, however, those ties had been murky at best.

*   *   *

Pop culture responded to the discord with a TV show that examined American social problems from a safe distance of light years.

"Beam me up, Scottie."

—Captain Kirk on *Star Trek*

This indefatigable show began on September 8 and attracted a cult following rivaled only by the Grateful Dead. "Space, the Final Frontier" was really about our tremulous world. This lowbrow space opera that bordered on camp humor inexplicably appealed to millions of viewers who cared next to nothing for science fiction. Boomers who cut their teeth on the *Magazine of Fantasy and Science Fiction, Analog* and *Galaxy* found the weekly morality plays unspeakably dull. They were a minority. *Star Trek* represented an attempt to rationalize the ferment of the period. Which was more than adequate proof of its merits.

Society wasn't going to assimilate this guy. For him there were no final frontiers. He found the very idea revolting.

"The Mask Man's a fag!"

—Lenny Bruce

On August 13, the master of crossing the line died of a heroin overdose. For challenging convention—as in his outrageous cartoon "Thank you, Mask Man"—he was persecuted and driven to self-destruction. Though he peaked in the 50s, Bruce's iconoclasm made him and comedians like W.C. Fields boomer heroes.

One of the themes Bruce and Fields explored was the effect of a repressive society on the individual. In *One Flew Over the Cuckoo's Nest*, Ken Kesey argued that insane asylum inmates had more humanity than their authoritarian keepers. Plays such as *Marat/Sade* and shrinks such as R.D. Laing portrayed the insane as more rational than the "sane." Nowhere was this better captured than in *the* cult movie of the day.

"The knight strikes at midnight."

—King of Hearts

This anti-war film examined the fine edge of insanity, questioning how sane our warrior societies really were. Alan Bates played a

Scottish soldier during World War I who happens upon a town occupied by lunatics escaped from the local asylum. They crown him king, and he saves the town from demolition at midnight. In the end he chooses the eccentric unreality of the asylum and joins his subjects, leaving the madly sane to run amok. The movie played nearly continuously for over five years at Central Square Theater in Cambridge, Massachusetts.

Art and portents of revolution made for great dorm room rap sessions, but reality had this persistent habit of sobering things up.

Born to Raise Hell

—Richard Speck

In the second half of the 60s, the asylum gates had opened—or the system was breaking down. Or both. Take your pick. Here are two reasons why. Richard Speck stunned the world by slaying eight nurses in a Chicago apartment. The lone surviving nurse identified him by his singular tattoo touting his destiny. A few weeks later, Charles Whitman climbed to the top of the clock tower on the University of Texas library and assassinated thirteen students, wounding thirty-one more. Both Whitman and Speck came from dysfunctional families. Whitman's sniping spree touched off a forty-year wave of mass murders. But it was Speck's butchery that shocked us most deeply.

Maybe hippies were right. Maybe they had a better way. Plenty of people thought so. Mass society and mass culture, the Cold War, and especially the War, brought us a reign of criminal terror to go with the cultural upheaval. Not only a new wave of street crime but violent crime with a twist: mass murders and serial killings. Although neither was completely new, by 1980 there was more than one of each per month.

Widespread gun ownership and copycat crimes didn't help matters. But the gun culture (and media exposure) was not responsible. These crimes would have happened anyway. So what was it? The "permissive society?" Had freedom become license? Had humanism undermined the divine role in our day-to-day lives? Had an increasingly materialistic, secular society turned away from God? The previous generation asked, "Where was God at Auschwitz?" This generation asked...

Is God Dead?

—*Time* magazine

Much misunderstood then and now, the so-called "Death of God" was a theological movement. As *Time's* cover story sought to explain, our concept of God had become irrelevant to today's world. Religion remained extremely important. "Christian atheists," many of whom were highly respected theologians, questioned the relevancy of the traditional anthropomorphic God to modern society. They were saying God as an omnipotent, omnipresent, bearded white guy up there in Heaven, sort of a 19th century British monarch presiding over his far flung empire, was dead. These Christian theologians argued that God in the image of man, "a personal loving God, who created the world and sustains it with his love," was dead.

These notions were vested in the theology of the twentieth century. The influence of the Holocaust, the Bomb and the mass slaughter of two world wars was obvious, whether acknowledged or not. To boomers, Vietnam and civil rights called God's beneficence and relevancy into question. God, that is, as filtered through the church.

Organized religion was part of the establishment. As such it had done little to help solve the terrible contradictions resounding through the country. Organized religion was part of the problem. The major Protestant denominations supported white supremacy for generations. A few major exceptions such as Quakers and Unitarians didn't mitigate that sad fact. By the 60s it was the fringe groups like Jehovah's Witnesses, many Pentecostals and radical sectarian churches led by people like Father Divine who were anti-racist. Not mainstream churches. Which may explain why boomers began to trickle into their services.

The 60s tested traditional faiths. All aspects of conventional society were subject to challenge, including religious beliefs. The century-long move toward a more secular society called traditional concepts of God, the Devil, good and evil to question. Protestant and Roman Catholic support of segregation certainly didn't help matters any. Clerics and scholars explored the relevance of an after-life to contemporary social and cultural tribulations. The "Death of God" became a convenient shorthand for the failure of traditional means of salvation, the failure of the church to confront our social problems. It didn't mean that, but that was its impact. To the devout, it provided a glaring indication of America going astray.

Notions of the "secular city" aside, widespread belief in God, church membership and attendance indicated the baby boomer generation was then and remains today deeply religious. And may ultimately prove the most devout generation since the Puritans.

*   *   *

Human Sexual Response
                    —Masters and Johnson

The published findings of two low-key, business-like scientists were refreshingly liberating—and to cultural conservatives sure proof of the continued deterioration of society. Humanism abounding, God "dead," and now this. To the few maybe. But William H. Masters and Virginia Johnson had conducted extensive experiments and published an intentionally dry inquiry into the physiology of sexual intercourse. They identified its four stages: excitement, plateau, orgasm and recovery. In doing so they dismantled long-held myths about sex. Namely, that women did not enjoy intercourse as much as men partly because they had trouble having an orgasm. Masters and Johnson also destroyed the myth that women were dependent upon men for vaginal orgasms, when in fact they could have multiple orgasms by clitoral stimulation. Shortly thereafter "frigid woman" joined the flat earth in the museum of discredited ideas.

This may sound quaint today. At mid-decade, it was as shocking. Their discoveries stimulated the sexual revolution that had already breached the walls of the sacrosanct sexual double standard. Their conclusion that homosexuality was closer to normal than abnormal was perhaps as influential as their iconoclastic assertions about heterosexuals.

Chapter 23

Make Love, Not War

1967. Two weeks after *Time* declared baby boomers its "Man" of the Year, 30,000 hippies met in San Francisco's Golden Gate Park to usher in the Age of Aquarius. The January 14 celebration...

A Gathering of the Tribes for the...
—Human Be-In

featured Timothy Leary, his former research associate at Harvard, Richard Alpert, who would soon feature himself as hippie guru Baba Ram Dass, Allen Ginsberg, Dick Gregory and Jerry Rubin, along with such local bands as the Dead and Jefferson Airplane. The idea was to bring hippies together with the political dissidents of the New Left. To the outside world they were indistinguishable. A local newspaper described it as "a union of love and activism previously separated by categorical dogma and label mongering."

Those involved were simpatico anyway. Leary saw politics as a power trip. "Turn on to the scene," he told the assembled flower children, "tune in to what is happening, and drop-out—of high school, college, grad school, junior executive—and follow me, the hard way." He and Ginsberg chanted while anti-war activist Jerry Rubin railed about politics. As Todd Gitlin described it,

"Off the platform, where most of the action characteristically was, twenty thousand young people, more or less, reveled, dropped acid, burned incense, tootled flutes, jingled tambourines, passed out flowers, admired one another, felt the immensity of their collective spectacle." The Hell's Angels provided their own form of edgy security. They were social outcasts and rebels just like the sons and daughters of the great gray middle class. Here in Golden Gate Park the twain had met, counterculture, political dissidents, and outlaw bikers.

The music, the drugs, the vibes celebrated "a new concert of human relations" that questioned authority in order to bring on a "Renaissance of compassion" in which all people lived fuller lives in a clean environment among like-minded, peaceable humans. As the Berkeley *Barb* waxed, "In unity we shall shower the country with waves of ecstasy and purification." Far out and groovy. To the straight world they were just a gaggle of weirdos hanging out with a pack of roughnecks. Dig it.

Make Love, Not War

—counterculture sentiment

When Jerry Rubin led a march on the Oakland army base back in October 1965, the then super-patriot Hell's Angels beat up many of the demonstrators. By '67 the times had changed so completely Angels were welcome fixtures in the Haight. (Perhaps due in part to the pacifying effects of LSD.) In any case, this slogan first appeared during the teach-ins of 1965 and two years later had gained widespread usage and acceptance.

By combining eros and pacifism with opposition to the War, the phrase completed the gestalt. Activists were as likely to show up at a Trips Festival or a concert at Bill Graham's Fillmore as hippies were at an anti-war rally. Various subcultures began to coalesce.

To be young in those days meant navigating a world of exciting ideas and new experiences. Equal parts sensual and cerebral exploration, all of it uncharted. No one had entered these waters before. The moment resonated into an ineffable feeling that all the forces of the universe were coming together to bestow upon us an entirely new world, shimmering with new realities and alive with better answers. It was up to each of us to...

Seize the Day,
Be Here, Now

—the time of the season

Now or not at all. One was a call to action. The other a plea to live life openly, honestly and in the present, to experience as much as you can while you can. Perhaps the spirit wasn't too far removed from that of John Winthrop aboard the Arbella gazing at the pristine New England shoreline and vowing to create a "City upon a Hill, the eyes of all people are upon us."

The counterculture flowered during the *Summer of Love* in Haight Ashbury, which began officially with the summer solstice, June 21, 1967. The Haight was already Mecca for some 15,000 hippies and was well known among the growing numbers of flower children across the country as the main point of light.

"If you're going to San Francisco,
be sure to wear some flowers in your hair."

—Scott McKenzie

Somewhere between fifty and seventy-five thousand young pilgrims showed up during the summer months. Many more who weren't able to split for the coast cast beams of longing. A bewitched news media saw in the tousled, beaded and blissed-out multitudes new hope for American society.

In the face of growing racial discord—for this was the Summer of Desperation in many ghettos—and a war without sense or sensibility, the alternatives of free love and peaceable toleration made more than a modicum of sense. For a brief shinning moment, it offered a positive alternative to violence and hatred. Besides that, doing your own thing in your own time was loads of fun. The Love Pageant Rally in the Panhandle of Golden Gate Park brought out a hippie Mardi Gras of thousands. True believers dismissed McKenzie's gentle pop tune as the work of a plastic hippie. Regardless, it captured the moment.

Monterey Pop
—the first rock festival

In mid-June, just before the solstice, 50,000 people paid six bucks a head to see Big Brother and the Holding Company, the Who, Otis Redding, Jimi Hendrix, the Byrds, the Mamas and the Papas, Country Joe and the Fish and of course the Dead. D.A. Pennybaker's film of the festival helped make Hendrix and Janis Joplin *rock stars*, a term not yet coined. When this movie hit theaters the following year, it became a calling card for the new age. A new day was aborning.

Keed Spills?
—The Fabulous Furry Freak Brothers

Underground cartoonist Gilbert Shelton's Freewheelin' Franklin, Fat Freddy, and Phineas; R. Crumb's Mr. Natural and Felix the Cat offered a mocking, sensuous look at this new society. Underground cartoonists and comic books stormed brazenly into places the now establishmentarian *Mad* magazine refused to go. This was especially so for *Zap Comix* by the counterculture's original twisted sister, cartoonist R. Crumb, who simultaneously spoofed and glorified the paranoia of the emerging underground drug culture.

But it was Shelton's Freak Brothers who asked the question of the day.

"Fat Freddy says:
Keed spills? Pill Skeeds? Skill Peeds?"

*   *   *

All the News that Fits

—Rolling Stone Magazine

The music would set us free and *Rolling Stone* would tell us all about it. Started with a $7500 investment, Jann Wenner's magazine hit the stands November 9. Its celebration of the music and the culture that went with it made an instant hit. Of all the counterculture publications, including dozens of underground newspapers, his was by far the most influential. By the time Wenner moved the operation from San Francisco to New York City, *Rolling Stone* had become the arbiter of pop culture.

Much of that pop culture was increasingly psychedelicized by bands such as Jefferson Airplane, Moby Grape, Grateful Dead, Jimi Hendrix. But it never really came together in a coherent way until...

Sgt. Pepper's Lonely Hearts Club Band

—the Beatles

They'd become the masters of their medium by the time they recorded the greatest album of all time. An eclectic mixture synthesized into vague themes about a performing band and laced with psychedelia, *Lucy in the Sky with Diamonds,* and a whiff of mysticism, *Within you, without you, Sgt. Pepper* set standards for excellence. At the same time, its experimentation signified a departure from rock 'n' roll basics. Pink Floyd was not far behind. Neither were other great albums, all of which stood in the shadow cast by John, Paul, George, Ringo in *Sgt. Pepper: Graceland, Tapestry, Axis Bold as Love, Pet Sounds, Surrealistic Pillow, Dark Side of the Moon,* and their own *Rubber Soul, White Album,* and *Abbey Road.*

*   *   *

Just a few months after rock came of age violence received a similar imprimatur. For good or for ill, both became part of the ethos. One belatedly, the other all too soon. Yet the essential truth rang as loud and clear as a "Day in the Life."

"Violence is as American as Cherry Pie."

—H. Rap Brown

Once dismissed as the ravings of a militant Black Powerist, these days it's cited as ironic gospel. H. Rappahannock Brown (now Jamil Abdullah al-Amin) was just trying to…

"Tell it like it is."

—soul power

When Brown succeeded Stokely Carmichael as the chairman of SNCC, he upped the ante. Which is saying something, considering his predecessor's fire-eating. Standing on the hood of a car in Cambridge, Maryland, on July 24, Brown told 400 local blacks:

> *"You better get you some guns...The only thing the honky respects is force...I mean, don't be trying to love that honky to death. Shoot him to death, brother, cause that's what he's out to do to you...The streets are yours. Take them."*

He was charged with inciting to riot. Later these charges were dropped. His real crime was threatening white people with a dose of their own medicine. "The white man won't get off our backs, so we're going to knock him off...America won't come around, so we're going to burn America down." Brown's revolutionary commitment proved to be a passing phase. He reverted to thuggery, always a possibility for the radical fringes. Some years later he got arrested for robbery and was sent to prison. Still later he converted to Islam, a truer reflection of his West African heritage than felony.

> ### *Up against the wall, motherfucker.*
> ### *(This is a stick-up)*
>
> ### —LeRoi Jones

Later calling himself Amari Baraka, this gifted black writer got caught up in the revolutionary fervor of the times. Baraka shrugged off his Beat background for Black Nationalism. After the Detroit riot, urban conditions dominated the racial dialogue—if it could be called a dialogue. It was more like simultaneous monologues. Elements of black leadership put down their integrationist ways for full-blown resistance. In doing so, some of them got the bright idea that armed-robbery and other felonies were legitimate acts of liberation. The system is racist; therefore, we get to hold up liquor stores. Right on, brother.

At any rate, it was time to stand up to the man. And that meant standing up to nearly naked aggression by a supposedly friendly police force. Before the Rodney King beating and the verdict in the O.J. Simpson case, white America didn't understand that most blacks viewed the police as an invading enemy sent there not to protect and serve but to keep them in their place. When, for the first time in American history, blacks formed a vigilante group to defend themselves, whites couldn't fathom the basis of its appeal.

Off the pigs
—Black Panther Party for Self-Defense

Huey Newton and Bobby Seale founded the Black Panthers in Oakland, California in 1967. Their ten point program stressed racial solidarity, self-help, community control and a few very 60s proposals such as the freeing of all political prisoners. They set up a breakfast program, a clinic and sought to develop other programs for the black community. Newton and other Panthers followed Oakland police around shouting out legal rights to black arrestees. Their image—armed and defiant, hardly endeared them to authorities. In fact, the Black Panthers were the first armed black organization in history formed for protection against whites. They grew into a national organization.

On May 2 thirty Panthers stormed into the California state capital carrying their rifles and shotguns in protest of gun control legislation. They took a wrong turn and ended up on the floor of the legislature, weapons in hand. To emphasize their defiance of white violence, the Panthers intentionally allowed themselves to be photographed holding weapons and exhibiting menacing scowls. This was what their posturing and occasional forays into violence got them: the public freaked out. So did J. Edgar

Hoover. Under his COINTELPRO (CounterIntelligence Program), law enforcement subverted the Panthers through arrest, harassment and murder. By the early 70s, they were reduced to a memory, maligned and misunderstood.

    *   *   *

Domestically, the 60s were the twentieth century's most violent decade. The violence at home was in part a product of the divisive war abroad, a war that was falling into its nadir.

Search and destroy
—American strategy in Vietnam

Where was God in Southeast Asia? The Vietcong were murderous cutthroats masquerading as Marxist/Leninist revolutionaries. Did that fact justify the American presence? Was an out of the way Third World nation really worth thousands of dead Americans? As journalist Strobe Talbot wrote, "America was thinking globally, acting locally and getting it wrong on both counts." The shabby hunt and kill strategy underscored the shabby morality of our involvement. The brass regularly inflated the number of enemy dead by 30% or more. By the end of this year, the Pentagon was reporting 220,000 NLF and NVA dead. This strategy placed greater emphasis on body count than territorial and political objectives and was as vague as the lists of dead were high. As Philip Caputo wrote, "If it's dead and Vietnamese, it's VC, was a rule of thumb in the bush." Even considering the other side's unrelenting harshness, our war of attrition gave rise to acts that were far too brutal and inhumane for a nation such as ours. Vietnam had become the Interzone's version of a holocaust.

The average age of the grunts out in the shit was nineteen, far younger than their fathers, who'd averaged twenty-six during the

Second World War. Fresh from high school, these men were thrust into a situation that bore no resemblance to that faced by hero G.I.s slogging across Europe. Ho Chi Minh wasn't Adolf Hitler. The Vietnamese peasants didn't feel any special need for liberation. So, our soldiers kept their heads down until "R 'n R" and hoped and prayed they got short in a hurry.

The light at the end of the tunnel
—General William Westmoreland

The commander of MACV kept saying we were winning the war—and asking for more men. Except for a handful of reporters in the field who eventually saw the sham and began to say so, most of us believed him. Westmoreland's remarks set him up for a big fall. Although he never used these exact words, *light at the end of the tunnel* resounded through the country like a "shot heard round the world." This time it was the sound of a self-inflicted wound.

Summoned home to reassure a fretful public, Westmoreland actually said, "I am very, very encouraged...We are making real progress." At the National Press Club on November 21, he elaborated, "We have reached an important point where the end begins to come into view." Troop withdrawal could begin, he hinted, in two years.

Credibility Gap
—lies our leaders told us

They were so numerous we came to expect them. Not only did the military inflate the body count, they also misrepresented their activities in Laos and Cambodia, where they'd been conducting illegal military operations, concealed from the people and their elected representatives in Congress.

As more boys came home in body bags and the War seemed to be going nowhere, opposition began to spread. So long as it stayed on a few campuses on either coast and in a few large cities, it was no more than troubling. But with the demonstration at the Pentagon on October 21 by 35,000 anti-war protesters (100,000 total counting those attending the rally at the Lincoln Memorial), the anti-war movement worked its way into the public consciousness.

Armies of the Night
—by Norman Mailer

Mailer immortalized the events surrounding this wild weekend. Part sideshow, part teach-in and part riot, it became a happening. Hippie protesters, which should have been an oxymoron, attempted to levitate the Pentagon. Others tried to stuff flowers into the barrels of the M-14s carried by the 2500 soldiers protecting the Pentagon. Mailer spoke, got himself arrested along with 681 others including Abbie Hoffman and Jerry Rubin. So did poet Robert Lowell and Dr. Benjamin Spock. For boomers a prime source of outrage was the draft. More than any other single factor, including the dubious reasons for being in Southeast Asia, the draft made this a generational issue. Thirteen thousand Americans had already died in Vietnam with many more to come, and a growing number were wondering why. The protest at the Pentagon launched the three-year nationwide wave of large, noisy and angry anti-war demonstrations.

"I ain't gonna study war no more."
—Martin Luther King, Jr.

On April 4, Dr. King joined the fray. Claiming that black combat deaths were disproportionately high, he urged black men to become conscientious objectors. "The bombs in Vietnam," he claimed, "explode at home...They destroy the hopes and possibilities of a decent America...The promises of the Great Society have been shot down on the battlefield of Vietnam." King rejected pressures from LBJ and his own advisors to temper his rhetoric. Being the moral leader he was, he marched on. For every $500,000 spent to kill one VC, America spent a measly $35 on the poverty-stricken. King urged all Americans to rally around "our fighting men in Vietnam" by protesting against the War. In merging the Civil Rights Movement with the anti-war movement, he lost an enormous amount of white goodwill and financial support. One year later to the day, he was assassinated.

*   *   *

The country was polarizing between Hawks and Doves, the establishment and the counterculture, straights and freaks, young and old. People on both sides stopped talking and started shouting. Feeling out of sync was not limited to a generation or a political persuasion. The times were bewildering to everyone.

"One word, Benjamin. Plastics."
—The Graduate

Poor Benjamin was out of sync with the world. Estranged from his family, ill at ease with people his own age, he was the hapless schlemiel we all fear being. When his father gave him scuba gear for his birthday, he put it on and sank in dejected isolation to the bottom of his pool. He was Holden Caulfield in sunny LA. He knew only that he loved Elaine, or thought he did. (He had that over Holden). Other than that, he couldn't see his way clear to the future. Join the club,

Benjamin. It was called alienation. The movie helped create the anti-hero and make Dustin Hoffman a star.

*   *   *

Something unsettling happened to our country once the War started escalating. Perhaps another gear in the machinery shifted. Whatever it was, whatever caused it, these words expressed it best.

"What we have here is failure to communicate."
—Strother Martin in *Cool Hand Luke*

Paul Newman played a small time hood trapped in a tough southern prison farm. The prison guards brutalized the prisoners, set them against one another, and sapped their spirit. The prisoners fought back just to stay sane. In the end desperation ruled; resistance proved fruitless; the pervasive power of the establishment prevailed. Cool Hand Luke was shot dead trying to escape.

Actually, what we had was a profoundly enhanced ability to communicate. We were communicating more than ever. The problem was many people didn't like what was being communicated. Electronic media was already ubiquitous by the time Marshall McLuhan told us we'd been absorbed into its global web. That the world had become a Global Village.

The Medium is the Message
—Marshall McLuhan

The brave new medium was continually re-defining itself—and us along with it. On the nightly news, we watched the brutality of war and the grit of urban crime interspersed with "happy talk" and surreal commercials. The tube often tied the world together with uncomfortable results. "The environment that man created becomes the medium for his role in it." Or put another way: "We shape tools and they in turn shape us." Marshall McLuhan helped explain our increasingly inter-connected lives in the Global Village, which, he claimed, was now defined as much by the act of acquiring information as the actual content of that information.

The medium, or process, of our time—electric technology— it's reshaping and restructuring patterns of social interdependence and every aspect of our personal life...Forcing us to reconsider and re-evaluate every institution formerly taken for granted.

The world would never be the same. No corner of the planet was too remote, too exotic, too unimportant to be excluded from the daily ritual of information gathering. And mass media was gathering it like squaw wood. He predicted we'd possess more knowledge of each other than we could absorb. His ideas anticipated the assault on privacy and the insatiable lust for intimate personal details. Most of these cravings were justified as the people's right to know, when in fact it was more a case of the people's ability to find out.

McLuhan saw baby boomers as the agent for change. "Youth," he asserted, "instinctively understands the present environment— the electric drama...This is the reason for the great alienation between generations. Wars, revolutions, civil uprisings are interfaces within the new environment created by electric media."

Maybe so, but the counterculture was based upon the rejection of this interface. *Understanding Media* came out in 1964, followed by *The Medium is the Massage* in '67 and *War and Peace in the Global Village* the next year. Ironically, with his later books people stopped paying attention. His message had become so ingrained it was as if he died well before 1980. In any case, he departed the interface before personal computers and the Internet, which he blithely predicted and defined.

*   *   *

Twiggy

—fashion model

Not all media were electronic. A few became messages about the state of the culture. The message was medium. Neither high nor low, but middle, halfway between male and female, boy and girl, slim and dead.

With her 5'7" 92 lb. frame, her short blond hair with the school-boy part and large blue waif eyes, British model Leslie Hornsby represented the androgynous look that itself signified revolution. Twiggy might have been haute couture but she looked like God's first flower child. With her appearance in *Vogue*, the counterculture's growing influence took an astral flight from black-lit crash pads to Kleig-lit studios. Really thin was really in.

*   *   *

Except on the playing field, that is. Professional athletes were bigger and badder than ever. The biggest game in America appeared as the hurly-burly of football surpassed the summer Sundays of baseball as the national pastime. The hype, the overproduction, the glitz, the mass marketing, Howard Cosell— football hit the big time. Designer sportswear was but a few years away.

Green Bay Packers 35—Kansas City Chiefs 10

—the First Super Bowl

The big question was the quality of the American Football League. Could the upstart league play with the big boys? Packer coach Vince Lombardi wasn't so sure. Reflecting on the game after the victory, he allowed as how the Dallas Cowboys, whom the Pack defeated in the NFL championship, was "a better ball club." Two years later in Super Bowl III, New York Jets Quarterback Joe Namath confidently predicted victory over the Baltimore Colts which were favored by over two touchdowns. "I guarantee you we will win," said Namath—and they did. That victory legitimated the American Football League (soon to become the American Football Conference of the National Football League after consolidation in 1969) and helped make the Super Bowl the nation's top sports event, surpassing even the World Series and the Indy 500.

Chapter 24

"In Order to Liberate This Village We Had to Destroy it."

1968. This was the year that was, ranking with 1776, 1861, and 1941. Our country was blitzed by one tragedy after another, compounding the confusion and stretching an already flayed society on tenterhooks. It was the most chaotic year of the most chaotic decade of the century—to be saved at the last minute by NASA and the Book of Genesis.

> *"In order to liberate this village,*
> *we had to destroy it."*
>
> **—American officer at Bien Tre during Tet**

At the end of January, the Viet Cong struck simultaneously throughout South Vietnam. Hand-to-hand combat took place inside the US embassy compound in downtown Saigon. Ten VC sappers made it to the perimeter wire, within several dozen yards of Westmoreland's headquarters at Tan Son Nhut Air Base. VC lairs were only thirty miles away. The American public panicked.

At first the brass focused on the diversion against our base at Khe Sanh up in I Corps. They were determined Khe Sanh wouldn't become an American Dien Bien Phu. Once they caught on, our armed forces rallied magnificently. Heavy month-long fighting ended in the complete route of the VC and NVA. The trouble was, when Westmoreland claimed victory, Americans, including America's sagacious uncle, Walter Cronkite, refused to believe him. "What the hell is going on?" he rumbled. "I thought we were winning the war."

Westmoreland had said in DC a few months prior to the Tet Offensive, "The friendly picture gives rise to optimism for increased success in 1968." Chairman of the Joint Chiefs of Staff Earle Wheeler termed Tet a "very near thing." Militarily, however, the Tet Offensive was a disaster for the North Vietnamese Army and National Liberation Front. They suffered horrible losses: somewhere between forty and fifty thousand KIA. The VC was virtually eliminated as an effective fighting force in the South. Hereafter, the NVA took over the bulk of the fighting. Despite this, psychologically and politically—which was where it counted most—the American war effort never recovered from Tet.

The off-handed remark by an American major came to represent all that was wrong-headed and immoral about the War. The exact quote is lost (if indeed it was ever uttered). Originally, it was reported by AP reporter Peter Arnett, who was the only one to have heard it. Whether it was, "We had to destroy the town to save it," or probably the most accurate quote, "It became necessary to destroy the town to save it," this phrase distilled the contradictions of the War. Americans were killing tens of thousands of people and destroying a country to prevent a communist takeover. The ironic twist on "Better Dead Than Red" was there for the whole world to watch on television.

Tet dampened the light at the end of the tunnel. The ground war was nowhere close to ending. The communists were not close to defeat. The South Vietnamese government had little support from its people. And the three-year bombing campaign, Operation Rolling Thunder, had not halted the flow of men and supplies along the Ho Chi Minh Trail.

The confidence expressed in 1967 had been shattered. In light of the 12,000 American dead the following year, many Americans began to doubt the point of continuing an unwinable war. Republican Senator George Aiken from Vermont would later quip, we ought to "declare a victory and get out." The sentiment was widely shared by a viewing public that couldn't get past the brutal image of South Vietnamese General Nguyen Ngoc Loan holding his snub-nosed .38 to the head of a bound VC suspect and calmly squeezing off a round. The American population, unused in the extreme to the wanton violence of war, asked, Who were these monsters we were fighting and dying for?

This was a question LBJ should have taken care to answer. Rather, he and many other leaders, such as Secretary of Defense Robert McNamara, cynically manipulated the facts and lied outright about the nature of the War. When the deception surfaced, the Credibility Gap became a Credibility Chasm. The architect of the Great Society was already under fire from his own party. Anti-war senator from Minnesota Eugene McCarthy had given LBJ a scare with a close second in the New Hampshire primary as hundreds of idealistic young people got...

"Clean for Gene"

—anti-war boomers

They cut their shaggy hair, tried out coats and ties, and tramped the country roads of New Hampshire carrying McCarthy's "Out Now" message, criticizing the president for arrogance and aggression against a small Third World nation. We now know LBJ agonized dearly over the escalating tragedy. He wanted desperately to end the war, but didn't know how. If he went to the public in candor about what it would take to get out, he might win support at the expense of his beloved Great Society programs. He was unwilling to sacrifice his domestic agenda. So, he dissembled—and became the Tet Offensive's ultimate victim.

> *"I shall not seek, and I shall not accept*
> *the nomination of my party..."*
>
> **—LBJ**

Tet destroyed his presidency. On March 31, after calling a bombing halt in hopes of establishing peace negotiations, LBJ dropped out of the presidential race. The great liberal president, who wanted his Great Society to boost America to its true majesty, had become so vilified and so widely unpopular he limited his public appearances to military bases.

*   *   *

The Tet Offensive shifted public support away from the Hawks. Ironically, even as people turned against the war effort, they turned with greater vehemence against the anti-war movement. The more events confirmed the movement's charges, the more public wrath the protesters incurred. No wonder. Many of us took to the streets shouting slogans and making obscene gestures without evincing one scintilla of respect.

> *"Hey, hey, LBJ, how many kids did you kill today?"*
> *"Ho, Ho, Ho Chi Minh, the NLF is gonna win."*
>
> **—anti-war slogans**

These ugly phrases resounded throughout '66, '67 and into 1968. Most boomers steadfastly supported the War, especially those on small college campuses. Overall, the strongest support came from baby boomers. But you couldn't tell that from the number of longhairs in the streets with their middle fingers pointing at the sun. Demonstrators disrupted college classes, sat-in at draft boards and armed forces recruiters, held noisy rallies in major cities, and staged mass marches in DC. As the anti-war movement grew in size and fervor, its goals evolved from protest to resistance. It was a fateful change because it exacerbated opposition even as the public came to agree with its arguments.

The movement was a tenuous coalition of anti-establishment radicals, who opposed the racist, militarist, capitalist "system," pacifists, who opposed war, and anti-war liberals. These latter individuals were neither radical nor pacifist and comprised the strength of the movement. They saw the War as a violation of international law and the American Constitution. Liberal Cold Warriors, who had fought in World War II or Korea and at first supported the campaign in Southeast Asia, began to view the American strategy of devastation as immoral. War policies were misguided because we were backing a corrupt, virtual dictator-ship for reasons that had little to do with our national security or their national self-determination. In addition, they represented the sort of arrogant over-extension of power that brought down civilizations as far back as Athens. It was, as Robert McNamara's 1996 book *In Retrospect* would later prove, the doctrine of containment gone mad. And American men and women were dying because of it. Not to mention hundreds of thousands of Southeast Asians.

      *   *   *

The very same week Tet forced LBJ out of the presidential race, the country's greatest moral leader since Abraham Lincoln gave his full measure. His prestige and influence were already in sharp decline when he arrived in Memphis to offer support and guidance to striking garbage workers. There for the first time, he was unable to keep the demonstrations peaceful. His final speech was eerily prophetic.

> *"...I've been to the mountain top...*
> *and I've seen the Promised Land."*
>
> **—MLK, Jr.**

King reassured his followers that "I might not get there with you. But I want you to know tonight that we as a people will get to the Promised Land...." On April 4 he was blasted into martyrdom by a petty thief.

King's death left a legacy that cloaked his militancy. Indeed, his "I Have a Dream" speech, great as it was, was not all that typical. He often was much more militant in denouncing white racism and came to believe that whites were unconsciously and perhaps intractably racist. Despite what apologists now claim, he believed the country owed its black citizens some sort of just compensation for centuries of abuse. Since America had done "something special against the Negro for hundreds of years," he reasoned, it had to "do something special for him now, in order to balance the equation...." In his final years he talked not only about a "revolution of values" but of "a redistribution of economic power." King was after all very much a man of the Sixties.

His death was a loss of incalculable dimensions. He could not be replaced or, as it turned out, succeeded. Only he and RFK could speak to both races without changing the style or content of their speeches. That night announcing the assassination to a stunned black audience in Indianapolis, RFK quoted Aeschylus from memory: "In our sleep, pain which cannot forgive falls drop by drop upon the heart until, in our own despair, against our will, comes wisdom through the awful grace of God." No one since, with the possible exception of Bill Clinton, has been able to speak to both races.

We should also acknowledge that though a man of the cloth King was no saint. That he rose so spectacularly above his short-comings, makes his greatness all the more profound. He plagiarized parts of his doctoral dissertation and embraced extra-marital sex as indiscriminately as a rock star. He used to quip, "Fucking is the best therapy," and was taped by the FBI testifying during sexual delight, "Make me pure, Lord, but not yet."

The riots of despair and anger that swept the country at his murder left forty-six people dead, 3500 injured, and 21,000 under arrest. In all, 168 cities erupted in turbulence that reached within four blocks of the White House. In DC, the once vibrant center of local black culture at 14th and U streets was reduced to rubble. Few countries are blessed with a man like Dr. King. Fewer still express their gratitude with an assassin's bullet. His death left black America leaderless at a time of growing white backlash and rancor between nationalist radicals and more moderate integrationists. Militant nonviolence also died with him, as did hopes for a speedy solution to the problems of the color line.

Meanwhile, at FBI headquarters jubilant celebrations took place.

The violence of 1968 was so jarring that even mainstream politicians began to wonder about the soundness of society. For anti-establishment radicals, the proof of their beliefs was becoming too strong to stomach. Boomers came into the 60s believing that all things were possible. Look at the early successes. The Civil Rights

Movement, the Peace Corps, the Space Program, the Great Society. Eventually the violence against civil rights workers, the riots of the Long Hot Summers, a war that stressed the number of dead as a measure of success, the assassinations, the repressive backlash pushed many of us to the dark belief in the futility of hope.

> ***"Now, it's on to Chicago, and let's win there."***
>
> **—RFK**

As a carpetbag senator from New York, Bobby Kennedy established a presidency-in-waiting. The country knew it was only a matter of when, not if. His moving journey into the Mississippi Delta demonstrated not only the depth of poverty in our affluent nation, but the depth of change in this man. After JFK's death, to quote Roger Wilkins, "RFK became a man connected to the world's pain." This despite his being his brother's son-of-a-bitch who'd practiced the adage "Don't get mad get even." Until his "transformation," if indeed he was transformed and not a cynical opportunist, Bobby Kennedy had been a vengeful prick, a tough Irish ward heeler. Yet, he apparently left behind his father's prejudices, his brother's immorality, McCarthy's virulent anti-communism (he'd been a McCarthy aide) and emerged as the charismatic champion of the downtrodden. The world loved him for it.

Bobby entered the presidential race in March after LBJ's surprising withdrawal. He was the people's favorite, not his party's. Vice President Humphrey had a planeload of political IOU's and most likely would have beaten him anyhow. On June 5, moments after he uttered this challenge to his followers, Sirhan B. Sirhan shot him. He died the next day at 1:44 AM at age forty-two.

> *"You see things as they are and ask, 'Why?'*
> *I dream things as they never were and ask, 'Why not?'"*
> **—RFK quoting George Bernard Shaw**

Mark the beginning of the end of our common dreams from this point. R.I.P.: JFK, MLK, RFK. The country has yet to recover from these killings. At the time of his death, RFK was the only leader alive who could bring together blacks and blue collar whites. The idealism brought forth by his brother and the Civil Rights Movement gave way to fraction, rejection and rebellion. King, the Kennedys gave hope to alienated parts of society. Now they were gone and the dark forces of reaction and hate were about to take their place. The politics of assassination reigned.

Their deaths also became instrumental in the Republican rise to power. To be sure the GOP was already gaining momentum, and most likely would have made considerable inroads anyway. The liberal/Democratic coalition was shattering. But the sad— and unspoken—fact remains these shootings created a power and leadership vacuum that directly facilitated Republican triumphs. Murder is no way to create change, especially in a democracy, especially in the United States of America. But that's exactly what happened.

> *"Gestapo tactics in the streets of Chicago."*
> **—Abe Ribikoff**

What began as protest a few short years before erupted into rebellion at the Chicago Democratic Convention at the end of August. Acting on Mayor Richard Daley's orders, Chicago police raged out of control. With impunity they harassed, beat and arrested peaceful demonstrators. They placed 500 undercover agents among the demonstrators, acting as agent provocateurs, causing the trouble that invited police retaliation. They inflicted such wanton violence and mayhem their actions were condemned from the podium of the convention. Daley responded to Ribikoff by calling him a dirty Jew and giving him the finger. Said Hizzoner, "Gentlemen, remember one thing: the Chicago Police Department is not here to create disorder. It is here to preserve disorder (sic)." The investigating Walker Commission later called it a "police riot."

Such disorder was the GOP's vehicle to power. The Republicans built a presidential majority on it that held into the 90s. But the unpleasant news from the streets of Chicago that hot summer was the clear sign that the country had turned away from the cooperative spirit of King's Beloved Community. 1968 was the year and Chicago was the place where the promise and the possibilities inspired by the Declaration of Independence became too great a challenge. It was a tragedy beyond measure.

The whole world is watching!

—shouted on the streets of Chicago

Demonstrators taunted. TV lights blinked on and lighted a rat's nest of chaos. Cameras captured the bizarre scene of roving bands of blue-helmeted cops beating anyone who looked vaguely suspicious, including Roman Catholic nuns, school children from Canada and Hugh Hefner. Right wingers blamed TV crews for the violence. What a colossal lack of decency at a time when conciliation would have demonstrated their leadership. Instead, conservatives only made a bad situation worse. Listening to reactionary critics, one would have thought there'd been no rioting prior to the invention of televison. The right had a convenient whipping boy that allowed it to seize the day. Which it did, gloriously.

Regardless, the news media had managed to make themselves part of the story. They'd become players. Their coverage of the domestic crisis completed the process begun in previous decades. News media were now an integral part of the political culture. Television especially no longer simply conveyed information to the public. It now shaped the political process itself.

The arrest of eight of the so-called radical leaders resulted in a comic show trial before a prejudiced, incompetent judge named Julius Hoffman, who frequently turned away in his chair when defense attorney William Kunstler spoke. The Chicago 8: SDS leader Tom Hayden, anti-war organizer Rennie Davis, pacifist Dave Delinger, Yippies Abbie Hoffman and Jerry Rubin, Black Panther Bobby Seale and student activists, Lee Weiner and John Froines. Shouting matches in the courtroom drove Judge Hoffman to have Bobby Seale bound and gagged. Hoffman finally separated him from the proceedings to avoid a mistrial. Seale's crime was two short speeches he gave in Chicago before leaving town.

The Chicago 7
—Chicago Conspiracy Trial

The Chicago 7 represented a cross section of 60s' radicalism. The Justice Department, working what was essentially a legal scam through Hoover's COINTELPRO, created this "conspiracy" and fed it to Chicago authorities. Tom Hayden was charged with stealing hubcaps. Their convictions, inciting to riot and contempt, were overturned on appeal. The government never had a case.

But that wasn't the point. This trial and many like it (such as the Catonsville 9) served the government's purpose by sapping money and energy from a movement that was a fragile amalgamation of disparate groups often with competing agendas. In the end, legal pressure helped destroy the New Left and the anti-war movement.

       *   *   *

Sports is a salve. Through demonstrations of excellence, sports can also be an avenue for protest against prejudice. The most famous example of this was Jesse Owens' track wins in Munich in the 1938 Olympics. Hitler left in a huff rather than concede the righteousness of the victory. Athletes uplift the world by replacing bitterness with grace. They inspire. They give hope. At least they should.

Black Power
—the Mexico City Olympics

American track stars Tommie Smith and John Carlos placed first and third in the 200 meters. At the awards ceremony they raised black-gloved fists during the national anthem and were promptly dismissed from the team. No one with even a passing knowledge of history would deny the sins of the past, still visited upon the present. This act, however, was about as graceless a performance from world class athletes as could be found—then. From this time forward, undisciplined athletes began to destroy the dignity of sports.

This was also the last Olympics in which we defeated the Soviet Union, 95 medals to 61.

Black discontent was real even if the Olympic protest was misguided. Inner city problems were deepening. White America declared everything that needed to be done had been done and suggested blacks were soiling their own nests. Any unrest was the fault of a few malcontents (like Smith and Carlos) encouraged by liberal wimps too weak to call a spade a spade.

It will always be the gravest of misfortunes that LBJ's investigation into the Long Hot Summers was released to a nation of doubting Thomases.

"Our nation is moving toward two societies, one black, one white, separate and unequal."
—National Advisory Commission on Civil Disorders

In late February, the Kerner Commission rejected notions that the Long Hot Summers were the work of a communist conspiracy. Its report made clear that police brutality was igniting the already volatile streets. Empanelled in July 29, 1967 by LBJ in response to the terrible Detroit insurrection and chaired by Ohio Governor Otto Kerner, the commission issued a strikingly dire portrait of the future of race relations. It accused white America of fostering an "explosive mixture" of poverty, poor housing, dismal education and few job opportunities and then turning a blind eye to the police brutality used to maintain the ghetto. "…[W]hite institutions created it, white institutions maintain it, and white society condones it."

Ironically, the report was re-stating a warning issued a hundred thirty years previously by Alexis de Tocqueville. "The most formidable of all ills that threaten the future of the Union arises from the presence of a black population upon its territory." The commission urged the government to create new jobs, better housing, reduce segregation and provide a "national system of income supplement." Pie-in-the-sky in those increasingly reactionary times. LBJ ignored the suggestions and concentrated instead on beefing up urban police forces with more men and equipment, and better riot training.

Concern for the rural and urban poor was not always a priority, even among blacks. The Civil Rights Movement concentrated on middle class issues. The 1963 March on Washington for Jobs and Freedom mainly lobbied for the Civil Rights Act of 1964, which would have its greatest impact on the middle class. As core issues switched to black poverty and degradation, institutional racism became the target.

Yet, without a man like King to lead the attack, nothing much was accomplished. Like so many others, he'd retained a liberal faith in the power of the federal government to correct grave wrongs. History was on his side. The 13th Amendment ended slavery. No state, local or personal action could have done that. The same held true for Jim Crow, ended by federal legislation. What about institutional racism? King's death ended the possibility for a unified voice on this vital question.

Resurrection City

—Poor People's Campaign

All pretence of racial unity ended in the mud on the Mall. With King gone, his lieutenant Ralph Abernathy tried to lead the troubled march of 50,000 into DC. His efforts were severely weakened by a power grab by militant nationalists. Unlike its 1963 counterpart, it also lacked a concrete legislative agenda. The campaign foundered in torrential May rains. The 2,600 residents at Resurrection City, which looked like a Hooverville from the Great Depression, melted away to 124 lost souls, who were finally removed by police.

Something should have been done. Poverty was endemic. Jobs were scarce, housing rotten, and the establishment reluctant to open its doors. The opposite happened. Congress ended the War on Poverty and other Great Society programs. Not all of them worked. But damn few had the chance to prove themselves.

> ### *"If you're not part of the solution, you're part of the problem."*
>
> **—Eldridge Cleaver**

This gem from Cleaver's *Soul on Ice* summed up the dilemma. The status quo was the enemy. Much needed to be changed to alleviate the problems defined by the Kerner Commission. The more the problems were detailed, however, the stronger the resolve of those determined to block the solutions. The status quo was fighting back. It was called...

The Southern Strategy

—backlash

And it won the day. At a time of national crisis, the country got a president driven by suspicion, prejudice and resentment. In November Richard Nixon rode the backlash into the White House. From there he began re-shaping electoral politics around the South, turning white anger to his advantage. Taking his cue from George Wallace's wide national appeal, he devised his Southern Strategy that championed states' rights conservatism against liberal federal interventionism. He played white against black, middle class against poor, cynicism against idealism, old against young, and prejudice against toleration—torturing an already tortured nation. Ultimately, this would lead to the southernization of American politics, with the South itself becoming a solid base for the GOP. In the cruelest of all ironies, boomer activism and idealism wound up handing the country to the reactionaries.

*   *   *

Crushed idealism can be as great a catalyst for change as idealism itself. Schools were over-crowded. Educational facilities were stretched. College campuses lacked enough beds, classroom space and teachers. Even so, things other than beds were on the agenda.

The Year of the Student

—7 million boomers go to college

In 1955 just 2.7 million were in college. By 1968, counting up from elementary school, one third of the population was in school. Twenty-five universities had thirty thousand students each. College enrollment increased by 50% in five years.

Baby boomers were everywhere. And everywhere we made our presence felt.

Generation Gap

—cultural chasm

On April 23 and for a week thereafter, upwards of one thousand Columbia University students occupied several campus buildings, including the president's office, in protest of the school's eviction of black families from their homes to make way for a new gymnasium. Police wielding billyclubs forcibly removed them, arresting 692. Columbia ended its Spring semester early.

As much as this was about racism, opposition to institutional support of War and student anomie in a large school environment, this was also a generational uprising. Sheer weight of numbers meant we would have an impact no matter what we did. We had as infants, toddlers and children. Now as young adults. No one, not Dr. Spock, our parents, or even ourselves foresaw the grassroots youth movement that had reached both coasts and linked up in the heartland like a generational transcontinental railroad. Young hearts and minds united in the freshness of ideas and intensity of outrage at the condition of their world.

Overburdened by numbers and beset by angry students, centers of learning became the focal point of protest. Arguments that these schools, the pride and privilege of our democracy, were instruments of oppression were absurd. The real deal was something else. They happened to be where legions of baby boomers came together the first time they were away from their parents.

To the adults the phenomenon represented a rejection of their struggles and sacrifices through depression and war. To the students, their children, it was one generation taking another's hypocrisy to task. Hypocrisy in race and poverty. Hypocrisy in materialism. Hypocrisy in the loss of neighborliness that accompanied the rise of "plastic" consumer culture. Hypocrisy in championing liberty while fighting an immoral war. Raise kids to expect more and they will.

Colleges and universities were the closest targets, much as the police were for the ghetto poor. As such they bore the brunt of student anger. In December gun-toting black students seized an administration building at Cornell demanding more black studies courses. They appeared to believe "education came through the barrel of a gun." At San Francisco State University, agitating black students linked with the SDS to organize a student strike. At South Carolina State, police shot three demonstrating students dead. Protest south of the Mason-Dixon Line still carried more danger. The murders became known as the Orangeburg Massacre.

Universities are designed to be agents of change. By 1968 change couldn't come fast enough for a generation that found itself being roundly condemned for its high ideals and higher moral standards. It became the mantra of our parents that we were too idealistic, too high-minded.

The protests spread world-wide. For a time this worldwide revolt of the young reached as far as China's Cultural Revolution. In many ways it represented the first large-scale reaction to the shift from an industrial society that still favored island communities and autonomous neighborhoods to the postmodern society with little privacy and the diminished regional and cultural identity of McLuhan's Global Village. Because the world didn't reflect our upbringing and because we were a generation with remarkable unanimity, we reacted the way people often react to inexplicable, uncontrollable change.

We were everywhere.

The Merry Month of May
—international student movement

That spring students rioted in New York City, Berkeley, Toronto, London, Rome, Milan, Belgrade, Prague and other cities. In Paris they tore up pieces of the sidewalk to throw at the police, and almost brought down the government. Mexico City police killed 350 peacefully demonstrating students. In West Germany students rioted after an assassin wounded their leader Rudi Dutschke. Vietnam and racism were partial causes. However radical the protesting students were—and they were regardless of the country—all of them dwelled on their strangled sense of living in an impersonal society. The basic causes were strikingly similar:

intransigent bureaucracies serving antidemocratic institutions through inhumane technologies.

In one form or another, in one country or another, students were spewing...

"non-negotiable demands"

—student radicals

Demanding greater freedom, less parental control, more governmental action but less government oversight, they attacked the very authorities from whom they expected solutions. The fit of generational pique was monumental. The problems were legitimate, as were expectations for solutions. The nuclear arms race, the war in Southeast Asia, poverty, repression, free speech, ethnic prejudice—all were hardly issues of interest only to café society.

What so startled the watching world was the violence that met these protests. Far more of the turmoil came from the establishment than the counterculture.

    *   *   *

Prague Spring

—Czechoslovakian uprising

In August when Soviet tanks rolled across the Czech border to crush the reforms of leader Alexander Dubcek, a light went out in the firmament. The Soviets reversed Dubcek's mild liberalization, banned new political organizations, censored the press, and curtailed public gatherings—dashing hope with the bitter determination of a Bull Connor. This repression should have become a rallying point.

Instead, it was allowed to fade from view, proving that freedom is relative. Repression for the Berkeley Free Speech Movement would have been a paradise of openness for the students in Prague.

Americans were so preoccupied they hardly noticed. They could only pause to observe in horror. When anti-war movement leaders refused to criticize the Soviets, they lost more credibility than a thousand Chicago show trials. Chicago 7 attorney William Kunstler said infamously he made it policy "never to criticize socialist countries." His reasoning was every bit as faulty as our policies in Vietnam. America may have had problems, but these problems did not compare to communist totalitarianism.

Indifference to the crushing of the Prague Spring should have shown us that even movement leaders had feet of clay. We should have been in the streets in front of the Soviet embassy in DC and legations across the country shaking our fists and screaming epithets at those cold gray walls. To the movement's eternal discredit, the reaction was muted and typically self-absorbed.

*   *   *

While tanks rolled through the streets of Prague, feminists in the SDS journeyed to Atlantic City to protest a long-simmering issue.

Sisterhood is Powerful
—Women's Liberation

Women's Liberation burst onto the scene when movement women announced their intention to protest the September Miss America Pageant. Men in the New Left greeted them with catcalls, all they needed was to get laid. Activist women, as with their predecessors among the Abolitionists, felt constrained by male domination. They re-learned the lesson. Racial, ethnic, class egalitarianism stopped at the gender divide.

On the boardwalk in Atlantic City women tossed bras, girdles, high heels and "other items of oppression" into a "Freedom Trash Can." The "bra-burning" myth began when *The New York Times* compared these actions to anti-war protesters burning their draft cards. Women in the Civil Rights Movement and the New Left complained that their only access to leadership was through their boyfriends and husbands. King, Abernathy cut a wide swath through the corps of female supporters. Stokely Carmichael framed this attitude best when he said, "the only position for women in SNCC is the prone position."

Women's Liberation would change this in a hurry. As women began to share their experiences in *consciousness raising* groups, a groundswell surged with the power of nature herself. This remarkable change among middle class women, who had been raised to compete against one another for the best husband, transformed the so-called "war between the sexes."

Equality for women struck a responsive chord. Women, not blacks, were the true second-class citizens. As a practical and legal matter, blacks weren't really citizens until 1965. As early as that year two women members of SNCC and SDS had circulated a letter arguing the similarities "between treatment of Negroes and treatment of women in our society as a whole...It is a caste system which, at its worst, uses and exploits women." When movement men ridiculed these early charges, women began a journey that would lead to the conclusion that when it came to sex the movement was no different than the establishment. The "free love" advocated by the counterculture (and by anti-war radicals, "Girls say yes, to men who say no.") wherein women were supposed to reject the double standard by sleeping around, played into the hands of horny men who got more pussy with less responsibility for it.

Women took to the streets to demand an end to all forms of gender discrimination, including equal pay and promotion for equal work and fair credit requirements. Benefiting from the groundwork laid by the Civil Rights Movement, Women's Lib amassed broad support.

Nowadays it is hard to imagine a world in which sexual discrimination was more pervasive than racism. Yet, into the 70s women were not considered physically capable of rigorous sport and exercise. As a matter of course, they were excluded from men's clubs and bars. Moreover, their demands for equal treatment were dismissed as "penis envy." By nature, women were weak, passive and shy. How odd it all now sounds to our restructured perceptions. That's because of breathtaking change that turned such laughable ideas into anachronistic exceptions.

The women's movement became the most successful Sixties protest movement, dwarfing the significant gains made by blacks. Demands—and legislation—for gender equality spread rapidly, initially meeting far less resistance than either civil rights or opposition to the War.

   *   *   *

Aspects of the counterculture began to spread into mainstream America. The War was now the defining issue. It had so upset domestic equilibrium that change was not only possible, it was welcomed. And the mainstream momentarily flirted with the presumed alternatives.

"This is the dawning of the Age of Aquarius."

Hair, on Broadway

This "American Tribal Love-Rock Musical" caused a sensation. The nudity, the bad-mouthing, the rock 'n' roll had patrons lined up around the block. The play about the War, racial and social problems was more than mere sensationalism. It contained equal parts naivete and enthusiasm, which more or less characterized the era.

> *"Harmony and understanding,*
> *Sympathy and trust abounding*
> *No more falsehoods or derisions*
> *Golding living dreams of visions*
> *Mystical crystal revelation*
> *And the mind's true liberation.*
> *Aquarius!*
> *Aquarius!*

Broadway titillated through 1742 performances at the staid Biltmore Theater. As cast member Paul Jabara called out at the end of the first act, the audience could go home now, they'd caught the nude scene. The real impact aside from the spectacular music was greater acceptance of alternative ideas, especially free love and less restraint. That the country was ready to listen at all showed a general inclination to cast off the rigid conformity of the past.

Slow on the uptake, once Americans began the inexorable move towards the counterculture, they did so with the self-righteous glee of the convert. The next decade—not the 60s—would become the real dawning of the new age. The irony of *Hair* was that its stagy defiance of the straight world on the Great White Way amounted to a sellout of the very values it claimed to promote. For the counterculture it was a huge mistake. To be effective it had to remain outside the mainstream. It wasn't entirely the fault of youthful freaks. Madison Avenue ad execs knew a good thing when they saw it. Had the flower generation resisted, the results would have been pretty much the same. The counterculture would have been co-opted by the consumer culture. The Age of Aquarius was too good for business.

Revolutions succeed then fade. A 1977 revival of Hair closed after forty-three performances. Hippiedom's novelties had run their course. Milos Forman's faithful 1979 movie adaptation met with only moderate success.

But that was ten years down a long road. Meantime, fresh ideas were still flooding society. New ways of living, greater environmental awareness, much of which was simply old ways revivified. Teepees and wood stoves were re-born with long hair and sandals.

The Whole Earth Catalogue

—Stewart Brand

Reading like the Sears Catalogue from Strawberry Fields, this 128-page catalogue became the bible of alternative lifestyles. It featured natural foods, hand-made furniture, geodesic domes, camping equipment and other hippie accoutrements. By its third edition in 1970, it was a best seller, further indication that alternative values were moving into the mainstream.

*   *   *

For a brief period, even as protest movements splintered and sank into the insanity of revolutionary violence, the energy for positive change sparked a cultural renaissance.

the Unisex look

—counterculture fashion

Fashion worn by both sexes. Straight long hair, headbands, bell-bottom blue jeans, gauzy shirts, olive drab army surplus jackets, sandals, love beads, accentuated by lots of rings, bracelets and necklaces. Along with anything that smacked of eastern mysticism: caftans, tunics and Afghan coats—all of it reeking of incense. England added Mary Quant, who invented the mini-skirt (definitely not unisex), and the Carnaby Street look, which favored Edwardian velvet jackets and pants and ruffled shirts. Second hand clothes emphasized the down-to-earth, anti-materialistic approach to living—which made vintage clothiers big business. A year or two later unisex went mainstream.

As did counterculture irreverence.

Sock it to me!

—Rowan and Martin's Laugh-In

This humorous variety show offering off-beat (for those days) skits and humor replaced the Man from U.N.C.L.E. Goldie Hawn was a featured player. Artie Johnson was the dirty old man Tyrone C. Horni and the Nazi behind the bush, "Veeeerrry interesting." Ruth Buzzi played the old lady with the handbag. That famous stiff Richard Milhous Nixon, then running for president, showed up to pose the question, "Sock it to *me?*" No, but given a little room to maneuver, you might one day sock it to yourself, old boy.

*   *   *

How's this for absurd?

The Heidi Game

—Big Time Sports

On November 17, the Oakland Raiders played the New Jets in the 4 o'clock game. At seven with the Jets ahead and seconds to go, the geniuses at NBC cut away from the game. Why? To air on time a made-for-TV movie about a young Swiss milkmaid with pigtails. Millions of fans missed the Raiders rally for two touchdowns in nine seconds to win the game 43-32. Frenzied fans called in such numbers they blew out the NBC switchboard in New York. For days afterwards the apologetic network aired the final two minutes every chance it got. This was the last time anything would pre-empt sports.

Take another example of the saturation of the absurd.

In-A-Gadda-Da-Vida

—Iron Butterfly

Released on July 8 the album went platinum in a heartbeat. The title came from a drug-induced mispronunciation of "In the Garden of Eden." Its full-sided treatment of a lazy guitar riff and an instrumental solo that sounded like outtakes from a West Virginia sawmill defined the transcendent notion of *heavy*. This dumb tune was best played loud after inhaling large quantities of hell weed in a black-lighted room with grape incense wafting from the ashtray and an uncooperative date ransacking the kitchen for a 500 pound bag of Oreo cookies.

A few years later, this numbing eighteen minute walking rock 'n' roll corpse found its way onto the White House taping system, only to be erased by an hysterical president. He was thinking that the White House was the Garden of Eden and he was protected from getting it socked to him as he socked it to everyone he considered his enemy. And if you believe that, you've bogarted the joint, my friend.

*   *   *

Machines did have their moments, especially those of the thinking variety. We were at a stage of mistrust so profound that as computers came along, we saw them as agents of establishment oppression, yet another unfriendly aspect of technology turning our lives to molded plastic.

"Open the pod bay doors, please, Hal."
—Keir Dullea in *2001: A Space Odyssey*

Perhaps Hal was too busy grooving to "In-A-Gadda-Da-Vida."

Mysticism or fine film making? Yes. This epic introduced us to the wonders of computer-generated special effects and a plot line so short on exposition it prompted our minds to take high flight. Stanley Kubrick's leap of imagination was breathtaking. From before the Stone Age to well into the Space Age at the toss of a femur. HAL 9000 personified the anti-technology bent of the counterculture. "He" was portrayed as inhumane and only superficially friendly to mere mortals. But the trip through hyperspace was outta sight.

Dave's cosmic journey to "Jupiter and Beyond the Infinite" only to wind up in some alien museum did not exactly mimic the attraction of the open road. Had he not met such a Dantesque fate, Keir Dullea's character, Dave, might have become cinema's ultimate biker. As it turned out he became its ultimate museum piece. Not so, your typical biker back on Earth.

Born to be Wild

—Hell's Angels

The song may have been by the mediocre Steppenwolf, but it described public perceptions of this outlaw motorcycle gang, cruising the zeitgeist on their choppers. Their love for the freedom of the open road, their expertise with Harley Hogs, their vaguely martial style of dress, their flouting of convention—all these things made them counterculture icons.

Their apotheosis was short. In the end the thrill of the open road couldn't disguise the fact that this gang killed people, dealt drugs and were less civil than HAL 9000.

Whether social or political, the revolutions of the day often gave way to excess. The Beatles wrote a tune called Revolution castigating these excesses. "So if you're carrying posters of Chairman Mao, you ain't gonna make it with anyone anyhow." The riffs were good. Characteristically, "Revolution" became an anthem for...revolution.

"Why don't we do it in the road?"

—the Beatles

The *White Album* was another stellar achievement, one of their last. A strain of melancholy runs through this double set, even in John's humorous commentary on the immoderate aspects of the sexual revolution.

Were we sniffing our own mortality in the wind? The fervor with which society was going about its business gave at least one jaded observer the idea the country was on a perpetual Candid Camera and loving every minute of it.

*"In the future everybody will be world famous
for fifteen minutes."*

—Andy Warhol

Although the exact date this world famous phrase was coined
remains unknown, it first appeared in print in 1968. Signaling the
growing pervasiveness of the media, it was the signpost up ahead
warning of the growing lack of privacy in a publicity-crazed
twilight zone, where everything and everybody becomes subject
matter for intense, intrusive and unscrupulous scrutiny.

     *   *   *

Yet some public figures weren't scrutinized enough for their own
good.

The Mick

—the last of the fair-haired boys

Blue-eyed, blond-haired, handsome, talented and as self-
destructive as a Hell's Angel, on Memorial Day in Yankee Stadium
in his final year in baseball, he went five for five against the
Senators. The third time in his stellar career. He was 36, with legs
so damaged he was playing first base and hitting a poor .223. That
day he hit two home runs, a double and two singles.

Number 7 had more natural ability than almost anyone who
played the game. Like the boomers who idolized him, he seemed
determined to ignore his biological clock and his own frailties. He
hit a whole lot of home runs, some while seriously hung over, was a
deadly clutch hitter, the fastest man in baseball for a time, won the

triple crown and MVP (three times) and ended his life a burn-out beseeching kids not to do what he did.

Somewhere in the life of this consummate Yankee, a life of athletic triumph and national exaltation, of physical defeat and personal weakness, lies the perfect metaphor for his world and our times. Mickey Mantle was the last hero.

*   *   *

True heroes should not be sports figures. Heroism involves more than athletic prowess. It involves self-sacrifice and a commitment that rises beyond talent and intelligence. Ultimately, it involves total selflessness. The self must be thrown away. The feats performed by three men, who on December 21 rode aloft the largest rocket ever used to launch men into space, defined heroism and saved 1968 from ignominy. For the next three days they made the 238,857-mile lunar voyage, humankind's first, and on Christmas Eve went into orbit around the moon.

"God bless all of you...on the Good Earth."
—Frank Borman

That night with the country transfixed by the televised scenes of the gray lunarscape, command module pilot, Jim Lovell remarked, "The vast loneliness is awe-inspiring and it makes you realize just what you have back there on Earth." The three men then read the first ten verses of the Book of Genesis. "In the beginning God created the heaven and the earth...and God saw that it was good." The moment was humbling.

Mission Commander Borman concluded with healing words for a nation sorely tested during the century's most tumultuous year, a year that left us struck dumb by pain, yet still idealistic enough to awed by their achievement. "And from the crew of Apollo 8, we close with good night, good luck, a Merry Christmas, and God bless all of you—all of you on the good Earth."

Only a country as strong as ours could have survived 1968.

Chapter 25

"The New York State Freeway's Closed, Man."

1969. As the year came to a merciful close, time began to work its magic on the American attention span. Just a few months later, Neil Armstrong broadcast this message at 4:14PM EST on July 21 from the Sea of Tranquility on the Moon. "Tranquility Base. The Eagle has landed."

Tranquility; the American eagle. It was more like America had come back to Earth. Around 10PM, Neil Armstrong opened the hatch and became the first human being to set foot on another body in the universe. The images were grainy and unfocused. The slippery figure moved cautiously down a ladder on the side of the lunar module and launched itself onto the lunar surface. Nineteen minutes later Buzz Aldrin followed.

> *"That's one small step for man.*
> *One giant leap for mankind."*
>
> **—Neil Armstrong**

Humankind's greatest feat since Columbus opened the New World; the most significant event since the birth of Christ. When the space ship Eagle settled into the extraterrestrial dust, all the other problems plaguing our society, even those of race and war, should have assumed the temporary status they deserved. Apollo 11 should have given us perspective. In fact, it was just the reverse. The Apollo project turned out to be a momentary sigh of relief, a diversion rather than a new direction. Race and war were integral aspects of dynamic pressures that led to Neil Armstrong's transcendent steps.

> *Here men from the planet Earth*
> *first set foot upon the moon*
> *July, 1969 A.D.*
> *We came in peace for all mankind*

We went to the Moon to get there before the Soviets. That itself was not so unusual. Nationalistic competition had driven Europeans to the New World. The shame was we found it difficult to enjoy the beauty and the wonder. Walter Cronkite's comment edged this singular event into the ambivalence of the times. "How could anyone want to drop out of a society," he wondered, "that could put a man on the moon?" For all its faults, Abbie Hoffman was forced to admit the establishment had a great "Special Effects Department."

We were proud and humbled…and bored. Just a few short years later, Apollo 17 ended the Moon program after years of carping from "the Portuguese lobby." Space exploration cost too much money and didn't produce any tangible benefits. At the millennium, no one knows when we'll return to Tranquility Base, if ever. The conclusion was inescapable. Without the Cold War Neil Armstrong and Buzz Aldrin would never have taken the giant leap.

*   *   *

The forces at play in our lives were cosmic, difficult to translate into everyday comings and goings. We were all one people united for better or worse on a small blue planet. Hope for a better world shone like a star burst. From the warbled reading of Genesis to the ghost-like men on the moon, it was time to get together. Perhaps the Beloved Community wasn't such an intangible.

> *"Come on, people, now*
> *smile on your brother;*
> *Everybody get together.*
> *Try to love one another*
> *right now."*
>
> **—the Youngbloods**

Written by Chet Powers, originally performed by Jefferson Airplane, *Get Together* was re-released after appearing on the Youngbloods' first album. This one song defined the ethos of the 60s, it captured the spirit that was moving a generation. The plea for brotherly love and cooperation, the impatient cries for Freedom Now! Peace Now! Out Now! The yin and yang of our generation. Exuberant good will, charity and optimism mixed with the urgent belief that if things didn't improve overnight they wouldn't improve at all, and we would slip back into the primordial darkness.

Because we were the first generation in human history to face the real possibility we might be the last generation in human history, we came to believe change had to be immediate. That posed problems. All that change, all that social good would take a lot of work. The challenge to make the world a better place consumed an inordinate amount of time. And ran smack into entrenched power. It had been going on all decade, and would continue.

Berkeley had long been the focal point. All good works/extremism (take your pick) radiated from there. What began as the Berkeley Free Speech Movement in 1964 had a late-decade reawakening in May in a place called...

People's Park
—Community vs. Establishment

As early as 1957 University of California Board of Regents had designated land south of the Berkeley campus for development. It languished. During the 60s it became a "scene of hippie concentration and rising crime." The university tried to evict the squatters with the support of local merchants, who felt the eyesore was bad for business. Local activist Mike Delacour proposed a user-developed community park. On April 20, local people cleared ground of detritus, sowed grass, planted trees and flowers, and even set up playground equipment and distributed free food.

Berkeley's chancellor objected. After meeting with members of the People's Park Committee and giving them time to propose a workable plan for the park, he reneged. In the pre-dawn dark of what became known as Bloody Thursday, 250 law enforcement officers swept the park and an eight block surrounding area. Later that morning workers erected a chain link fence around it. Such peremptory actions produced the inevitable angry demonstration. To everyone's surprise sheriff's deputies fired on the unruly—but unarmed—demonstrators killing one man and blinding another.

Governor Reagan ordered in National Guard helicopters, which covered this largely residential area with tear gas. Such surreal imperviousness produced a sympathetic public reaction, forcing the powers to back off. After months, years actually, the university and activists worked out an agreement allowing People's Park to continue. It has since been designated an historic landmark.

The battle over the park emphasized the confusion of the 60s. The land was legitimately the property of the university to develop as it saw fit to serve university (and student) needs. The need for open space and a community gathering place was just as legitimate and more pressing a problem. Despite our tradition of squatters' rights, the law was clear. To uphold it authorities used force. People took to the streets. Both sides represented competing ideas for change. But where did community needs begin and established interests end? To what degree did Berkeley serve the immediate community, if at all? Was that the school's proper role? How much personal freedom was allowable before it threatened civic order? History favors power over people. The Sixties attempted to reconcile the two.

    *   *   **

Personal freedom has always mattered to Americans. Long before boomers, the self-sufficient loner had become an American archetype. Yet, how could you work for the betterment of society and still...

"Do your own thing in your own time."

—Peter Fonda in *Easy Rider*

The conflicting impulses could not be resolved easily. The romance of the road was never stronger than during the 60s. Although the yearning to experience life in all its variations was not new, it sure felt new. The times pulled us in opposing directions. The road offered the perfect opportunity for self-discovery. *Easy Rider*, the story of two hippies on choppers, didn't present escape so much as fulfillment—on one's own terms. That was the attraction of this quintessential 60s' phrase. Set your own terms and go for it. Don't be stifled by conformity. Explore the world. Pursue your own ideas—and to hell with everything else. The cataclysm at the end of the movie may have come at the hands of rednecks, audiences left the theaters in stunned silence, but the enemy was self-deception. "We blew it," said Peter Fonda at the end, and he was right.

Easy Rider espoused personal freedom and liberation and ended up conveying little more than paranoia. What did Captain America and his pal Billy get wrong? Weren't they just living out a Beat fantasy? Even the Beats recognized that the journey towards nirvana, a journey of self-discovery, wasn't a license to flout social and individual responsibility. The Sixties were never about license. "Do your own thing" didn't mean "Anything goes." Yet that was how it was often taken. And it was a sure-fire recipe for disaster.

In her brilliant dissection of the late 60s, Joan Didion wrote, "…the Sixties ended abruptly on August 9, 1969, ended at the exact moment when word of the murders on Cielo Drive traveled like brushfire through the community (LA), and in a sense this is true. The tension broke that day. The paranoia was fulfilled."

Helter Skelter

—Charles Manson

As events unraveled the feeling of inevitability swirled up from the mud. Bad things were happening and there was nothing to be done about it. Just as the Age of Aquarius reached its zenith in the mountain meadows of upstate New York, a twisted emissary from the nadir reached up and latched onto its ankles.

Although Manson himself didn't participate directly in the mass murder at the estate of Roman Polanski, his followers were acting on his belief in the imminence of a race war when they murdered pregnant actress Sharon Tate and her houseguests, mutilated their corpses and scrawled inflammatory words across the walls in blood. Two days later, with Manson in the lead, they broke into the home of Leon Labianca and committed similarly depraved acts on the man and his wife. Five members of the Manson family, including Manson himself, got life without parole.

Was the Manson family part of Woodstock Nation? They considered themselves hippies, did they not? They lived on a commune and paid lip service to alternate lifestyles. To the masses who went to Woodstock, they were part of a depraved world created by the establishment. To our parents, the Manson family represented their worst nightmares: liberty breeding license, desires replacing standards, their sons and daughters becoming cult killers or victims, or both. For obvious reasons, no generation wanted to claim Charles Manson.

For the moment and despite *Life* magazine's cover photo of the drug-crazed Manson, the Tate murders could be dismissed as more strange doings from kookie California, especially the perpetually strange environs of Hollywood. In the long term, there's no denying Manson's looming presence on the outer fringes of hippiedom. He wasn't the only cult leader of the time. Many more would follow during the cultural anarchy of the next decade.

He struck as DJ's were playing *Get Together* like there was no tomorrow, and there was word on the underground radio stations WHFS in DC, KDNA in St. Louis, KMPX and KSAN in San Francisco, and KPPC in LA of a huge rock festival in Woodstock, New York. It was to be a real happening, the Big Kahuna of all rock festivals, where peace would finally be given a chance. And—get this—Dylan was coming!

"The New York State Freeway's closed, man. Far out."

—Arlo Guthrie at Woodstock

Three days of peace and love and music in conditions that would have tested anyone's resolve. The masses assembled on Max Yasgur's farm outside White Lake in upstate New York by the hundreds of thousands. (The good folks at Woodstock had gotten an injunction.) So many that the fences were overrun and it became a free event. The stage revolved to allow one band to be set up while another played. The spirit was magical. The grounds a swamp. The weather did not cooperate. It didn't matter. Virtually every big name was there except Dylan, the Rolling Stones and the Beatles. The music was wonderful, the spirit of co-operation in the face of disaster was nearly universal, even from the establishment, which saved the weekend with food, water and medical services. For a brief, precious weekend, Woodstock Nation, as Abbie Hoffman dubbed it, made believers out of our parents, and ourselves.

"Good morning, what we have in mind is breakfast in bed for 400,000."

—Wavy Gravy

He of the Hog Farm and lately Ben and Jerry's Ice Cream. Affiliated with the Merry Pranksters, this commune came to Woodstock and whipped up food for the masses forced to sleep on the vast hillside in front of the stage. There was no place else to go. Too many people, not enough space. For a decade the Farm maintained a commune in Tennessee that was self-sufficient right down to home birthing and home schooling. But they will always be remembered best for Wavy Gravy's own tripped-out take on life.

Rollo May saw Woodstock as a "symptomatic event of our time that showed the tremendous hunger, need, and yearning for community." Maybe a million people dropped out and spent time on communes. Alternate lifestyles became an expression of the need for community.

*   *   *

Others seized the day and protested.

Hell no, we won't go.

—the Moratoriums

Moratorium Day took place on October 15. Across the country a million people rallied. One hundred thousand in Boston. In DC Coretta Scott King led a silent march of 45,000 people past the White House. Marchers held a lighted candle in one hand and the peace sign aloft with the other. A poll indicated 55% of the country sympathized with the protests. If true, it was seriously misleading.

The Peace Sign dates from the anti-nuclear movement in Britain. A combination of the semaphore for 'N' & 'D': Nuclear Disarmament. Ultimately it also indicated opposition to the War.

Into the early 70s as the country continued its reluctant turn against the war, it turned with growing vehemence against the anti-war movement. Vice President Agnew's characterization of the demonstrators was applauded by a majority of Americans.

"...an effete corps of impudent snobs who characterize themselves as intellectuals."

—Spiro Agnew

In mid-November the New Mobe, the New Mobilization Committee to End the War in Vietnam, organized another anti-war moratorium. Somewhere between 250,000 and 800,000 impudent snobs (depending upon whose estimate you believe. It was probably under 500,000), most of whom were young, middle class whites, showed up in DC. The dramatic 40-hour March Against Death across Memorial Bridge involved 46,000 people carrying placards each bearing the name of an American soldier killed in Vietnam.

The Moratorium was the largest demonstration in the history of the country to date, anti-war or otherwise. In spite of increased antipathy for the movement, the steady groundswell of opposition to the war was palpable even to died-in-the-wool Hawks. Dr. Benjamin Spock spoke to the crowd, comprised mostly of Spock babies, as did Senator George McGovern, Coretta Scott King and many others.

On November 13 as the Moratorium was getting started, to widespread news coverage, Agnew blasted the press corps, especially the three networks and *The New York Times* and *The Washington Post*, who, he claimed, were critical of the War and uncritical of the anti-war movement. "The views of the majority of this fraternity do not—and I repeat not—represent the views of America." His criticism of the movement and mocking of the press "as nattering nabobs of negativity" struck a responsive chord with the public. While the majority of Americans supported the war effort and the vast majority of news media did likewise, large city newspapers tended to oppose it, as did a visible minority of reporters. What Agnew and the public were reacting to, and they reacted strongly, was the patently elitist mentality of television reportage, regardless of the story.

Not that there weren't a few loud-mouthed, impudent snobs around. Better an impudent snob than a bribe-taking vice president, heh, Spiro?

Days of Rage

—Weatherman

These assholes were worlds worse than Spiro Agnew, the state of Maryland's simpering contribution to the zeitgeist. The Weathermen sought to bring 20,000 "angry youths" to Chicago on October 8 for "Four Days of Rage" to "bring the war home" and "smash the state." The Weather Underground (changed from its original name to overcome sexism) was a fantasy-radical offshoot of the SDS whose members fancied themselves urban guerillas. Most anti-war demonstrators did not share the ideology at all. They simply wanted the War to end. The few who did were as ardent as they were extreme. About 300 showed up in Lincoln Park wearing football helmets and gas masks. Seeing they had no support, even from more radical elements of the various protest groups, these lame nihilists ran through the streets breaking windows, bumping into people and shouting epithets—tactics designed to bring down the establishment, like *fer schur*.

Then they ran into the cops, who gave them the thrashing they deserved, arresting 100. Days of Stupidity would have been closer to the truth. Two months earlier over 400,000 "angry youths" had gone to Woodstock. In another month a million citizens would participate in the Moratorium. The Days of Rage and other such deluded acts carried out by this maladjusted gaggle of spoiled malcontents permanently discredited the movement's worthy goals. The Weather Underground was more out of touch with the spirit of the times than *any* of its establishment enemies. As Todd Gitlin, a former president of the SDS, said of them, "The world having failed their analysis, they rejected it." They also rejected such bourgeois traditions as couples. Everyone was supposed to sleep with whomever they pleased, forcing homosexuality on the unwilling for the sake of political correctness. When this insanity failed, they tried enforced celibacy. Perhaps it never crossed their fevered minds that some traditions last because they organize society in the most rational of ways. That's why Vietnam was a failure of policy. That's why the Weathermen were out of their collective minds.

Although more Moratoria followed in succeeding months, they failed in their prime goal. Well organized, peaceful demonstrations may have gathered the anti-war movement under a more presentable banner, giving it greater strength and respectability, but they failed to change American war policy. They did not stop the war.

Other traditions such as racial discrimination, widespread poverty, and hide-bound status worship have long histories. They become traditions because so many people benefit from them. Sad but true. The flip side of oppression is comfort, often of the many at the expense of the few. In a democracy this can become a certain tyranny of the majority, who have little reason to complain.

The October Moratorium so rattled President Nixon, who lurked behind the blinds during the march past the White House, he struck back with a masterstroke. On November 3, he warned the nation that "North Vietnam cannot humiliate the United States. Only Americans can do that." He appealed to the great sprawling middle classes to see him and his policies through. A precipitous withdrawal, he claimed, would result in a bloodbath. You have to wonder what exactly he considered 58,000 dead GIs and hundreds of thousands of dead Vietnamese.

The Great Silent Majority

—Richard Nixon

When the Silent Majority responded with broad support, Nixon concluded, "We've got those liberal bastards on the run now. And we've got to keep them on the run." Nixon proved himself one of the shrewdest politicians around. How else could this petty, prejudiced, and deeply resentful man have gotten himself elected president of the United States twice? He saw straight to the heart of the matter. Most voters were neither young, nor black, nor poor. They were white and middle class—and they were angry. *Time* made them its Man of the Year. Nixon appealed to race and class prejudice disguised in code words such as "Law and Order" and "the Permissive Society." In doing so, he left an already polarized society deeply riven. Rather than "Bring Us Together" as his campaign slogan promised, he drove us farther apart.

He lied outright during the presidential campaign when he claimed to have a "secret plan" to end the War. What he was really wanted from the Silent Majority was a free hand to continue the slaughter in Southeast Asia in hopes of forcing the NLF and the NVA to come to terms.

One would tend to forget grave moral issues surrounded the War.

"...well planned, well-executed, and successful."
—U.S. Army report on the My Lai Massacre

On March 12, 1968, an infantry company under Lt. William Calley killed at least 109 Vietnamese villagers. The number was probably closer to 400, some of whom were raped and scalped and had their tongues cut out. The story didn't surface until the following year. Talk about a firestorm.

At first the public refused to believe the indelibly grotesque pictures of piles of dead bodies published in *Life* and broadcast on the news. When it did, it felt Calley was a scapegoat who didn't deserve his life sentence. Ever the ethical relativist, Nixon interpreted outrage about American atrocities as an attack on his administration. He released Calley to house arrest during his appeal, which he promised to review personally. The sentence was later reduced to twenty years. In 1975 his conviction was modified to parole. Although 278 American soldiers were convicted for war crimes in Southeast Asia, Calley was the only person ever punished for the My Lai Massacre. The VC and NVA committed similar monstrous atrocities but that sort of justification stultified a country that prided itself on its stellar moral standards.

The country generally fell in line behind Nixon and Calley. Americans so wanted to persist in their belief that this was a good and great nation they turned a blind eye to My Lai. The public never fully overcame the notion that uncovering and reporting this war crime was somehow worse than the event itself.

"We have met the enemy and he is us."

—Pogo

Walt Kelly's famous line summed up the confusion many Americans harbored about the deepening divisions in society and about a nightmare war that was hauling our morals through the rice paddies. Considering all the rancor, this observation by cartoonist and social critic Walt Kelly was right on the mark.

Democracy's self-destructive impulses were not news. Jean-Francois Revel had written eloquently of the "variety of cultures" splintering "democratic societies into separate groups, each battling for advantage and caring little for the interests of others or society as a whole." Since those days, right through the turn of the century, the country has been ariot with disparate interest groups, each wanting to do their own thing at the expense of others. American democracy seemed hell-bent on destroying itself. But we survived the Civil War. We survived the violence and chaos of the 1890s. We would survive this.

*   *   *

There was enough comic relief around to keep everyone sane—and distracted (by distraction). Our ability to manufacture freaks and turn them into stars served to underscore the teeming nature of our endlessly changing culture. Ours was a society that could commit and ignore a My Lai while at the same time producing and embracing a Tiny Tim. Somewhere in the vast and gloriously mushy middle, sanity and stability awaited their turns in the spotlight.

"Tiptoe through the tulips with me."

—Tiny Tim

Forty-eight million people tuned in to watch the marriage of the forty-something Tim to seventeen year old Miss Vickie on the Tonight Show. Named variously Derry Dover and Larry Love, Tiny Tim was, in one way or another, a tad light in the loafers, with his flour-faced, ukulele-strumming, falsetto-voiced, effeminate-gesturing one man sideshow. Born Herbert Khaury, Tim came to national attention on *Rowan and Martin's Laugh-In.* He was the first of our postmodern human cartoons. Tiny Tim's singular presence made the surreal qualities of Farrah Fawcett, Michael Jackson, and Boy George possible. He parodied something, perhaps nothing more than his own bizarre ways.

Tiny Tim was the mainstream's contribution to the era's moveable theater of the absurd. It didn't stop there. On college campuses, on the FM underground, a ridiculous rumor sprouted and found fertile soil in the boomer imagination.

Paul is dead

—drug-induced rumor

It began as a prank at the University of Illinois. For a few months speculation raged that Paul died in a 1966 car crash. We sought clues about this by playing our Beatles records backwards and reading into the symbolism on the covers of *Sgt. Pepper* and *Abbey Road*. "Strawberry Fields Forever" backwards had John saying, "I buried Paul." "Revolution No. 9" chanted, "Turn me on, dead man." Had we smoked a little more pot, maybe he'd risen from the grave on Johnny Carson and married Doc Severinson. Paul turned out to be among the living, although you couldn't prove it from his subsequent music. Protested he to *Life*, "Can you spread it around that I am just an ordinary person and want to live in peace?" Yeah, sure.

"See me, feel, touch, heal me."

—*Tommy*, the Who

You know the dialectic is seriously askew when Paul McCartney claims to be alienated. So why not turn this generational ethic into an opera? Better still a rock opera? God knows there was a lot from which to be alienated.

A rock opera? Sure enough. The Who's Pete Townsend came up with a series of anthems to the day. This grand experiment with the most flexible of all music forms also predicted the cultism that flourished in the 70s. The words of the little lost boy cut off from the world, his damaged senses unable to filter the information into any usable form, spoke to weary hearts and minds. Alvin Tofler called it "overchoice." Most of us called it confusing. The search for sense and sensibility would produce profound cultural changes, not all of which were especially appetizing.

Yet stabilizing influences came along. Thanks to the Great Society's insistence upon noncommercial public broadcasting, a friendly, educational program aired at the end of this tumultuous decade that offered a wholesome morning refuge. Its famous host was none other than...

Big Bird

—Sesame Street

It was a place kids could go to keep the world that produced Tommies at bay. A marvelous place called Sesame Street, where they could sing and play along with Jim Henson's Muppets. Henson had been working with puppets since his freshman year of college, perfecting the funky humor and technical proficiency that became his hallmark. The Muppets were already nationally known by the time PBS asked Henson to develop characters for its new children's show.

These included Ernie and Bert, Oscar the Grouch, Grover, the Cookie Monster, and of course the 8-foot-2-inch Big Bird. The Muppets became the centerpiece of the show that used short entertaining pieces to teach the alphabet, reading, counting and other concepts. Children loved it. So did their parents. At the very least, it was something safe in perplexing times.

*   *   *

Sesame Street stood virtually alone for a time. Acts of flesh and fraud did little to shore up faith in the leadership, especially when venality came from one of the supposed good guys. The Kennedy legacy began its dispiriting decline on a hot day in mid-July. While the nation and the world had their eyes on the Apollo 11 mission to the Moon, we were reminded that indulgence and arrogance might forever restrain our soaring aspirations. That the Kennedys, whose historical legacy promised to rival that of the Adams, would suffer such tragedies during the 60s and the decades that followed, served the ever-painful reminder that no one, not even the people we loved and admired, could escape blows of circumstance, especially those brought on by our own frailties.

"I panicked."

—Teddy Kennedy

What he was really saying was "I got caught." His companion Mary Jo Kopechne drowned in the backseat of his car after he drove off a bridge on Chappaquiddick Island off Martha's Vineyard. Kennedy swam to safety and ten hours later reported the accident. He got a two month suspended sentence for failing to report an accident, but lost his credibility and any real hopes for the presidency. The results of the coroner's inquest were sealed. Rumors of money changing hands have never gone away.

*   *   *

The Civil Rights Movement spawned a dozen protest movements that included the student movement, the New Left, the anti-war movement, the Counterculture, Black Nationalism, the Chicano movement, Women's Liberation, the Gray Panthers, Consumer Rights, Ecology, and the American Indian Movement. Two met with considerably more than raised eyebrows: radical feminism and...

The Stonewall Riots

—Gay Liberation

The 60s forced toleration on a conservative country. A surprising amount of reform met with quick approval. More worked its way into the system over the next decade. Yet toleration and acceptance had their limits. To this day, the public remains uncomfortable with gay rights.

For the once hidden minority, the campaign began on June 17. "Hundreds of young men went on a rampage in Greenwich Village after a force of Plainclothes policeman raided [the Stonewall Inn] that the police said was well known for its homosexual clientele," wrote *The New York Times*. This time homosexuals were moved to stand up against the harassment. Four hundred gay men and women showered the police the following night with bottles and coins when they returned for another sweep of the area. The police rioted; homosexuals shouted, "Gay Power!"

Although a few gay rights organizations had existed since the 50s, this incident proved to be the starting point for political activism that sought to remove the long-standing stigma attached to homosexuality. Of immediate concern was ending physical violence. "Rolling queers" had been a long-standing practice.

Average Americans rejected the street round-ups and repressive violence, but they refused to welcome gays into Normal Neighborhood. Despite this, in several cities and in both the Democratic and Republican parties, gays and lesbians increased their presence and in some cases began to wield real power. Like feminism and abortion, gay rights ran up against a stone wall of consensus, as though the country were saying, This much and no more. Still, the changes wrought were enormous.

*   *   *

Just when you'd think excess had no more bounds, the establishment kicked in with a dose of its own that justified much of the paranoia now flooding the culture.

COINTELPRO

—J. Edgar Hoover

The Bill of Rights meant little to America's Minister of State Security. Hoover's Counter Intelligence Program encouraged, if it did not actually authorize, the pre-dawn, December 4th raid of the Chicago headquarters of the Black Panthers. He considered them as great a threat to national security as communism and made sure they were heavily infiltrated. Using a floor plan supplied by a paid informant, police officers stormed in and killed dynamic leaders Fred Hampton and Mark Clark while they lay in bed. Hampton was asleep beside his pregnant girlfriend. Four days later in LA, police officers engaged in a gun battle with Panthers.

COINTELPRO was the eminence grise behind both actions, supplying intelligence and guidance. Chicago police tried to falsify their account until ballistics experts proved they'd fired ninety-nine shots to the Panthers' one. All charges against the Panthers were dropped. They hadn't violated the law. Their true offense was militant race pride. While no police officers were ever indicted, the FBI was held criminally complicit and forced to pay almost $2 million to the families of the dead and wounded. It didn't matter. COINTELPRO succeeded in decapitating the Panthers, Hoover's goal all along.

By the end of the year, most Panther leaders were dead (twenty-eight), in jail or out of the country. An ill-conceived merger with SNCC and the erratic leadership of Stokely Carmichael, the new organization's Prime Minister, further hastened their demise. With the leadership dead, gone, or so radicalized they no longer related to their followers, the Panthers were finished.

Hoover unleashed COINTELPRO on the New Left/anti-war movement as well. He left them alone until 1968, then he initiated a program of dirty tricks that included harassment, disinformation, fake letters, break-ins, wire taps, agents provocateurs and informers. The Army already had such a program underway. In addition to the murder of the Black Panther leaders in Chicago, perhaps the most famous example of the sort of damage Hoover's KGB-style repression wrought was the death of ex-patriot actress Jean Seberg. Although living in Paris, both she and her husband had been actively opposed to the War. COINTELPRO operatives planted the false story in *Newsweek* that Seberg was pregnant by a Black Panther leader. Her white baby was stillborn; Seberg suffered an emotional breakdown, and after several failed attempts, killed herself in 1979 on the anniversary of her baby's death. Her husband sued *Newsweek* for libel and won.

*   *   *

Sympathy for the Devil

—the Rolling Stones

In December the Stones held a free all-day concert at Altamont Raceway in California to honor guitarist Brian Jones, who'd drowned in his own swimming pool. They hit upon the brilliant scheme of paying the Hell's Angels about $500 worth of beer to provide "security," something they'd done from time to time in the past. The Angels kept order through murder and mayhem. While the Stones were playing "Sympathy for the Devil," an Angel knifed a man to death in front of the stage. The murder was caught on film in *Gimme Shelter* and later judged justifiable homicide. But the damage was done. From the heady highs of Woodstock in August to the speed-driven downs of Altamont, the Age of Aquarius, Woodstock Nation lasted less than half a year. Politics and hedonism did not mix, did not produce a better world. Drugs, self-indulgence and extreme radicalism doomed what held the conflicting aspects of the counter-culture together—a desire to make things better. Elements of the various protest movements and countercultures hung together as long as the freshness of the era permitted. In the end, they had little more in common than contempt for the adult world.

Meanwhile, a budding and equally disillusioned contingent of radically conservative boomers was waiting in the wings for the opportunity to champion many of those same anti-establishment views. In many ways the right was more revolutionary in its assault on values than all but the most wild-eyed left wing head cases. But their day had not yet arrived. The 1960s had ended, but the Sixties were not yet over.

PART IV

Polyester and prevarications...

And now for something completely different
—Monty Python

1970–1980. When people talk of the 60s, they're really thinking of the 70s. For this was when the social and cultural revolutions we associate with the era reached Main Street.

The 60's stirred dreams, raised hopes and spun out of control. The 70's defined *ugly*. Experimentation, mandates for change degenerated. We dragged ourselves through the gutter of self-esteem and human growth movements, bad clothes, worse music, sleazy sex, tawdry cocaine dens called discos, and paperback gurus telling us everything we needed to know about things we didn't need to know about. The prosperity that made reform possible ended with the Arab Oil Embargoes. In place of cheap gas, we got gas lines, soaring prices, and an economy that sputtered and stalled. Inflation drove prices up and optimism down. Both parents had to work. Suddenly it was an era of diminished expectations. Tough going for a generation that expected things to get better simply because they always had. Boomers, who always had so much, were now told to expect much less. It wasn't a popular notion. Tom Wolfe dubbed it the "Me Decade." The decade of me, myself and I.

Those starting a family did so either through naive optimism or desperate desire to escape the swift currents of cultural change. Politically, we witnessed the confirmation of many of our charges, domestic and foreign. Watergate proved we shouldn't trust anyone over thirty. The most self-absorbed person of the decade turned out not to be Timothy Leary, Abbie Hoffman, or a dope-smoking longhair languishing on a commune but the President of the United States, the over-maligned and under-vilified Richard Milhous Nixon. He turned out to be corrupt in a way that seriously damaged the establishment he purported to defend. His corruption wasn't a matter of sex or money. It was a matter of political process. The CIA turned out to be a rogue elephant, stomping on small nations as though they were part of America's private hunt club. As for government, the best advice came from indicted Nixon aide, Gordon Strachan. "Stay away" from Washington, he warned.

And we did. Life was for the individual. The establishment was Mr. Hyde in a double knit suit with the ethics of a coke dealer. Speaking of which, the callow hype of marijuana and LSD gave way to the cynical decadence of Quaaludes and cocaine. While blacks began joining the mainstream, the women's movement, which had sprung from the hypocrisy of other protest movements, brought changes more revolutionary than anything ever envisioned by Martin Luther King, Jr., Malcolm X and especially Stokely Carmichael.

Towards the end of the decade, another significant movement emerged, populated and pushed largely by boomers, promulgated by television, characterized by Christian fundamentalism and called the Fourth Great Awakening. To a generation with hopes blunted by gas shortages, diminished prosperity and Third World levels of inflation, Jesus Freaks made an ironic coda to the alienation our expectant generation had raised to an art form.

Chapter 26

"Four Dead in O-HI-O."

1970. Disaffection was at an all time high. Another Ivy League professor was touting the correct way to achieve a fuller life. What's more, in a collection of articles serialized in *The New Yorker*, he tried to show "How the Youth Revolution is Trying to Make America Liveable." As a book it became a phenomenal best seller.

The Greening of America
—Charles Reich

In Consciousness III, we reject the Protestant Work Ethic of Consciousness I and the power grab, competitive corporate statism of Consciousness II in favor of brotherly love, communal lifestyles and a more realistic sexual morality.

Reich claimed our industrial, consumer-driven culture contributed to the loss of self, an absence of community, loss of democracy and general social disorder. That a liberated consciousness would rise "out of the wasteland of the Corporate State, like flowers pushing up through the concrete pavement." The previous year in *The Making of a Counter Culture*, Theodore Roszak articulated a generational anti-technology revolt "at the non-intellective level of personality," the personal having become obsessively political. Like many others, he perhaps mistook flower children for a permanent fixture. British historian Arnold Toynbee merely considered them a "red warning light of doom for Western Civilization."

Nevertheless, Reich saw and felt the special hunger to create a decent, caring society "notably unaggressive, nonviolent, uninterested in the political game." He gave voice to ideals. We didn't notice that this sort of apolitical approach to reform diverted attention from the political reforms essential to re-creating the world. At the same time journalist David Halberstam took a much tougher stand. "Good-by to all that," he wrote in *McCall's*, "to the Sixties, to all that hope and expectation. It started so well, belief that...all the pieces would come together for a golden era of American social and cultural progress, victory over the darker side of our nature, victory over injustice. It ended in pain, disillusionment, bitterness, our eyes expert in watching televised funerals."

Despite this chilly if all too accurate assessment, what is amazing is the extent to which the public embraced Reich's somewhat spaced-out nostrums. Considering the breadth and depth of the backlash, a surprising amount took hold, at least for a while. "Consciousness III postulates the absolute worth of every human being—every self. Consciousness III does not believe in the antagonistic or competitive doctrine of life." One great example was the growing concern for the world in which we lived.

Save the Planet

—Earth Day

Coming at the time of the fateful Apollo 13 mission, the first Earth Day brought together millions concerned with the effects of rampant industrialization and over-consumption on the environment. The modern ecology movement considered the War part of the same abuse of power by a heedless corporate system that was destroying the environment as well as people and nations in its quest for profits.

Wisconsin Democratic Senator Gaylord Nelson and California Republican representative Pete McCloskey proposed it. Denis Allen Hayes organized it. "It was Earth Day," according *The New York Times*, "and like Mother's Day no man in public office could be against it." Though dominated by boomers, E-Day brought together 20 million Americans from all parts of society. Cities, states and Congress passed legislation supporting stronger measures against pollution and in favor of environmental awareness. The Green Revolution had begun. Earth Day appeared for a brief sunny moment to bring a troubled nation solace. At last most of us could agree upon something. *Most* of us.

*   *   *

Nixon had his own answer to Earth Day. Eight days later, after watching the movie *Patton* twice, he went on television to announce...

The Cambodian Incursion
—America invades a neutral country

Notice the Newspeak, incursion, not invasion. Nixon informed us that a joint US/South Vietnamese operation was going after North Vietnamese sanctuaries inside Cambodia. The nation was outraged. Nixon defended US actions in what was probably the clearest explanation for our presence in Southeast Asia given thus far. "If, when the chips are down, the world's most powerful nation, the United States of America, acts like a pitiful, helpless giant, the forces of totalitarianism and anarchy will threaten free nations and free institutions throughout the world." He offered no answer to American violation of international law. Cambodia was a sovereign nation, and we were invading it. Instead, he pined, "I would rather be a one-term president and do what I believe was right than to be a two-term president at the cost of seeing America become a second-rate power."

The invasion was a failure. We didn't locate the so-called sanctuaries or the much ballyhooed NVA "nerve center." The operation also failed to put a significant crimp in the flow of arms coming down the Ho Chi Minh Trail. The invasion also signaled what was an already well-established fact. This was Nixon's war now. He may have inherited an untenable situation from LBJ, and North Vietnamese violated Cambodian sovereignty first, but his bellicose and illegal tactics in Cambodia and Laos stepped up the fighting even in the face of the withdrawal of American troops.

Cambodia was a non-belligerent nation when Nixon chose to invade it. Although it made clear military sense to attack the NVA supply bases there, Americans were brought up believing their country didn't invade prostrate neutral nations. The American public, slow to anger and even slower to turn against established order, now felt the war was a mistake, that the U.S. ought to withdrawal even if it meant defeat. The ignominious invasion of sleepy, backward, peasant Cambodia pushed a majority of Americans into the negative on the so-called "mistake" question. Pollsters asked, Was the war a mistake? Yes, it was. Should we continue it? No, we shouldn't.

Demonstrations erupted all across the country. Student strikes spread from major universities to small colleges in the heartland, which had steadfastly supported the war effort. ROTC buildings became targets for campus outrage. Possibly twenty-five percent of American university students participated, maybe two million all together. Demonstrations produced such havoc seventy-five campuses closed early for the summer. Protests broke out in most major cities, involving the middle class and blue collar workers, people not part of the anti-war movement.

Reacting to the convulsion, Nixon lashed out against anti-war protesters, "these bums, you know, blowin' up the campuses." Such intemperance gave just enough official approval to cause a violent counter-reaction. Agnew followed with talk of "positive polariza-tion," that is separating the troublemakers "from our society—with no more regret than we should feel over discarding rotten apples from a barrel." In California Governor Ronald Reagan suggested removing the campus radicals from society. "If it takes a bloodbath, let's get it over with. No more appeasement." His aides backtracked, but his outburst reflected Attorney General John Mitchell's cogent prediction. "This country is going so far right you are not even going to recognize it." The right wing counter attack was underway. The consequences were deadly.

"Four Dead in O-hi-o"

—Kent State Massacre

The event that tipped the balance in public opinion took place four days into the "incursion." On May 4, Ohio National Guardsmen fired their M-1 rifles indiscriminately into a crowd of student protesters at Kent State University, smack in the middle of America's heartland. They wounded nine, killed four. A presiden-tial Commission on Student Unrest called the murders "unneces-sary, unwarranted and inexcusable." Typical of the ambivalence brought home by the war, most Americans defended the Guardsmen even as they opposed the operation in Cambodia. Subsequent investigations and lawsuits cleared the Guardsmen of the most serious charges despite evidence indicating these actions *might* have been deliberate and pre-meditated. Even Spiro Agnew called it murder.

Most poignant was the tear-racked reaction of Alison Krause's father. She was one of the slain students. The day before she was gunned down, she put flowers in the barrels of National Guard rifles, saying, "Flowers are better than bullets." Naïve it's true, but hardly cause for murder. Her distraught father was hysterical with grief at the slaying. "My daughter's not a bum," he sobbed to the media from the front porch of his home in Silver Spring, Maryland. The scene shook the country. But the killing didn't stop.

Ten days later, Mississippi police fired into a women's dorm at all-black Jackson State University during a chaotic night of protest, killing two, wounding nine. Though largely ignored, these additional slayings added to national unrest over the War and Nixon's lack of concern.

Cambodia and Kent State and Jackson State temporarily reinvigorated a moribund anti-war movement. Within days of the invasion, millions of people took to the streets against this brazen act of international lawlessness and the domestic tragedies it produced. Thousands of people: professionals, corporate executives, educators, even fifty Foreign Service officers lobbied for an immediate end to the War. Henry Kissinger later wrote that "the very fabric of government was falling apart. The Executive Branch was shell-shocked. After all, their children and their friends' children took part in the demonstrations." By the end of the week a million people had arrived in DC to stage what remains the largest protest in the city's history. Although the country was horrified by the slayings, fifty-eight percent of Americans thought the students were to blame. The polarization continued.

In some sort of half-baked campaign of revolutionary revenge, deluded fools in the Weather Underground vowed to strike back. They bombed fourteen government and military buildings between

1969 and 1974.* On March 6 three of these geniuses crossed the wrong wires in a Greenwich Village townhouse and bade the establishment fond farewell. Two others ran screaming naked from the burning townhouse next door to Dustin Hoffman's, who barely managed to get his paintings off the walls ahead of the smoke and water. In August four terrorists parked a truck bomb by the Army mathematics research center at the University of Wisconsin killing a grad student, who was undoubtedly part of some fascist cabal.

The problem with the fantasies of these spoiled, immature and addle-brained radicals and their random, ill-conceived, half-thought out schemes was that innocent people got killed in the name of intellectual consistency and political correctness. All they succeeded in doing was handing the country over to the very people John Mitchell predicted would come to power. Eventually, they grew up. After the damage was done.

Still, Kent State was unforgivable. The nation mourned. In New York City Mayor John Lindsay ordered the American flag lowered to half-staff over City Hall. This was too much for the right wing to swallow. A resentful Nixon, who'd traveled to the DC Mall early in the morning to talk to demonstrators and ended up lamely trying to talk sports, struck back.

America, love it or leave it.

—the Hard Hat Riot

Organized at his behest by construction union official Peter Brennan, a counter-demonstration (an anti anti-war movement) in New York City pitted wrench-wielding construction workers

---

* 250 bombings in all.

against anti-war demonstrators. As thousands of peaceful demonstrators assembled in front of City Hall at noon on May 8 to hold a vigil for the Kent State casualties, 200 construction workers descended on them. The police stood by. Sound like Birmingham?

When a postal worker raised the flag to full staff, an aide to the mayor re-lowered it. Incensed, the hard hats rioted. Swarming past the police, over parked cars, chanting, "Kill the Commie bastards" and "All the way with the USA," they singled out long-haired males, whom they thought were sissies and female wannabes who had betrayed the tough, patriotic frontier image of what it meant to be a man. They drove the demonstrators off the plaza, going through them "like Sherman went through Atlanta," as someone noted. With order gone, the rioters moved to the close-by campus of Pace College randomly attacking students, injuring seventy-five seriously enough to put them in the hospital. Nixon rewarded Brennan by appointing him Secretary of Labor.

Hard hats also attacked anti-war demonstrators in St Louis. All part of Nixon's successful war on the movement. That's not to say, as Herbert Marcuse claimed, that the movement didn't die but was murdered. The movement was already fractured from within. The irrational radicalism of factions such as the Weather Underground and indiscriminant feminist attacks on men weakened it to the point that for many it just didn't seem worthwhile anymore. They were burned out. The SDS fell apart in 1969. According to Todd Gitlin, it had already "degenerated into a caricature of everything idealists find alienating about politics-as-usual: cynicism, sloganeering, manipulation." When it traded morality for violence, revolution for reform, resistance for protest, it stuck a knife in its own heart. Repression from the Nixon administration delivered the coup de grace.

*　　　　　　　　　*　　　　　　　　　*

One group gained momentum.

Don't Iron while the Strike is Hot

—Women's Strike for Equality

On a suggestion by Betty Friedan, NOW declared a nationwide commemoration of the 50th anniversary of the ratification of the 19th Amendment. On August 26th thousands of women boycotted work, housework, or brought the kids to Dad at his workplace. On the surface, this was a joyous celebration of something long overdue. "It made all women feel beautiful. It made me feel ten feet tall," said one feminist. Kate Millet told a gathering of 40,000 in New York City, "Today is the beginning of a new movement." Women's Liberation had come of age. Indeed, many states responded with corrective legislation. Twenty-six states still kept women from certain jobs. Twenty limited them to eight-hour days. Congress would follow suit in 1972 by passing the Equal Rights Amendment and sending it to the states for ratification. Abortion rights soon came before the courts. Popular culture responded with *The Mary Tyler Moore Show*, spinning off *Rhoda* and *Maude* two years later. All shows portrayed women as much more independent and less wedded to men and tradition.

Unfortunately, just as other movements had gone off the deep end, some feminists couldn't resist. Although a distinct minority, radical feminists turned on men with vehemence equal to the New Left's anti-establishment rhetoric. All men were the same as far as they were concerned. They were all...

male chauvinist pigs

—"patriarchal male oppression"

Relationships were bourgeois. Marriage was slavery. Sexual intercourse was rape. True, New Left men got a healthy dose of their own medicine. But in embracing ludicrous positions that were blatantly irrational, these feminists crippled their own movement at the peak of its power.

As radical feminists gained status within the women's movement, they pushed such issues as lesbian rights, bisexuality and women as another colonized minority. Such vitriol forced mainstream feminists to accept such outré notions as political lesbianism, a nonsexual version of homosexuality. NOW was moved to endorse gay rights, where Betty Friedan once considered lesbians the "lavender menace." Its new president, who was married with children, bragged about having a girlfriend on the side. The sainted Gloria Steinem gloated, "A woman needs a man like a fish needs a bicycle." The organization's new slogan was, "Out of the mainstream, into the revolution."

These controversial ideas accelerated a backlash that may well have arisen anyway. Radical feminists attacked all men, whom they considered oppressors, without regard for their station in life and attributed to them all things evil: war, racism, poverty, the class structure, you name it.

"Goodbye to All That," wrote Robin Morgan in an all-feminist issue of *Rat,* an underground newspaper, "Goodbye, Goodbye forever, counterfeit left, male-dominated cracked-glass-mirror reflection of the Amerikan nightmare. Women are the real left." This after male radicals hooted down women speakers at the January 19 counter-inaugural. They didn't want to listen to feminist rhetoric. In newspapers such as *Off Our Backs* and *Notes from the First Year* that featured articles and position papers like *"The Myth of the Vaginal Orgasm," "The Politics of Housework"* and *"The Personal is Political,"* they championed a society not only dominated by feminist thought, but by women.

Not only men reacted negatively. Most women did as well. Most women—fundamentalist Christians excluded—wanted political, social and economic opportunity. Not an exchange of one tyranny for another. After all, tens of thousands of boomer women were entering the workplace. Radical attacks against male chauvinism only alienated natural supporters and isolated the movement from the once receptive mainstream. By launching wild-eyed broadsides against all things male, all things traditional—and by insisting that women were as oppressed as blacks—radical feminists destroyed their own credibility. They turned a worthwhile reform movement into a caricature of self-indulgent solipsism. As black feminist bell hooks wrote, "Feminists praise self-centeredness and call it liberation." The Personal is Political had become the personal at the expense of the commonweal. In fact, feminism reached a point where it ridiculed the commonweal.

Now under attack from former allies, many activists found reason to discontinue their support. Indeed, as reporter Sally Quinn would write in 1992, "Many women have come to see the feminist movement as anti-male, anti-child, anti-family, anti-feminine. And therefore it has nothing to do with us."

*   *   *

The thing was, a whole lot more than feminism had less and less to do with "us." Disenchantment with the slow, bureaucratic and too often unyielding nature of change in America turned into a game of Truth or Dare—even among the Beautiful People. With all the sincerity of a Doris Day epic, Park Avenue salons began to open their rarefied doors to revolutionary radicalism.

Radical Chic

—Tom Wolfe

When thirteen Black Panthers strolled warily through the doors of the Leonard Bernstein's New York apartment on January 14, a society matron exclaimed, "These are no civil-rights Negroes wearing gray suits three sizes too big—these are real men!" Like she knew. As real men and real radicals, they spouted real cant to a really attentive audience that included Barbara Walters and Otto Preminger, assembled to raise money for the Panther 21, yet another group of real, incarcerated radicals. Neither the Panthers nor their esteemed hosts or guests had ever put their lives on the line during the Mississippi Freedom Summer, either.

This wasn't really "elegant slumming," a criticism Leonard and his wife went to great lengths to deny. Some of the Beautiful People were bound to be concerned and involved. No, this was indolence of the sort that would produce in other quarters the hedonistic excesses that gave the Moral Majority credibility. In fact, there had been several radical chic fetes. Previous events aided various radicals, including Friends of the Earth, Bernadette Devlin, and the Young Lords, a Puerto Rican gang that was felt to approximate the Black Panthers.

Ray "Masai" Hewitt, Black Panther Minister of Education, gave his spiel denouncing, as Wolfe wrote,

> *"that motherfucker Nixon (to general approval) and advocate that as Maoist Revolutionaries they were dedicated to overthrowing the Establishment, by force if necessary, (which he thought it was, and to general skepticism), one of the Beautiful People suggested, 'He's a magnificent man, but suppose some simple-minded schmucks take all that business about burning down buildings seriously?' As an art gallery owner got up to leave, he asked the closest Panther in dead earnest 'Who do you call to give a party?'"*

The revolution died that cold bright, chi-chi evening in January.

*   *   *

A turn away from political protest was inevitable. In doing so, we sought to make leaders out of people who'd escaped the mundanity of daily life. People who'd dropped out by rising above and seemed to live unconstrained lives. We vested rock musicians with qualities worlds beyond their ability to stand and deliver. Given the power and freedom exhibited by the new cultural phenomenon known as Rock Stars, we tried to make them political experts, cultural sages and moral guardians—with predictable results.

"Take a piece of my heart now, baby."

—more dead rock stars

Our assumption of their wisdom, our uncritical adulation of their every witless remark underscored their limitations and fueled their excesses. We made heroes out of musicians, people not known for their restraint or sense of responsibility. Just four and a half years after leaving Austin, TX, Janis Joplin overdosed on heroin— two weeks after Jimi Hendrix drowned in his own vomit. Appearing on the *Tonight Show* he'd been asked to discuss religious significance of his music. He responded, "That's heavy...I'm stoned, man." Replied befuddled guest-host, Flip Wilson, "I can dig it." The following year Jim Morrison died in Paris, a physical and mental burn-out. Other rock stars followed. Bob Dylan came perilously close. In 1977 the King himself crapped-out after years of self-abuse.

*   *   *

It was beginning of an ugly decade. Failed leaders, war, mindless excess, narcissism, drugs, disco and hideous clothes—wantonly hideous clothes. Fashion described the self-destructive bent upon which we'd embarked.

Polyester

—fashion statement

For the first time polyester passed cotton in the textile market, 41% to 40%. With it came cheesy double knits, garishly patterned clothes, ultra wide bell-bottoms, hip huggers, designer blue jeans, and stacked heels, all of which played well at the local disco. The fashions of the 70s were tacky—matching the times perfectly. The mini skirt gave way to the midi as women entering the workplace found the short, panty-flashing minis a bit unpractical. On Earth Day in Denmark, Anna Kalso released the pumpkin-colored Earth Shoe. The clunky, practical shoes, designed after the heel below toe imprint the foot makes in the sand, went well with the sideburns and moustaches men began wearing.

What was needed was a dose of the old fashion.

     *   *   *

The most repeated line of the decade. *Time* hailed it as a return to romance.

"Love means never having to say you're sorry."

—Ali McGraw in *Love Story*

Parental insensitivity was a vital ingredient of Erich Segal's huge 115-page novel that sold 21 million copies in 33 languages. Maybe it was banal, as William Styron huffed, but it struck a chord. In the faithful movie adaptation, also by Segal, Ryan O'Neal played the drippy Oliver Barrett IV, who was loosely based on Al Gore. His class-conscious WASP of a father refused to accept his young déclassé wife. In the end he apologizes. But, as Jenny dying from leukemia, Ali McGraw gets the last word. An updated, more sensitive but dimwitted version, of "Frankly, my dear, I don't give a damn."

*   *   *

The new sensitive male was still a few years away. Meantime, the macho man of football threw in his cleats.

> ### *"Winning isn't everything— it's the only thing."*
> ### —Vince Lombardi

He led—or rather browbeat—the Green Bay Packers into one of football's greatest dynasties, winning six divisional and five NFL titles. But it was his hard-nosed, root-hog-or-die attitude that made him a legend. Stressing the fundamentals of blocking and tackling, he claimed, "Statistics are for losers." Winning and nothing else defined competition. Vince Lombardi personified its narcotic effect on the national psyche. After a brief and restive retirement, he came back the year before he died to give the patsies known as the Washington Redskins its first winning season in fourteen years.

Chapter 27

Have a Nice Day

1971. In response to military action in Laos, the Weather Underground set off a bomb in the Senate wing of the United States Capitol at 1:31 AM on March 1. The bomb destroyed a bathroom and injured no one. Their communiqué said in part:

> We have attacked the Capitol because it is, along with the White House and the Pentagon, the worldwide symbol of the government which is now attacking Indochina. To millions of people here and in Latin America, Africa, and Asia, it is a monument to U.S. domination over the planet. The invaders of Laos will not have peace in this country.

Suspecting she knew one or more of the bombers, the FBI detained one young woman for days grilling her for information. She knew nothing. That was as close as they ever got to arrests. The explosion's shrill message echoed well beyond the marble hallways. Desecration of this shrine of freedom wasn't protest. It wasn't resistance. This was terrorism, and rather counterproductive terrorism at that. The sympathy candle many Americans had reluctantly lighted to end the war flickered in this ill wind. A few months later it went out entirely.

"Close down the government!"
—May Day demonstrations

Beginning April 24, 200,000 demonstrators converged on DC for what was to be the anti-war movement's last gasp. Vowing to prevent the government from operating, these now full-fledged rejectionists, spread through downtown areas like two-legged cockroaches. Random groups of demonstrators fleeing from head-smashing Civil Disturbance Units along K Street broke an occasional window and looked more like juvenile delinquents than political dissidents. As members of the Peoples Coalition for Peace and Justice and the radical May Day Tribe blocked traffic, slashed tires and made a general nuisance of themselves, many citizens pleaded with them to try a little common sense. "You're alienating me," they exclaimed. Rain falling on damaged waters.

Seeking to forestall further violence, DC police and federal troops swept West Potomac Park where 30,000 protesters were camped. It was a brilliant, though legally dubious preemptive move. (The pretext was rampant drug use.) Police violated civil rights without compunction. They crammed many of the 7,000 arrestees into a fenced-in retaining pen on the Redskins' practice field next to RFK Stadium. The courts threw out all but 200 cases. Almost all had committed no crime. A little over a month later Nixon revived the Subversive Activities Control Board, dormant for twenty years. Terrorism led to even more repression. Nixon needn't have bothered. Although the radical impulse still had some strength, the divisions among the remains of the New Left were deep. Subversion by the Nixon administration had been too effective.

Vietnam Veterans Against the War joined these demonstrations. Founded in 1967, the VVAW had by this time become the most influential anti-war group. People who loathed the anti-war movement would listen to these men and women who'd been there, many of them out in the shit for thirteen months. Vets testified before Congress that the My Lai Massacre had not been an aberration. On April 27, in perhaps the saddest day of the entire war, over one thousand threw their battle medals onto the steps of the Capitol. Numb from years of demonstrations and violence, the country was nevertheless moved by the sight of ex-GIs expressing their sense of betrayal.

"The History of U.S. Decision-Making Process in Vietnam"
—the Pentagon Papers

Resistance had taken on subtler more effective forms. Insiders opposed to the war embraced some or all of the anti-war reformist ideology. Their actions had important consequences. On June 13, *The New York Times* began publishing excerpts of this study commissioned in 1967 by then Secretary of Defense Robert McNamara. *The Washington Post* and other papers followed in close order. The revelations about government duplicity shocked the nation. Historian John Morton Blum, claimed the papers, "revealed a depressing record of mistaken assumptions, prevarication, and flawed judgments" that cost tens of thousands of American lives.

Although the study covered only the years LBJ was president, 1964-68, Nixon mistakenly believed Daniel Ellsberg and Anthony Russo, the former Defense Department employees who leaked the documents, were in league with the Democrats to discredit him (it was the Me Decade after all). He sought to block further publication. The Supreme Court ruled in favor of freedom of the press.

To stop further leaks, the paranoid president authorized aide Egil Krogh to set up the Plumbers. This secret White House black-bag team included former CIA operative E. Howard Hunt and former FBI agent G. Gordon Liddy, both of whom would soon go to jail for Watergate crimes. Hoping to discredit Ellsberg, the Plumbers broke into his psychiatrist's office. They found nothing and succeeded only in destroying the criminal case against him.

*   *   *

The disillusioned declaimed, just a bit too eagerly, "The system is breaking down." It wasn't. But it was showing a certain creakiness at the joints. A decade of rapid and occasionally unwise social and political change plus an out-of-control war had deleterious effects. "Law and Order" was the mantra being chanted from state houses to the nation's capital. It meant more than maintaining order in the streets. It justified a crackdown on any kind of protest, most especially that having to do with the ghetto. In this vein it amounted to little more than code for opposing further racial progress. Such inflexibility seemed to confirm dire assessments of "the system" by producing even more chaos.

A Time to Die

—Attica

In September, made desperate by stifling, overcrowded and unhealthful living conditions, inmates at the Attica Correctional Facility in New York, sixty percent of whom were black and Latino, sought change through the grievance system. When prison officials blew them off, 1,000 of the inmates rioted and took hostages. They released eleven injured guards and held thirty-nine others to exchange for negotiations. Governor Nelson Rockefeller refused to negotiate and, when one of the released guards died from his injuries, ordered 1,500 state troopers and police to assault the prison. Ten prisoners and twenty-nine hostages died in the wild shooting spree. No prisoners had firearms. The police killed all thirty-nine. Eighty-nine others were wounded.

Subsequent investigatory panels criticized authorities for America's bloodiest prison riot, where conditions proved far below acceptable levels even for the hardest of hard-line penal authorities. Twenty-five years later, the state of New York settled the inmates' lawsuits for multiple millions of dollars. The Weather Underground detonated a bomb in a state government building in Albany to show "solidarity" with Attica prisoners.

*   *   *

Attica appeared to confirm the worst suspicions of both sides of our divided nation. The riot and subsequent massacre proved the society was falling apart either from permissive excess or excessive repression. Either way, violence had become endemic.

"A little of the old ultra-violence."

—A Clockwork Orange

This brilliant and chilling movie, based on Anthony Burgess' novel, depicted the dark side of the future plagued by dystopic urban landscapes overrun by violent gangs. *Looking Backward* 1970s style. Although set in millennial London, the violence that so appalled audiences was already commonplace in parts of urban America, right down to roving gangs of murderous, thrill-seeking adolescents.

In Kubrick's satiric vision society might rid itself of the problem through the Ludovico Technique, a none-too-subtle swipe at B. F. Skinner's notion of conditioning. A good way to drive away free will in the name of an orderly society. Here was a better way.

Smile, Big Brother's watching you. Well, maybe Big Brother's little brother.

Have a nice day

—☺

Big Brother's insidious new look. Mass advertising, mass marketing, and mass entertainment promulgated the suffocating uniformity of modern technological society. This insipid phrase pretended to promote the general well being when it really represented resignation. If we can't live up to our ideals, at least we can enjoy the day. Maybe living for today was wiser—or at least more practical. The vapid yellow doily threatened to "nice" us into submission, as it put a face on Marcuse's nonterroristic totalitarianism. Everything done would be for our own good. Our faces on credit cards. Accessible private databases that knew more about individual Americans than they themselves knew. Even a personal identity card and an official identification number—our driver's license and social security number. All of it important to efficiency and order so that "we" may serve you better. This was the real dystopian dream. Have a good one.

*   *   *

Resistance to sameness was indeed possible. You didn't have to look far to discover wild diversity. It was all around. When David Crosby sang of "letting your freak flag fly," he sang to the few. When Ruth Gordon sang, she addressed the many.

"If you wanna be free, be free."

—Harold and Maude

A love affair between a repressed young man and a free-spirited woman on the verge of eighty. Here was a movie that explored the yearning for fulfillment that was as endemic as protest and rebellion. You can be anything you want. The movie offered a more positive way of coping than the conditioning of *A Clockwork Orange*.

At the other extreme was self-indulgence and poisonous excess. Societies tend to lose their moral boundaries during wartime. Vietnam plus the corruption and repression coming from the Nixon Administration produced some rather funky ideas.

If it feels good, do it

—counterculture sentiment

The personal is political, as the saying went. Unfortunately the personal began to replace the political. As we moved from radical politics to the sexual revolution, the personal became the goal. Partly out of frustration, partly inevitably, partly due to the arrival of Quaaludes and other downs on the drug scene, lots of boomers shifted towards hedonism and carried it into mainstream America.

"If you can't be with the one you love, love the one you're with."

—Steven Stills

The uninhibited notion from Steven Still's first solo album (1970) made sense at the time, capturing as it did the last threads of free-spirited innocence left over from the patchwork of Sixties' ideas. Except the sexual revolution had reached the point where people joked they first did it, then they became friends, not to mention exchanged last names after the morning after. The bouncy tune became a top 40 hit.

The bass player for the Rolling Stones coined a term to describe the girls who threw themselves at musicians, doing anything for them—anything—in groups or by themselves, and in front of anybody.

Groupies

—Bill Wyman

His claims of sleeping with hundreds more groupies than either Mick Jagger or Keith Richards still causes one to scratch his head. But he put his finger on a real phenomenon. These were not mere stage-door-johnnys. These were women (and a few men) who made a career of offering themselves up on a platter. Thousands of young and not so young girls gave it all up for the opportunity to sleep with their favorite musicians, as though it were a shot at stardom, a temporary reprieve from their humdrum lives. As stories spread of orgies and wild times, some groupies became legendary for the number of players they seduced, or the way in which they seduced them. It produced people such as Cynthia PlasterCaster, who molded erect rock 'n' roll penises for her bookshelf, Pamela Des Barres, who turned her exploits into a best seller, and Sweet Connie, who even showed up in rock lyrics. Rock 'n' roll's adoring fans couldn't help but be influenced. In a real sense, we all became groupies, at least for a while.

The problem came when the adult middle class flirted with the sexual revolution. It was one thing for unmarried, unattached, uncommitted young people to glory in the spirit of personal freedom and experimentation. To a degree it was healthy. But when society as a whole began to frolic in the meadows of license, you got swinging, open marriage, and wife swapping parties that were frankly and openly decadent.

*   *   *

Caught hugging the corner at a DC reception, Nixon's National Security advisor on the cusp of fame and celebrity was asked why he wasn't taking part in the sexual revolution. His response was a classic.

"I'm a secret swinger."

—Henry Kissinger

The shy Harvard professor was in the process of transforming himself from a lumpy professor lurching through a Georgetown salon during power cocktails into globe-spanning Super K. He secretly negotiated rapprochement with Red China, leading to the presidential visit the following year. The Arab nations came to trust his word, which helped détente in the Middle East. His amoral, value-free approach to geo-politics, quite in keeping with the cultural tenor of the time, angered many conservatives who saw the world in the stark terms of good and evil. Averred Henry, "Nations don't have permanent enemies, only permanent interests."

Compare his amoral foreign policy with the amorality of the new morality.

The new morality was no morality. The line between revolution and nihilism blurred until it became indistinguishable from chaos. The suicidal jump from the idles of *Harold and Maude* to the "give a fuck" philosophy of Gonzo journalism was breathless in the extreme.

"As your attorney, I advise you to drive 100 miles an hour."

—Dr. Gonzo in *Fear and Loathing in Las Vegas*

Hunter S. Thompson held that mainstream society was so hopelessly corrupt the only way to address it was fully loaded.

Might just as well party hearty. His hip, hyperbolic journalism raised the good Dr. Thompson to demi-godhood. He wrote of splitting a cap of black acid with John Chancellor, dragging Nixon aide Chuck Colson down Pennsylvania Avenue by his balls, and showing up at a sheriff's convention in Vegas blitzed on drugs and attitude. His *Fear and Loathing on the Campaign Trail '72* probably told more truth about the maimed state of the nation than any other journalistic work of the time. His early comparison of Richard Nixon to Adolf Hitler struck most of his fans as extreme until Nixon's venomous hatred began to uncoil. No one else so accurately captured the zeitgeist of heedless excess in the face of heedless lawlessness.

With a man like Nixon in the White House, it was no wonder that unusual crimes began to creep onto the national TV screen. From White House dirty tricks to this breathtaking hijacking, the 70s began to show its dark side with one weird crime after another.

D. B. Cooper

—a skyjacker

This hijacker became a folk hero and an urban legend. Bespectacled and middle-aged (and perhaps in disguise), he hijacked a Northwest Orient plane and demanded $200,000 or he would blow up the plane. After landing in Seattle, swapping thirty-six hostages for ransom money, D.B. Cooper took off for Reno, Nevada, whereupon he parachuted out the back of the plane.

The perfect crime, almost. He was never caught. Many months later children discovered some of the marked money along the Columbia River. Cooper and the rest slipped away. Authorities reasoned he had frozen to death during the descent through freezing rain and both he and the money blew out to sea. Er...something like that.

*   *   *

"What's Goin' On"

—Marvin Gaye

This concept album, one of two he produced in the early 70's, captured the spirit of the times. His R&B detractors accused him of selling out to the hippies. But at heart Marvin Gaye always had a social conscience, even if sex was his thing. He covered the gamut of issues plaguing black America from the War to drugs to crime and violence and the already frightening tendency towards self-destruction.

The other major entertainment medium produced its own peculiar and popular form of social commentary. A TV show about a man with contempt for just about everything.

Dingbat!

—All in the Family

Archie Bunker was America's "lovable" bigot, calling his hippie son-in-law *meathead*, and his "oppressed" but loving wife a *dingbat*, while railing against the *colored*. Whether it was healthy to trivialize such deep social traumas was debated for a time and forgotten. Many Americans saw parts of themselves in this unruly working class family from Queens caught up in a world changing so fast they could only hang on and hope for the best. Although the ironies of Archie's faith in mythical golden days of America's past when "girls were girls and men were men" might occasionally have been lost, this was the first TV show to bring social controversy to the surreal world of the television sitcom.

Chapter 28

A Third-Rate Burglary

1972. On May 15 in the parking lot of a suburban Maryland shopping center, the next misfit loner to blast his way into history pointed his pistol at George Corley Wallace, who was running again for president. Arthur Bremer, an out-of-work busboy, shot the bantam weight Alabama governor, paralyzing him from the waist down and taking him out of the race. Just as he recorded in his diary about driving fast, stalking presidential candidates seemed to excite him. "Speed limit—70 m.p.h. I did over 90 once or twice...

"...danger gave me an erection."

—Arthur Bremer

Wallace was much more than simply a racist southern governor. He had become the point man for alienated blue collar workers and middle class men and women from all sections of the country who felt put upon, if not vilified, by the era's shifting values. LBJ's speechwriter Horace Busby foresaw this as far back as 1964. "America's real majority is suffering minority complex of neglect," he warned. "They have become the real foes of Negro rights, foreign aid, etc., because...they feel forgotten."

Many of them turned to George Wallace in 1968 and again in '72. Wallace offered himself as the voice not only for ridiculed rednecks, but for those many horrified by left-wing politics, "free-love" and hippie excess. His popularity among disaffected whites remained radiant until the shooting. Ironically, the assassination attempt gave him legitimacy, even respectability as an establishment politician. Something his racist background had prevented.

Wallace's vile demagoguery does not explain a national appeal that extended beyond race. Although he lost both his protest presidential bids, his was the first outcry against the challenge to tradition. George Wallace made white backlash politically respectable. Both Richard Nixon and Ronald Reagan were able to capitalize upon it in major ways. It is seriously misleading to view all his supporters as racist. By 1972 class resentments played a more important role. Concern about social chaos and a break down of social order and civil respect drove many citizens to him. For all that though, he hovered at the fringe as something of a radical crank until he was shot. Years later he would once again be elected governor of Alabama, this time with heavy black support.

Bremer had actually stalked Nixon all over the country hoping to cure his own impotence by killing the incumbent president. Security proved too tight; he couldn't get close enough. So he settled on Wallace, shooting him four times, wounding a Secret Service agent, a bodyguard and a campaign worker—and thereby insuring Nixon's re-election, whose Southern Strategy meant to capitalize on Wallace's growing constituency. Those angry Wallace voters turned to Nixon, not the Democratic Senator from South Dakota, George McGovern. To the judge at his sentencing Bremer said, "Looking back on my life, I would have liked it if society had protected me from myself."

*   *   *

Mercifully, successful political shootings of the tumultuous era ended with Wallace. Unfortunately, the politics of assassination gave way to the politics of scandal.

> ***"I won't comment on a third-rate burglary."***
>
> **—Ron Ziegler**

Nixon called the Watergate break-in "a crappy little thing that didn't work." But as this crappy affair unfolded it became clear that it sank all the way into the well-hidden sewer of our political culture. The President of the United States set his operatives to the task of wire tapping conversations, opening mail, conducting black bag jobs against those he considered his enemies. His Attorney General John Mitchell claimed the government had the right to wiretap "domestic subversives" without court approval. And so they increased 100% from 1969 to 1970 alone. The Cubans who got caught breaking into the Democratic National headquarters in the Watergate had connections to the CIA and the White House. The trail they left, which was about as obvious as Gretel's bread crumbs, led to one unavoidable conclusion. The president violated his oath of office and subverted the Constitution not through carelessness or ineptness, but with criminal intent.

We should never believe Richard Nixon suffered more for his crimes than the country he was sworn to serve.

On June 17, Frank Wills, a night watchman at the Watergate office building, discovered tape over the lock of a door, starting off the final event of the Sixties era. *Washington Post* reporters Carl Bernstein and Bob Woodward uncovered a program of political espionage and sabotage that included dirty tricks, forgery, disinformation, burglaries, wiretaps, and millions of dollars of laundered money. Directed from the White House, Nixon's operatives destroyed the Democratic presidential candidates he feared, especially Maine Senator Edmund Muskie, while aiding the nomination of the weakest candidate they could find, George McGovern. In doing so, they rigged the election on a scale not seen since the stolen election of 1876.

Despite the widening scandal, Richard Nixon cruised to a triumphant landslide over the forlorn McGovern, who dropped his first vice-presidential running mate, Thomas Eagleton, when Eagleton's electro-shock treatments for depression became known. Nixon carried 49 states and received 521 electoral votes. The hapless McGovern, carrying only Massachusetts and the District of Columbia, promised a precipitous withdrawal from Vietnam and a host of already discredited liberal programs. Voters found him wimpy and Liberace-like. Nixon's Committee to Re-Elect the President, which even Republicans referred to as CREEP, spread the word that a vote for the liberal senator was a vote for "Acid, Abortion and Amnesty."

Nixon had an October Surprise in line just in case his illegal tactics failed. Less than two weeks before the election, radio Hanoi announced a preliminary agreement on a peace plan. In Washington, the National Security Advisor told the Washington press corps...

Peace is at Hand

—Henry Kissinger

Campaign ploy? Undoubtedly. The country was so desperate for "Peace with Honor," peace of any kind, that it greeted Nixon's latest cynical manipulation with euphoria. Despite Kissinger's declaration, peace was not at hand. Vast differences remained between the US and North Vietnam. Even more important, South Vietnam was bristling with objections to the preliminary agreement. The plan fell through shortly after the election. In December

Nixon announced a resumption of the bombing of North Vietnam "until such time as a settlement is arrived at." The new round of bombing was the heaviest in the history of warfare. The air campaign continued until the Paris Peace Accords were signed and the war was Vietnamized.

Hanoi Jane
—a prominent anti-war activist

In July Jane Fonda showed up in Hanoi. Wearing a coolie hat, she made a photo opportunity sitting in an anti-aircraft gun and went on Hanoi radio to address the GIs, "I implore you, I beg you to reconsider what you are doing."

Outrage at these treasonous acts was more than understandable. She'd won an Oscar in April for Best Actress for her role as a prostitute in *Klute*. Whoring her poorly thought-through ideas in the country killing American soldiers wasn't likely to win her the Presidential Medal of Freedoom. She earned the hatred she received.

Eventually, she apologized to Vietnam veterans and to the country. She confessed that her tactics, as those of the anti-war movement in general, were shrill and misguided. But, she insisted, the movement had been right all along about the War.

Jane Fonda's mistakes lay in more than her tactics. Her analysis of the war missed on an essential factor. Her mistakes and some transgressions of the anti-war movement flowed from that. Anti-war protest should have focused on the policy makers, most of them civilian, and on their non-government co-conspirators and apologists, and stayed there. Attacking our armed forces, the grunt in the field or even the bulk of the military brass, who were trying to do their duty, was wrong. It amounted to stupidity as monumental as her journey to North Vietnam.

Hanoi Jane's depredations, gratuitous insults against Vietnam vets such as spitting on them in airports (which may prove to be near total myth) and shouted slogans like "FTA" ("Fuck the Army") were symptomatic. As was granting the NLF the moral high ground. This was as flawed as the policies it criticized. America was wrong in Vietnam; therefore, all those opposed to the U.S. were good. An immediate consequence was a tip of the hat to international terrorism. Painting the world in black and white, gave terrorists of the world a boost in stature they never deserved. America was not the world's bad guy.

Black September

—Palestinian terrorists

Pre-dawn, September 5, the Olympic Village at Munich, Germany. Eight Palestinian terrorists stormed the quarters of the Israeli Olympic team. Their goal was to hold Israeli Olympians hostage to secure the release of 200 of their comrades in Israeli jails. The wrestling coach and a weight lifter held the door closed while six others escaped. The two were killed; nine more were taken hostage, forcing the Munich games into suspension. In the rescue attempt the captives were killed along with five terrorists and a West German policeman. With this act Arab terrorists forced themselves into our awareness like never before. It was an awareness rife with scorn. ABC commentator Jim McKay, haggard and grieving, expressed the contempt and sadness best: "My father once told me when I was kid that our greatest hopes and worst fears are seldom realized. Our worst fears are realized tonight. They're gone, they're all gone."

In those days the Israelis still held the moral high ground. And that tended to cloud our judgment. Palestinian terrorists did nothing to disperse those clouds. The 1948 UN mandate creating the Jewish state displaced thousands of Palestinians, ultimately taking away their country. The plight of the Palestinian people should have caused concern among Americans. Terrorist violence may have come from desperation, but explanation was not justification. While this wanton act and the dozens of airline hijackings grabbed the world by the throat and made it pay attention, the terrorists lost the world's support before they ever had a chance to make their case.

*   *   *

All this at the once sacrosanct Olympic Games, the place of gods and immortal feats. After a memorial service, the Games resumed. But they were largely overshadowed by cognitive dissonance thundering over the events. Spectacular sports triumphs provided a melancholy interlude and not much more. Soviet gymnast Olga Korbut won the world's heart. But the man of the hour was an American swimmer.

> ***"I just pretended a beautiful blond
> was waiting at the end of each lap."***
>
> **—Mark Spitz**

The handsome swimmer won seven gold medals, four individual and three team. He was the first Olympian ever to achieve such a feat. He was a poster boy for about six months. Although his comeback in the butterfly at age forty-five for the 1996 Olympics failed, his accomplishments will last much longer.

*   *   *

A handful of European leftists bought the same monolithic analysis as Jane Fonda. Many were committed communists. Many more were reformers who'd lost their sense of proportion. They willfully, often gleefully joined the growing international terrorist network that included not only the Palestinians but the Irish Republican Army, Italy's Red Brigades, Peru's Shining Path, Uruguay's Tupamaros and the best known of them all:

The Baader-Meinhof Group
—West German terrorists

After a gun battle in downtown Frankfurt, police captured Andreas Baader. The narcissistic leader of the most feared terrorist band of the day, a band that once included the world's best known terrorist, one Ramirez Ilich Sanchez, aka Carlos the Jackal, wound up in jail two weeks ahead of his revolutionary co-conspirator, Ulrike Meinhof. He was 29, she 37. Both got life without parole. Neither lived much longer. Hearing Baader had died in his cell, Meinhof committed suicide. Or, so the highly suspicious story goes.

Terrorism was a long way from dead. With a patron like the Soviet Union seeking to exploit the chaos, and with enough grievances to last yet another half century, it wasn't going away any time soon. Back home in the states, our radical left spun off such a pathetic bunch of losers into terrorist cells that not much damage occurred. They managed to ignite themselves rather than society. Our damage was spiritual. Coming to grips with a pervasive sense of dissatisfaction proved difficult, but it didn't produce much terrorism.

*   *   *

National Black Political Agenda
—Black Nationalism

In March black leaders met in convention in Gary, Indiana, to discuss post-civil rights strategies. Widely reported upon and heavily attended, this was the last time blacks showed anything close to the unity of purpose of the Civil Rights Movement. The Black Nationalist tide crested here with demands for reparations in the form of cash payments to correct generations of slavery and enforced poverty, and land for The Republic of New Africa. A National Black Assembly would oversee the construction of this black Palestine out of the American Israel. The Agenda also supported "the struggle of Palestine for self-determination."

Barely masking its anger, the Agenda accused America of "world-wide military imperialism," and advocated several thoughtful (and many ludicrous) remedies to our painful racial problems. "We need a permanent political movement that addresses itself to the basic control and reshaping of American institutions that currently exploit Black America and threaten the whole society." The Agenda also demanded political and economic empowerment as well as a national plebiscite of blacks to determine if they wanted to become independent or "wish to remain under the captive sovereignty of the United States."

In June a jury acquitted intellectual Angela Davis of complicity in the 1970 murder of a California judge. Using her guns, black terrorists from Soledad Prison had seized him as they attempted an escape. Angela Davis went on the lam for two months after a gun battle in which three of the Soledad Brothers were also killed. Once captured she spent sixteen months in jail. Herbert Marcuse claimed she was his most brilliant student and a promising scholar. She also entertained connections with the Black Panthers and SNCC. The University of California refused to re-hire her. Her Marxism and radical connections were too much. But Angela Davis easily found work in academia, where she remains to this day.

Her career path—not her radicalism—underscored the wrong-headedness of the National Black Political Agenda. America's complicated society welcomed many blacks, finally. Political empowerment through civil rights legislation began to show results. All over the country, thousands of black men and women started winning elections. More important, hundreds of thousands of blacks entered the middle class and the great American shopping mall of opportunity.

Like their white counterparts, black Americans were seduced and empowered by material prosperity. Hope for revolutionary separation was never great, or wise for that matter. Fortunately for the well-being of ordinary people, such radicalism faced bleak prospects. Besides, there had already been significant change in American race relations—brought to you courtesy of free market capitalism. Racism, it turned out, wasn't good for business.

*   *   *

Ferment at home mirrored ferment abroad. American popular culture depended on things that could be sold for profit, like movies, music, books—or sex. The sexual revolution hit the mainstream in ways never imagined. Responsibility, commitment, morality gave way to the market place of situation ethics and moral relativism.

Open Marriage:
—A New Life Style for Couples

Authors Nena and George O'Neill dreamed up the ridiculous notion that you could be married, raise a family and still have an active dating life. Rigorous conformity always produces rebellion. In that context, they made one healthy point. In our parents' world conformist pressure ruled out having close friends of the opposite sex. A platonic relationship was suspect and unseemly. It just wasn't socially acceptable, consequently everyone suffered.

> *"Open marriage means an honest and open relationship between two people, based on the equal freedom and identity of both partners. It involves a verbal, intellectual and emotional commitment to the right of each to grow as an individual within the marriage."*

Had the O'Neill's limited their suggestions to more equitable arrangements through expanding individual opportunities and widening the circle of acceptable friends, they would have done a great service. They didn't. In pure Sixties fashion, they went overboard—way overboard.

When they came up for air, they were in the land of license. Never mind the adults who followed these cult-like rules. In a way they deserved the unhappiness they produced. "We are not recommending outside sex, but we are not saying that it should be avoided, either." How's that again? "In an open marriage, in which each partner is secure in his own identity and trusts in the other, new possibilities for additional relationships exist, and open (as opposed to limited) love can expand to include others." Oh.

This tract amounted to a 269-page justification for screwing around. Did these people ever hear of the word stability? Or commitment. Or children, for pity's sake? Their children suffered immeasurably. Just ask any late boomer or early Gen-Xer what it was like growing up in the 70s with hip parents who smoked dope and tried to practice this nonsense.

In their alcoholic embrace of sexual convenience, the O'Neill's and myriad other pop philosophers like Robert *Looking Out for Number One* Ringer threatened the structure of the very world they were trying to improve. The point of the Sixties was to make America a moral place, not to turn it into a national bathhouse. Failure to raise

American morals made terrorist fools of some, witless hedonists of others. In the end, no one gained. And children lost the most to the parental quest for new bodies. One flawed set of morals was plundered to create a newer one with even deeper flaws.

A Gourmet Guide to Love Making
—The Joy of Sex by Alex Comfort

Somewhere along the line we developed a fetish for how-to books. This manual and *Everything You Always Wanted to Know About Sex But Were Afraid to Ask, explained by David R. Reuben* marked the beginning of a tidal wave of self-help, self-improvement books addressing every conceivable aspect of our lives—and then some. Leave it to us boomers, technically proficient, spiritually adrift, to reduce life's greatest pleasure to an easy-to-read instruction manual, complete with diagrams and pictures.

*   *   *

With corruption ranging from the family room to the Oval Office, one might legitimately wonder if society had fallen into a slithering pit. With drug stores selling anything from skin books showing the pink to dildos and rolling papers, the conclusion might be inescapable. But not quite. Hollywood came to the rescue. Here was a well crafted bestseller made into a masterpiece film about family, loyalty, honor and self-sacrifice. But it came from a very strange place. A tough guy was about to show us the meaning of integrity, American style.

"I'm going to make him an offer he can't refuse."
—Marlon Brando as Don Vito Corleone

Leave it to Francis Coppola to turn the Mafia into a symbol of family values. *The Godfather* created an American archetype. In terms of style, it became the *Casablanca* of its era. The film and its sequel rank among the best American movies ever, restoring as they did, personal honor and family respect to the pantheon of our national character. Its benchmark opening line: "I believe in America." Honor and violence, how American can you get?

An even better movie that year, this adventure, based on James Dickey's novel of violence, became *Easy Rider* to hordes of back-packers that were leaving their crash pads for hiking trails and white-water adventures. Camping, natural foods were about to come into their own (Celestial Seasonings Tea began business this year). But there was danger in them thar woods.

"Weee...weee...wee."

—Ned Beatty in *Deliverance*

The revival of interest in the great out-of-doors caught on big among boomers as a way to clear the lungs of all that incense—and to preserve the youth we suspected was slipping away. Camping was part of the back to nature movement and offered a refreshing alternative to revolutionary streets. However, the indelicate scenes of a de-pantsed Ned Beatty and a scraggly, ridge-running pervert not only sent chills up our class conscious spines, it gave a new meaning to the tune we sang as kids...and made us wonder at the Supreme Court's June decision to ban the death penalty.

If you go out in the woods today, you're in for a big surprise.
If you go out in the woods today, you'd better go in disguise.
Cause every bear that ever there was
is gathered there for certain because
Today's the day the teddy bears have their pic-nic!

*   *   *

Relax, you could always stay home and play with this latest new-fangled invention. More than murderous rednecks, here was the true shape of things to come.

Hi-Tech

—the calculator

The first rumble of the hi-tech avalanche that was about to bury us came in the form of a hand-held, pocket calculator. Imagine where we *wouldn't* be today had it stopped there. The mid-priced models went for $300.

Chapter 29

Out of Gas

1973. You have to wonder about the role of technology even in political scandal. Would Watergate have played out the way it did without the televised Watergate hearings? If the Watergate burglars had not sought to replace defective bugs? Had the president not taped himself breaking the law? The answer seems obvious. The affair took place on television, not in rooms stuffy with blue cigar smoke.

Watergate consumed most of this year and the next. It was already such a big deal the country barely acknowledged the Paris Accords ending our involvement in Vietnam. This came just seven days after the most expensive inaugural celebration in our history. Nixon and Agnew began their second term, protected by troops and National Guardsmen to ward off 100,000 protesters. Yet, dissent was not the problem these men needed fear.

In Vietnam, a truce began at 8:00 AM the 28th of January. The United States agreed to withdraw its remaining troops. In return, the North Vietnamese agreed to repatriate American POWs. By Christmas only fifty GIs remained in country, as embassy guards. Fighting continued between the North and South, but for the first time since 1965, Americans were not fighting, or dying.

There were no celebrations.

Neither was there much ado about America's participation in the coup in Chile. Mused Henry Kissinger, "I don't see why we need to stand by and watch a country go communist due to the irresponsibility of its own people." So we helped overthrow democratically elected Marxist president Salvadore Allende and install that great humanitarian Augusto Pinochet. The Nixon administration refused to countenance Allende's socialist reforms. Understandable—except here was yet another example of America imperiously denying the right of national self-determination in Latin America.

Americans were too preoccupied to notice. In November Nixon sought to use television to appeal directly to the hearts and minds of the people. Even though Watergate had gotten down to cases, he still had a better than even chance of surving it. In a nationally televised question and answer session from Disney World, a cynical play to middle America, he felt compelled to give us this bit of reassurance. "People have got to know whether or not their president is a crook. Well...

"I am not a crook."

—Richard Milhous Nixon

What a pitiful statement for a president of the United States to make. Yet, Tricky Dick had no one but himself to blame. In 1969 he authorized illegal actions against the anti-war demonstrators and other radicals. In 1970 he approved the Houston plan to employ government intelligence agencies to sow the seeds of destruction of the New Left and Black Nationalists. He gave rise to these sorts of questions, and paved the way for his own destruction. He later rescinded approval of the Houston Plan—because of its illegality. Instead, he used his own operatives.

At the sentencing of the seven original Watergate operatives, Judge John Sirica, a Nixon appointee, read a letter by burglar James McCord implicating higher ups in the White House. "Maximum John" had been dissatisfied with the investigation. Claiming both prosecution and defense failed to do an adequate job, he personally questioned several witnesses and uncovered a $199,000 payment to Gordon Liddy.

By April the president's press secretary was forced to declare that previous White House statements denying involvement were "inoperative." Shortly thereafter Chief of Staff Bob Haldeman and domestic advisor John Erlichman resigned. Both ended up in jail. Nixon maintained his own innocence, but growing public outrage prompted a Senatorial investigation. What prompted Nixon's claims of innocence were the revelations of the Senate Watergate hearings.

"I'm just a country lawyer."

—Sam Ervin

No one better exemplified national outrage at the duplicitous manipulation, the illegal and unconstitutional acts of Richard Nixon than the senator from North Carolina. The wily old gent proved a great deal shrewder than the "country lawyer" he called himself. The televised Watergate hearings began May 17. When Nixon's arrogant men presented themselves before his Watergate Committee, this southern mossback, who had opposed civil rights legislation in the 60's, dismantled their defenses and exposed them for the heedless bounders and mincing poltroons they were. His sagacious little backwoods tales endeared him to the public. Even the hapless Acting-FBI Director, L. Patrick Gray, (the most likely candidate for Deep Throat) admitted burning evidence taken from E. Howard Hunt's safe, and resigned.

The Nixon administration was rotten to its very core.

The public found out how rotten when former White House counsel John Dean spent four days reading his 245-page testimony to the committee and a riveted TV audience.

> *"There's a cancer on the presidency."*
>
> **—John Dean**

Dean was in his mid-thirties with unkempt hair (for the Nixon White House. Nixon thought he "looked hippie"). Before he testified, he fished an old pair of horn-rimmed glasses out of a dresser, wore them instead of his customary contacts and got his hair cut short and neat. His image of the straight-laced product of private schools was manufactured for his testimony. His unflappable monotone coupled with his beautiful blond wife Mo seated behind him, who looked like the citified cousin of the American Gothic daughter, worked like a charm. He was utterly convincing. There was a lesson buried in there for defiant longhairs who thumbed their collective noses at convention: credibility.

With deference and assurance, Dean recounted his conversations in the Oval Office during which he warned Nixon that Watergate was closing in on him. Dean's low key testimony proved to be devastatingly accurate in its condemnation of Nixon's actions and attitudes. He placed most of the responsibility on Haldeman and Erlichman for the widespread campaign of illegality. But he flatly said Nixon himself discussed paying hush money to the burglars and other conspirators.

Republicans on the committee pressed Dean unmercifully, as they should have. They were unable to rattle him or undermine his credibility. Dean countered by revealing just how craven Nixon was.

"Opponents List and Political Enemies Project"
—the Enemies List

Nixon considered Joe Namath, Bill Cosby, Paul Newman, Daniel Shore, Jane Fonda, Dick Gregory, plus numerous Democrats such as Teddy Kennedy, Edmund Muskie, and Walter Mondale to be his personal enemies. Besides them he added the presidents of Yale, Harvard Law School, MIT, the World Bank, the Ford Foundation, the Rand Corporation, the NEA, Phillip Morris, and the National Cleaning Contractors. The list featured four of his former cabinet members, two ex-ambassadors, a Nobel prizewinner and fifty-seven members of the media, including right winger Roland Evans. And let's not forget Gregory Peck, Steve McQueen, and Carol Channing! John Erlichman hired an ex-New York cop, John Caulfield and the sleazy J. Anthony Ulasewicz to go undercover against them.

This degree of paranoia can only be described as Nixonian.

Most Americans, including loyal Republicans, were dumbfounded at the depths to which their president had sunk. Nixon was turning out far worse than even his harshest critics in the New Left and anti-war movement had made him out to be. Fortunately, an even-handed—Republican—voice emerged to reduce Watergate to its bare essence. From the ranking minority member of the Watergate Committee came…

"What did the president know, and when did he know it?"
—Senator Howard Baker

Republican senator and Nixon supporter posed the gut question. The nation wanted to know precisely that. The answers to Baker's twin questions were, "Most everything, and from the very beginning."

Slowly, inexorably Nixon's house of cards began to crumble. Too many men had to go to the wall for him for it to stand. Faced with the opprobrium of family and nation—faced with jail—a handful of the president's men found the integrity to refuse the lie. With visible pain, witnesses before the committee began to confess their misdeeds, shamefully forced upon them by White House superiors. Dwight Chapin, the president's appointments secretary, who had just received an Outstanding Young American Award, admitted to hiring an old college roommate, Donald Segretti to wage a campaign of illegal dirty tricks against the Democrats. Segretti concocted a letter, for example, accusing a Democratic presidential candidate of fathering an illegitimate daughter, and supplying the name. Both Chapin and Segretti did time in the slammer. The breadth of the crimes committed to advance Nixon's career shocked even the most cynical political veterans.

In mid-July one of the president's men, an Air Force veteran, provided access to the ultimate dirty trick. The one Nixon played on himself. It would lead to the smoking gun.

"I was hoping you fellows wouldn't ask me about that."

—Alexander Butterfield

In 1971 Nixon ordered a secret taping system installed in the Oval Office, his private office in the Executive Office Building, and elsewhere. The tapes of his conversations about Watergate (and many other matters) were revealed by Butterfield, the man who administered the system. Here might lie proof of the president's veracity. Yet, despite Nixon's persistent denials of involvement in Watergate, for some strange reason he resisted releasing the tapes.

When they were finally released, the first shocker was Nixon's profanity. Here was a man asserting his moral leadership by castigating movies such as *Love Story* for its foul language, cussing like a collegiate. You had to hand it to him. He had a way with sexual innuendoes, coining adolescent phrases to describe his tactics. He wasn't going to go the *hang out* route. If his enemies had the balls of a brass monkey, well so would he. He would *stonewall* it. When that situation became untenable, he tried a *limited hangout*. When that didn't work he adopted a *modified limited hang out*. That didn't work either.

In light of the vile statements recorded on his own taping system, even ardent supporters could no longer deny this man's deep malice. Len Garment, himself a Jew albeit a favorite of Nixon, referred to him as "a champion hater," who was particularly anti-Semitic. "Most Jews are disloyal," said Nixon, "You can't trust the bastards. They turn on you."

Arguments that Nixon is best understood as a war time president facing domestic turmoil are utter rationalization. Would any of Nixon's supporters wish to see such activities by any administration again, under any circumstances?

Far worse for the president was the possibility the tapes held incriminating evidence. John Dean was delighted to hear about them. He was positive they would vindicate him, which they ultimately did. The June 20, 1972 tape contained an 18 ½ minute gap. That was just three days after the break-in. Subsequent tests showed the gap to have been the result of five separate manual erasures. Nixon's personal secretary Rose Mary Woods said she may have accidentally erased the Oval Office meeting between Nixon and Haldeman. Indications, however, were that Nixon himself had erased the crucial conversation.

Archibald Cox, who'd been appointed Watergate Special Prosecutor, wanted the tapes. Nixon refused. A bloody battle ensued. Nixon first claimed it would "jeopardize the independence of the three branches of government." After trying and failing to hide behind national security and executive privilege, he agreed to release edited transcripts of the tapes. Then Nixon ordered the Ivy League patrician Cox, whom he detested, fired.

The Saturday Night Massacre

—newspaper headlines

Attorney General Eliot Richardson refused to fire Cox and resigned. Undersecretary William Ruckleshaus also refused. Nixon fired him. Solicitor General Robert Bork agreed to fire Cox. A national firestorm resulted.

Angry callers besieged the White House. Even Republican loyalists began to question Nixon's role in the affair, puzzling before the cameras why he just didn't tell the people that had overwhelmingly re-elected him exactly what the hell happened and ask their forgiveness. They may well have forgiven him. But Nixon's criminal mind would never allow a confession. Perhaps the most damning condemnation came the morning after the Massacre when the head of the American Bar Association issued a terse statement calling for Nixon's resignation that began, "No man is above the law." Nixon's approval ratings hit 27%, the lowest ever for any president since polling started.

Honk if you think he's guilty

—bumper sticker

Even before the bumper stickers could be printed, people actually began writing this on cardboard and sticking it in their rear windows. Cars drove slowly past the White House, laying on the horn. The din in front of 1600 Pennsylvania was louder than any anti-war demonstration.

     *   *   *

In the midst of this uproar, the Vice President of the United States ran afoul of the law. Like Nixon's, this one was entirely of his own making. Spiro Agnew, it seemed, was a petty white collar criminal. In disbarring Agnew the following year, the Maryland Court of Appeals called him "morally obtuse."

Nolo contendere

—Spiro Agnew

The vice president's cluelessness had been the subject of many White House jokes. Low level staffers used to call him to meetings to which no one else would show up. That was good clean fun. He was effective in his role as Nixon's attack dog, castigating news media and protesters alike for their lack of patriotism. Unfortunately, Spiro had been taking bribes. Since his days as Baltimore County executive, contractors had been paying him off in sums between one and two thousand dollars. The payments followed him into the vice presidency, handed to him across his desk. He stuffed the cash-filled envelopes into his breast pocket and went about the business of defending American virtue against radical liberals. What was most surprising was the paltry amount of the bribes. But then this was the man who specialized in attacking a (perhaps nonexistent) liberal media, which, he claimed, did not—repeat not—represent the views of most Americans.

Agnew's moral sky was bleaker than any relativistic liberal's he so resolutely scorned. Ten days before the Saturday Night Massacre, and after extensive plea bargaining to avoid going to jail, he pled no contest to tax evasion and resigned from office, one bright and shining hypocrite. Nixon replaced him with House Minority Leader Gerald Ford under the Twenty-Fifth Amendment. After Nixon resigned, Ford appointed former New York Governor Nelson Rockefeller to fill the vacated vice-presidency, making them the first president and vice president elected to neither office.

*   *   *

With Watergate occupying the national mind, this wild entertaining book detailing the surreal post-World War II experiences of one Tyrone Slothrop defined the universal paranoid delusion then rampant.

"A screaming comes across the sky."

—Gravity's Rainbow by Thomas Pynchon

During the war a German V-2 rocket landed wherever Slothrop got laid. "Just because you're paranoid doesn't mean they're not after you." Or as Thomas Pynchon also wrote, "They're embracing possibilities far far beyond Nazi Germany." Whoever *they* were.

Thomas Pynchon was unusual for an increasingly publicity mad public. Like J. D. Salinger, he refused interviews, correspondence, phone calls, everything. No one knew where he lived. He shunned publicity, refused even to attend awards ceremonies or pick up his National Book Award. Like his creator, Tyrone Slothrop was consumed by paranoia. He was sort of a 60s' version of Tom Clancy's Jack Ryan, filibustering across post-war Europe dressed as Rocket Man.

In the end, Slothrop learned his paranoia was no fantasy. He actually discovered the little man in the room who was controlling a centuries long conspiracy against his family by Royal Dutch Shell.

*   *   *

How odd it might seem today that a multi-national like Royal Dutch Shell would care a fig for one person, even if it was Tyrone Slothrop. Early in the decade, gasoline, or more to the point, petroleum became a critical factor in geo-politics. The result of the new factor proved as revolutionary as anything proposed by the SDS. Hastily written signs posted at gas stations told a tale of a shifting balance of power in the world.

Out of gas

—Arab oil embargo

On October 17, Arab leaders struck back at the West with a 25% cut in oil production and an embargo on oil exports to the U.S. This came in response to western support for Israel during the Six-Day War of '67 and the Yom Kippur War that began on October 6. We relied on OPEC for a fourth of our oil; Europe 72%; Japan 82%. In addition, OPEC began raising the price of its crude. As a result, we sat in long gas lines to buy gas that cost more with each fill-up. The embargo produced double digit inflation and an energy crisis. In a few years the cheap gas and muscle cars of our youth would be gone, gone, gone. Gas jumped to 55 cents the following year, nearly a 60% increase.

In 1979 in response to the Camp David Accords, a second oil embargo led to the nation's first gas riot, appropriately enough, in Levittown, NY, where cars got torched and 195 people got busted. America would never be quite the same. Soon to be gone were the days of a single income family. Gone were the guarantees of each succeeding generation attaining a higher living standard than its parents. New realities descended over post-Vietnam America, adding a final economic insult to the injury of war.

*   *   *

If oil was now a critical international issue, abortion was about to become the defining issue at home. And it all began with a measly Supreme Court decision. Even before the Baby Boom Generation, American women had lots of kids. They averaged seven children in the early 1800's. That number fell to four by the end of the century, then three, and two by our own era. The main means of preventing births were abstinence, crude contraception, and abortion. The Third Great Awakening and Christian Fundamentalism ended legal abortions earlier this century.

The women's movement considered reproductive freedom essential to its liberation from *kinder, küche, kirche* that defined women's subordinated lives. Based on the right to privacy, the split decision, written by Justice Harry Blackmun, overturned state bans, allowing abortion on demand during the first trimester. Combined with improved contraception, for the first time in history women could now exercise the sort of control over their reproductive systems that men always took for granted. They'd lacked this power since Eve. It was a critical right, belatedly won. But *Roe* also touched off legitimate outrage over the immorality of killing unborn babies.

Reproductive rights

—Roe v. Wade

Ideological battle lines as tough as any ever drawn between Hawks and Doves split this country at its already frayed seams.

With a few exceptions, the wrenching separation over abortion mirrored the pro/anti-war, conservative/liberal split. The new guise was Pro-Life versus Pro-Choice. In the years to come it would lead to social violence and death. For now *Roe vs. Wade* sounded a call to arms for social and religious conservatives who felt abortion would turn America into a Sodom of license and atheism. It was the final tear.

Pro-Lifers considered abortion murder. Feminists considered it essential for full equality. The decades-long culture war that resulted grew to encompass other issues, but abortion lay at its center. Like Vietnam, it pulled at the heart of what it meant to be an American.

Baby boomers, though active in the Pro-Life movement, which was dominated by men from the very start, generally supported abortion rights, as did most Americans. Boomer women were the first generation significantly affected by the availability of legal abortions. They were approaching thirty now and had already decided to put off marriage and children in favor of all these newly available careers. Abortion was critical to the career track, both as a symbol of equality in the workplace and as a real escape hatch from traditional role of wife and mother. Here was the next great war between traditionalism and modernism. Here was Scopes played out to a national audience through many venues including church, Congress, court, and commerce. For a time it looked as though abortion rights and feminism would win hands down.

Especially after Billie Jean King triumphed over a ludicrous Male Chauvinist Pig, who claimed to be defending male superiority, in a sideshow worthy of the tawdry 70s.

The Battle of the Sexes
—Billie Jean King vs. Bobbie Riggs

The taunting little Riggs wasted number one ranked Margaret Court in what was termed the Mother's Day Massacre, forcing Billie Jean King to change her mind about playing him. She'd been turning him down for months. So they met in the Houston Astrodome before 30,000 people and several million more on television. She wafted into the arena on a feathery divan born by hunky Neanderthals. Riggs entered in a Rickshaw pulled by "Bobby's Bosom Buddies." Overconfident in the extreme, he didn't even bother to take off his Sugar Daddy windbreaker during the first set. He needn't have bothered. The match was over with King's first daring passing shot, at which the outwitted, out-gunned and over-matched Riggs could only point as it sliced past him. The twenty-nine year old Billie Jean King thrashed and humiliated the fifty-five year old Riggs, while up in the broadcast booth, headband-wearing Rosie Casals blithely ridiculed his body, his hair, the way he walked (like a duck), most everything about his physical appearance, much to the consternation of the always dignified, low-key Howard Cosell.

Next to no one would have predicted a farce like this would change history. But it did. Not only women's tennis but female athleticism took on an entirely new dimension, that of worthy competitor. The challenge match turned out to be a watershed.

```
*******************************
*   More women are now enrolled  *
*      in college than men (50.3%)    *
*******************************
```

In the meantime, more than tennis matches was in the works. A book appeared that amounted to a feminist declaration of independence from the confining aspects of tradition. "Our image of ourselves is on a firmer base, we can be better friends and better lovers, better *people*, more self-confident, more autonomous, stronger and more whole."

Our Bodies, Ourselves
—Boston Women's Health Collective

Before it got out of hand, Women's Liberation and the sexual revolution freed both men and women from confining and often hypocritical gender roles. "Until very recently pregnancies were all but inevitable, biology was our destiny—that is, because our bodies are designed to get pregnant and give birth and lactate, that is what all or most of us did." This book opened the door for women to take an active role in their own health, sexuality and well being. The ultimate goal was to enable women "to enter into equal and satisfying relationships with other people" through better self-awareness and less reliance on male-dominated institutions and male physicians. "Body education is core education." This widely read book encouraged revolutionary practices such as vaginal self-examinations and bold ideas that women voice their opinions about their personal health care to their doctors.

Boomer women embraced this book as their mothers had Dr. Spock.

In the meantime, men, mostly younger, were responding to these new realities. They might snicker at Bobbie Riggs' antics and admire the surreal bodies in *Playboy* and its burgeoning imitators, but in fact, as Norman Mailer was forced to concede in *Prisoner of Sex*, it was high time to start helping out around the house. In addition, economic necessity had put Mom in the workplace where men were going to have to learn to deal with them as equals.

The new sensitive male

—gender revolution

Phil Donahue was in his heyday exploring the nuances of the new manhood. In attempt to show they weren't male chauvinist pigs, many guys went with the flow. Men who'd been schooled by their fathers on the firm handshake and the square-look-in-the-eye measure of the man started hugging. White guys tried to mimic the black power handclasp: fraternity and sensitivity rolled into one muscular act. But did you do it at waist level like a handshake, or at chest level with your bicep curled pulling the other fellow gut close? Bad enough Women's Liberation had forced macho men to bring out a softer side—well, some men—without having to go through this tortuous rigmarole. It was way too close for comfort. How do you hug and be hip at the same time? Hard enough to clasp hands and not look phony.

While men were valiantly trying to suppress lust in the name of this brave new way of looking at the world, women stepped in to fill the vacuum in the ethos of sexuality with defiant promises of more and better sex. One naughty sorority girl wrote about every good girl's inner desires—and came off sounding just like the old, insensitive male of the species.

Zipless Fuck

—*Fear of Flying* by Erica Jong

You mean girls think the same way about sex that boys do? Yup, right down to the obsessive horniness. At least they did in the 70's.

Zipless, you see, not because...men have button-flies rather than zipper-flies, and not because the participants are so

devastatingly attractive, but because the incident has all
the swift compression of a dream and is seemingly free of
all remorse and guilt...The zipless fuck is absolutely pure.
It is free of ulterior motives. There is no power game. The
man is not "taking" and the woman is not "giving."

(Guys called this getting laid.)

*   *   *

In its salient way, *Fear of Flying* was every bit the revolutionary
manifesto as *Our Bodies, Ourselves*. The two fit neatly into the
package of New Feminism and cultural revolution, assaulting the
masculine parameters of the American middle class. Pent-up desires
now being regularly liberated into the unblushing light of day.

And of course, the assault was viewable on TV, as sort of a
domestic version of Vietnam.

An American Family

—the Louds

We were transfixed by this 12-hour PBS documentary depict-
ing the slow and painful disintegration of an upper middle-class
family from Santa Barbara, California. This occasionally pruri-
ent exploration of the troubled American Dream turned a mirror
on Our Lives, Ourselves as it magnified to excruciating detail the
effects of cultural upheaval and rapid social change on a prosperous and once typical family that had "made it." Comparing the
Louds to Sloan Wilson's fictional Rath family made the tremendous distance of cultural change seemed like a never-ending
journey. The Raths struggled to maintain the family unit against
the assault by materialism. The Louds sought to free themselves

of the restrictions of familial responsibility. By this time son Lance didn't have to worry too much about coming out. And Pat Loud knew life wasn't over for a divorced, middle aged woman. When husband Bill returned from a business trip, she handed him her lawyer's card. "I'd like to have you move out." Responded Bill, "Well, that's a fair deal." Sure, Bill.

*   *   *

It might be a little clearer now why so many boomers were disillusioned. By 1973, many erstwhile radicals were more interested in partying than politics. Out of despair, defeat, or passing fancy, reform had gone the way of cheap gas.

One of the largest, and one of the last, rock festivals took place at the historic Watkins Glen race track in upstate New York at the end of July. Attended by over 600,000 (only 150,000 were expected), the all-day affair featured the Dead, the Band and the Allman Brothers.

Keep on Truckin'

Grateful Dead

Traffic was tied up as far south as central Pennsylvania. After this, localities banned rock festivals drawing over 5,000 and they all but disappeared. Downers had become the drug of choice for many. They transformed the euphoric festival spirit into hard core, blitzed-out revelry. It wasn't drugs alone, not by a long shot.

The music had begun to lose its unity, too. The king of the hard rock, pre-metal bands, Led Zeppelin, had been the best band around for some years. They showed up in '69 as the opening act for the Who and transformed the way rock 'n' roll approached

American Blues. They played it with an edge and a kick that seemed its destiny.

The Allman Brothers represented the spreading popularity of country influenced rock. The Dead were hitting their peak. They had continued the traditions of Moby Grape and other bands such as the ego-driven Buffalo Springfield. Country rockers like Lynyrd Skynyrd and the Marshall Tucker Band continued meat and potatoes rock 'n' roll, with a country twang thrown in.

With the appearance of Kiss in 1974, those face-painted lizards and lovers and cats and space men, rock as entertainment, as arena-filling extravaganza would create huge indoor concerts, involving tractor and trailer entourages and seriously expensive pyrotechnic-filled productions. Kiss and the glitter, glam and arena rockers, Alice Cooper, David Bowie and the wonderfully creative Pink Floyd turned rock into the White Elephant that sparked the punk rock reaction.

*   *   *

Sad state of affairs when we have to depend upon athletes for our inspiration. Corrupt politicians like Nixon and Agnew were such failures as moral and inspirational leaders we had to turn to the natural second choice. But oh what a sublime choice it was.

Say, Hey!

—Willie Mays

Rookie of the Year in 1951, the Say Hey Kid was the best player of his era. For twenty-two years, from the time he smacked one out off Warren Spahn in his first home at bat through his 660 homers (third in the all time list behind Aaron and Ruth) and his .302 lifetime batting average, he was one of the best fielders, base runners and clutch hitters. Vic Wertz wasn't the only player humbled by his athletic prowess. Everyone who ever played against Willie Mays found himself in the same category. Grace and finesse underlay his enthusiasm and ability. The Say Hey Kid was easily one of the four or five best players ever to play the game.

Chapter 30

"Our Long National Nightmare is Over."

1974. Another cataclysmic year in a succession of years of disaster and divisiveness. The country underwent something as unprecedented as the Civil War, survived it with its institutions still standing but deeply altered. The year didn't start out with much promise. In fact it took on the appearance of the next version of 1968. The good news was that with the resignation of Richard Nixon the Sixties mercifully came to an end.

Not without a parting gesture.

*   *   *

Symbionese Liberation Army
—Terrorist kidnappers of Patty Hearst

On February 5, this interracial terrorist group kidnapped Patty Hearst. Nineteen years old and sharing an apartment with her sententious boyfriend Steven Weed, the newspaper heiress changed her name to "Tanya" and joined the SLA "to stay and fight for the freedom of the oppressed people." Had this sideshow not developed such deadly consequences, it would have been parody from start to finish. The SLA Robin Hoods, who proved more Hoods than

Robins, made a defiant gesture "for the people." They demanded the Hearst family fork over $6 million to feed the poor. The Hearsts gave up $2 million for what turned into a Third World grab fest off the backs of trucks. You have to admit forcing the family of a famous tycoon to feed the poor had a certain flair, even if it turned into a debacle.

Meanwhile, Tanya showed up on a security camera participating in a bank robbery. In May police cornered the SLA in a nationally televised, realtime 1,000 round shootout in an LA suburb. Tanya's body was not among the revolutionary dead. Police caught up with her a year later and she was sentenced to six years for her crimes, chief among which seemed to have been getting kidnapped. Jimmy Carter pardoned her after two, implicitly acknowledging what everyone should have granted from the outset, that Patty was suffering from Stockholm Syndrome. Everything about her life said she wasn't strong and didn't possess William Randolph Hearst's domineering personality.

The trial and time "Tanya" endured revealed an unsavory societal grudge against the rich, in its way mirroring the SLA's non-negotiable demands on behalf of the poor. When it was all said and done, the entire ordeal proved merely a temporary if entrancing diversion from the real terrorism of the day: Nixon's near hijacking of the law. It might have been different had Watergate been a mere policy crisis or an attempt to reorient society towards compassion. But it wasn't. This was petty politics gone haywire. Once again the personal proved political during the Me Decade.

*   *   *

the Smoking Gun

—White House tapes

This June 23, 1972 recording of Nixon's Oval Office conversation with H.R. Haldeman revealed him approving the cover up of White House involvement in the Watergate break-in. The President of the United States was captured on tape obstructing justice and violating his oath of office. Nixon had suggested Haldeman call CIA deputy Director Vernon "Walters and have Walters call [acting FBI head L.] Pat[trick] Gray and just say, 'stay the hell out of this—this is, ah, business here we don't want you to go any further on it.'" Haldeman agreed and it cost both him and his boss their jobs. Following the release of this tape, the House Judiciary Committee voted three articles of impeachment.

All the President's Men
—by Carl Bernstein and Bob Woodward

They were Mutt and Jeff, the loose Jew and the stiff WASP, who made it big—really big. Through incredibly hard work, lucid insight and fortunate connections, they broke the early stages of the Big Story. But not without its downside. Fame ruined Bernstein's prodigious talent (after all he and Woodward were played by Dustin Hoffman and Robert Redford). Worse, their achievements spawned a generation of cynical, suspicious, self-seeking journalists who dreamed of their own glory and cared next to nothing about the commonweal. For a good while afterwards, young reporters cutting their teeth on suburban school boards and neighborhood barbecues paraded through the nation's newsrooms declaiming cover-ups, turning preliminary negotiations into completed scandal, occasionally forging stories and mocking public trust while evincing a nearly total lack of perspective and conviction. Credibility and respect will forever remain twin victims of Watergate.

"Our long national nightmare is over."

—Gerald Ford

Facing certain impeachment and conviction, the other victim Richard M. Nixon resigned on August 9. In a rambling, wrenching speech before his staffers in the East Room of the White House, Nixon summed up his faults when he said, "Others may hate you, but they don't win unless you hate them back. And then you destroy yourself." A fitting epitaph.

After being sworn in, Gerald Ford reassured us the worst was over. "Our Constitution works. Our great republic is a government of laws and not of men. Here, the people rule." (Except for the mere thirty years of recrimination while the GOP lay in wait to exact its revenge.)

The sense of disappointment and defeat was pervasive, even among dissenters. It mattered little that they had been vindicated. Whether we admitted it or not, all generations of Americans were united in grief over an irretrievable loss. It was like suffering the death of one's parents. The ultimate irony in the era of the generation gap was that Nixon's resignation hit young people like a betrayal by a respected parent. Much generational cynicism stemmed directly from Nixon's monumental moral lapse. It told young people that no matter how much you care, no matter how dedicated you are, dark forces will be there to destroy your idealism in the name of personal self-interest.

The loss was of more than innocence. Watergate was not the coming of age ritual that perhaps Vietnam had proven to be. Other presidents had played it fast and loose, and would again soon. Fast Eddie Felson was nothing new to American politics. Nixon's corruption went far deeper. It made America so painfully ordinary. People realized that, at least in their lifetime, America would not regain its strength of character. Richard Nixon had betrayed the sense of honor of which this nation had always been so justifiably proud. If you take away a nation's honor, its institutions become suspect. If its institutions are suspect, its reason for being comes into question. After Watergate, America seemed anything but a City on a Hill

*   *   *

By the 1990s people had forgotten that the 60s' began as a quest for values. The reclusive Robert M. Pirsig's lyrical, fictional account of a journey Phaedrus, the narrator, and his eleven year old son Chris took through America was all about values.

Zen and the Art of Motorcycle Maintenance
—an Inquiry into Values

Although the book's title comes from *Zen in the Art of Archery*, superficially it recalled *On the Road*, and in scope perhaps *Moby Dick*, as *The New Yorker* suggested. Both works represented quests for self-discovery and fulfillment, and truth in self. At every stop, around every corner, in all parts of the country, in all seasons and weather conditions, Phraedus' pilgrimage produced wonder and enlightenment. One could learn to accept and grow from within.

The author approached over 100 publishers before one finally took him on. What resulted was a colossal best seller. The unlikely book about an unlikely subject struck a high note in the Me Decade's unhappy symphony. The book confronted the problem boomers faced—or thought they faced—at that point their lives. Namely, why technology had alienated individuals from each other and from society. That being so, how can we live? How can we survive? Pirsig's answers helped point the way.

He called his book "a moving, roving Chautauqua," after the touring tent seminars of the mid-19th century that educated and entertained. Except this time the audience toured on motorcycle. "On a cycle, the frame is gone…You're in the scene, not just watching it anymore, and the sense of presence is overwhelming."

It was a way to divorce the romantic from the classical, to unify the cold realm of technology with the warm realm of humanism. His solution, the Zen solution, was to merge with activity, the surroundings, even the motorcycle, to experience all on a romantic level. Music to an aging hippie's ears.

*   *   *

Great reading. Unusual because in America, the only thing that overcomes western subject/object duality in the way of Zen, is the champion athlete, who seems totally at one within his or her element. Such sublime physical eloquence was as rare for a Westerner as nirvana was for the Easterner.

715

—Henry Aaron

In 1974, on the first day of the season, Henry Aaron tied Babe Ruth's home run record. Then at home in Atlanta on April 8, he hit Al Downing's first pitch into the left field bullpen. He retired several years later with 755 career home runs. Perhaps it is making too much of disparate events. But the same year an American president resigned in disgrace and a book searching for the Zen experience on the back of a motorcycle became a mega-best seller, came a feat of magnificence that championed physical and mental struggle as the way—the Western Way?—to overcome centuries of subject/object duality between the races. In any case, Aaron's feat carried at least as much lasting significance as Nixon's. And that was a good thing.

*   *   *

The Brady Bunch
—another American family

Here was a studied contrast to the Loud family whose fraying reflected the tensions within American society. If the Louds were plagued by the changes that led to their undoing, the Brady Bunch was largely...happy, despite the way two single parents with three kids each came together. From Sept. 16, 1969 to Aug. 30, 1974, over five seasons of 116 half-hour episodes and a pilot, the family and Alice the housekeeper, who refereed the loving chaos, laughed and wise-cracked through a never-ending series of domestic and social issues. The Bunch provided weekly swatches of "Ozzie and Harriet"-type wholesome family fun at a time when a little sureal suburbia was exactly what the nation needed.

Chapter 31

"A Rogue Elephant"

1975. It has become customary to refer to the Sixties as a time of left wing excess. Without denying the irresponsible excesses of the far left, the actions of the establishment weighed far more heavily on society. The Pentagon Papers detailed the duplicity of LBJ's war policies. Subsequent studies, including those by military men, such as Harry Summers' *On Strategy*, detailed the sheer wrong-headedness of the war effort. Beyond that the lawlessness of such programs as COINTELPRO, the deceit, the hatred and corruption coming especially from the Nixon administration were more destructive than the fires of dissent and protest.

Violent repression and anti-democratic activities from the establishment fomented most of the problems associated with the 60s—and for that reason must, at least, share the reproach. Those wanting to blame all America's current ills on the 60s would do well to remember that it was also the era of LBJ, a world class narcissist, and Richard Nixon, a man of intemperate morals and voluptuous hatreds.

Sex, drugs and rock 'n' roll

—**bumper sticker**

Even with the Age of Aquarius reduced to a bitter pipe dream, this little mantra was not the intended legacy of so idealistic an era of reform. Sex clubs, group sex, hip bisexuality, homosexuality, drugs for partying—historic standards thrown out the window. All of it justified by one of the most counterfeit notions we ever came up with.

Who's to say what's normal?

—pop "wisdom"

A negative phrase that signified so much. For a generation all too aware of what was wrong with society, this flirtation with license was a disappointing cop-out. The justification? Society was so beyond redemption we might just as well get it on. By the mid-70s, in spirit and in outlook, America was a defeated nation. Vietnam and Watergate dumped immorality upon the ashes of hope.

Although to check out the nocturnal activities on campus, one might have concluded it was just good clean f-u-n.

Streaking

—campus fad

Trailing out of the devil-may-care laxity of the age, students were now showing their contempt for the uptight world of the establishment by running naked across campus, even across the dais at graduation. Streaking even went nation-wide when in 1974 a man "who went to great lengths to show his shortcomings" (according to host David Niven) scampered across the stage at the Oscars. Compared to all the other chaos, most people were inclined to view it with relief, recalling as it did the cherished Golden Age of phone booth stuffing and goldfish swallowing—and laugh it off.

Streaking was just a fad, not a bellwether, wasn't it? Perhaps. It was a time of fads. In the fall of 1975 the Pet Rock got its fifteen minutes of fame. Five million people actually paid $5.00 for a polished beach stone nestled in excelsior cradled in a cardboard box. An instruction booklet told the owner that this pet didn't need to be fed or house-broken. People stupid enough to buy one probably threw down $3.00 for a Mood Ring that changed colors with the wearer's emotions. They probably wore it dressed in a leisure suit and platform shoes while sitting with an encounter group partner (dressed in hot pants, no doubt) at an *est* meeting with their Pet Rock in its box beside the Lava Lamp. Top end Mood rings went for as much as $250.

"Let's do the Time Warp again."

—The Rocky Horror Picture Show

Normal? The transvestite Transylvanian Dr. Frank 'N Furter didn't know from normal.

> *"I'm just a sweet transvestite, from Transsexual Transylvania...Give yourself over to absolute pleasure. Swim the warm waters of sins of the flesh-erotic nightmares beyond any measure, and sensual daydreams to treasure forever. Can't you just see it? Don't dream it, be it."*

The movie was a cult hit. *The* cult hit of all times...and a long, long way from the Age of Aquarius. By 1975 America was as far from the benign and naïve days of "peace and love" as those days were from the idealism of "I have a dream" or "Ask not what your country can do for you...."

For years at midnight, boomers dressed in costume to see this flick, shout dialogue at the screen, call Janet a slut and Brad an asshole every time they appeared, flash flashlights, shoot each other with water pistols, get up and dance the Time Warp in front of the screen. Invariably someone rode a motorcycle through the theater at the appropriate moment. "No matter how you slice it, it's still meatloaf."

"Jane, you ignorant slut."
—Dan Ackroyd on *Saturday Night Live*

The counterculture's offbeat, anti-establishment humor found its way into the mainstream through the backdoor of late night television. Many of the antics of the Not Ready For Prime Players were drug-inspired and a decided stretch beyond the satire of *That Was the Week that Was* of the early 60s and *Laugh-In* of the latter. The first crew of Gilda Radner, Chevy Chase, John Belushi, Lorraine Newman, Dan Ackroyd, Jane Curtin and Garret Morris brought inventive talent to inventive skits. They were the Mickey Mouse Club all grownup but still as full of themselves as ever. The show added Bill Murray and later such future stars as Eddie Murphy, Dana Carvey, Mike Myers and Chris Farley. But it was the original cast and crew of writers who gave the show its lasting significance.

The opening prat-fall, "Live from New York, it's Saturday Night," the news, "I'm Chevy Chase and you're not" and the musical talent and semi-permanent host Steve Martin—all announced a new generation of comedians that said one thing: We have no Gods before us. The show challenged, then changed, the very nature of humor. The Players became stars in their own right. John Belushi, the most talented of them all, followed an almost predictable course of self-destruction through drugs and profligate living in 1982.

*   *   *

Wait a minute, some of the rejection humor had a basis in fact. That other Transylvanian castle—the one up on Capitol Hill in DC—was doing its own version of the time warp.

"...like a rogue elephant on the rampage."
—Church Committee report on the CIA

By its magnitude and implications, Watergate brought demands (that were more akin to howls of outrage) to find out what else the American government had been up to behind the public's back. An investigation of the Central Intelligence Agency revealed it had been relentlessly violating the civil rights of Americans within the United States and abroad by tapping their phones, breaking into their homes, opening their mail and tailing them. In addition to infiltrating illegally into radical groups, the agency assassinated foreign leaders, staged coups and traded arms on the black market. Nice list for an arm of the American government. Sanctioned or not by various presidents, all of it violated federal law. The FBI and the even more secret NSA had committed similar actions. Despite the evidence no one ever suffered indictment or trial.

The exigencies of the Cold War may explain these actions, but it failed to justify them. Every petty dictator and rapacious tyrant has at some point told his subjects that if they didn't constrain his actions, he would get them what they wanted. The people invariably went along. But this was America—our country—that had created a roving arm of repression and used it without compunction or restraint. Revelations such as those from the Church Committee's inquiry substantiated a great deal of the now defunct New Left's attack on the establishment's modus operandi. The ends may justify the means in Soviet Union or Communist China, but it wasn't supposed to happen here. If you throw in the

Pentagon Papers and the Watergate tapes, the results make a compelling case for the high road to tyranny.

A grateful nation ought to pause a moment to thank all the activists from civil rights to anti-war that we never quite got there.

*   *   *

Inescapably though, the full truth meant that the counterculture also spawned hell-seeds. Although fewer and farther between and not nearly so dangerous as the leeching of the powerful, they became more visible. The unasked question of the day was this. Which posed the graver threat to the social fabric, the CIA or the Manson family? Doubtless, the generation one belongs to will influence the answer. One aberration was political, the other cultural. Eventually the two had to meet.

The Manson family (and it *was* an aberration of the counterculture) cultivated sociopaths like mushrooms. One emerged from underground to point a pistol at Gerald Ford. Gerry Ford! A most likable and necessary man. More than the assassinations of the previous era, an attack on this uncharismatic man was an act of nihilistic madness. And she was just the first.

Squeaky

—failed presidential assassin

Now serving a life sentence, Lynette Fromme pointed an uncocked .45 at the president in Sacramento on September 5. This twenty-six year old member of the Manson family was joined in her failure later in the month by Sara Jane Moore, who actually managed to jerk off a round from across the street. Moore had been an FBI and police informant and was vague about her grievances. She got life, too. Gerry Ford was such an unobjectionable man, unless you consider physical awkwardness and slowness of wit grounds for assassination. 'Inexplicable' comes to mind.

*   *   *

More explicable, if no less difficult to suppress, were the economic woes the country had lurched into.

Whip Inflation Now

—"stagflation"

The oil shock began the rude decline of America's transcendent standard of living. Economic stagnation and double-digit inflation pushed it down further and stood on it. Despite the growing wealth of the few, the many found it difficult to keep up. Wives went to work when their husband's salaries were no longer adequate. Families unused to such things found themselves conserving energy and everyday living expenditures just to maintain. Favoring laissez-faire, Gerry Ford proposed a limp voluntary program to keep the relentless rise in the price of food, fuel and other necessities at bay. The excesses of the War came home all in a dark gray flock ending the days of carefree cruising in gas-guzzling cars with eight-cylinder engines and huge backseats. They were no longer affordable. Gone like a "hot rod Ford and a two dollar bill."

*   *   *

Apollo-Soyuz

—last flight of the Apollo Program

The spectacular space program wound down along with prosperity. National vision seemed to dull as the national pocketbook lightened. On July 17, Apollo 18 and Soyuz 19 docked in space. Astronauts met Cosmonauts in a symbolic act of détente between the United States and the Soviet Union. Criticized as a public relations stunt and so mundane as to leave an already bored public changing channels, it accomplished the important technological advance of successfully linking up two disparate spacecrafts. The mission also gave Deke Slayton, an original Mercury Astronaut, an opportunity to go into space. A heart murmur held him back until then. This was our last manned space flight until the Space Shuttle. For the next decade, America and Americans strove mightily to re-focus inward. Our concerns had always been mostly domestic anyway. Now they shrank even more.

Chapter 32

The Me Decade

```
************************
*    The First Wave hits   *
*        the big Three-O    *
************************
```

1976. Ideas of deferred gratification and temperance for the greater good slipped away. Boomers wanted it now, and they wanted to "feel good about themselves" as they got it. Self-fulfillment and self-actualizing, exercise and jogging, natural foods and macrobiotic diets—hey, whatever. Turning thirty was tough. The much feared barrier we had steadfastly ignored was upon us. One by one, year after year, another wave of boomers crossed over as though being called home. Some handled it with grace. Others with total denial. They would spend years trying to look and act younger. It couldn't be happening to us—and so soon.

Ultimately this translated into an emphasis on living the good life. Glorification of youth when combined with the egoism of disenchantment resulted in the cult of the *self*. In grand paradox it became something of a social movement.

The "ME" Decade

—Tom Wolfe

New York magazine had the right idea when it featured the "ME" of its cover story in very large, bold type. The conclusions drawn from the "lessons of the 60s" were more sentiment than rigorous analysis. Arguments that the U.S. was hopelessly corrupt and beyond redemption were as emotional as they were empty. These notions were so woefully incomplete and half thought-out as to be adolescent folly. But this cynical creed was surprisingly pervasive. All institutions from schools to government to corporations were toxic to the individual. The establishment destroyed what was good about people—and nothing could be done to correct it. The goals of social justice gave way to the goal of self-improvement. Self over society.

What an appropriate thirtieth birthday present for baby boomers.

By dropping out, at least spiritually, of the political world, you could become a better person in hopes of rising above the irretrievable depravity of institutional America. The path to a better world wound through the fitness center. Change might come through attrition, the old ways giving way to the fulfilled spirit of the young. Then again, it might not. Meanwhile, self-fulfillment powered the many. Singles bars, singles-only high-rise apartments proliferated like macrobiotic diets and hot tubs.

With self-fulfillment movements popping up all over the place and an Indian guru preaching TM (transcendental meditation), boomers spent the self-absorbed 70s obsessing about their inner child. They embraced the Human Potential Movement in its multifarious aspects such as transactional analysis, gestalt therapy, rebirthing, primal scream, encounter groups, free sex, including sex clubs such as Plato's Retreat, and ultimately religious sects from

Hare Krishna to Zen Buddhism to Charismatic Christianity. Used-car salesman Werner Erhard's *est* (Erhard Seminars Training) and other approaches to spirituality considered rationalism a cause rather than cure. Trouble was, he offered little in its place. Ultimately, est and all the others failed to offer even a sympathetic ear. Encounter groups became vehicles for sexual license.

In the *Culture of Narcissism*, historian Christopher Lasch attacked America's "hedonism, narcissism, cult of the self." No if, ands or buts (as our parents might have put it) about it, boomers were its mainstay. Parents despaired for their kids' future while those kids learned the art of sensual massage, talked about three-somes, and dodged de-programmers, convincing themselves the world would be a better place if they chose the correct massage oil.

Americans would soon jam into fitness clubs the way they once jammed the streets in protest. Now they protested against nature as it made war on their own bodies. Health spas sprang up everywhere, offering indoor jogging tracks, racquetball courts, workouts and aerobic dance A 1968 book on aerobic exercise sold in the millions.

The quest for the *self* had a powerful spiritual manifestation. Although they will object passionately at being lumped together, religious cults and charismatic and Pentecostal forms of Christianity were a clear result of the social drift of the 70s. The spiritual loss America suffered from Vietnam, Watergate and the pervasiveness of racial rancor drove many millions to various forms of religion for solace.

Gurus such as the 15-year-old Hindu mystic Maharaj Ji and his Divine Light Mission and Maharishi Mahesh Yogi offered yoga as the way to achieve spiritual peace. The Maharishi attracted the Beatles, the Beach Boys, Stevie Wonder. Ji held a mass convocation in the Houston Astrodome in 1973 with part of the parking lot reserved for UFOs. When none showed his movement suffered. Eventually Ji got ulcers from the stress.

Far more important than the phalanxes of passive aggressive Hare Krishnas in airports or Moonies selling flowers at intersections was the rise of fundamentalist Christianity preaching traditionalisms, a literal interpretation of the Bible and a passionate rejection of modernism and postmodernism. In Virginia, to cite two examples, Fundamentalist Baptist minister Jerry Falwell became the leading televangelist while Pentecostal Pat Robertson's Christian Broadcasting Network zoomed from four stations to 130 affiliates by the end of the decade.

All offered refuge from the vulgarity of a secular culture that had lost its focus. This religious revival would coalesce into a social and political uprising known as the Fourth Great Awakening. Once again, boomers would become the shock troops of a vast reform movement. A harbinger of the future came in the November presidential election when Christians of many denominations and sects turned out to vote, being rallied by their ministers for a candidate that was quite open about having accepted Jesus as his personal savior and becoming a Born-Again Christian.

"I'll never lie to you."

—Jimmy Carter

I'll never lead you either. He was the most devout president ever and the most conservative Democrat in the White House since Grover Cleveland. This might have worked to his advantage had he been a more imposing figure. The public craved dynamic leadership. Wanted him to take charge. But his modest, humble ways, admirable though they were...

"I have looked on a lot of women with lust. I've committed adultery in my heart many times. God recognizes I will do this and forgives me."

...did not suit the presidency well. Inflation, a stagnant economy that developed under Nixon and continued through Ford, hit the hapless Carter smack in the face. Perhaps no man could have led effectively through those dark, double-knit days. But it was Jimmy Carter's watch and he failed it.

Despite his emphasize on humans rights, his visionary energy conservation policy and the Camp David Accords that brought real peace to the Middle East, history conspired to insure a failed presidency. At this point, the country was inclined to distrust its leaders, even a man as honorable as Jimmy Carter. He was the first president whose word was automatically doubted.

*   *   *

The 70s specialized in bad attitudes. The rage abroad in the land, the disgust with institutions and to some degree with each other found its representation in a fictional TV news anchor named Howard Beale.

"I'm mad as hell and I'm not taking it anymore."

—Network

His ranting so captivated his fictional audience his network gave him his own talk show. The joke, though, was on the left. Most people, especially the makers of this movie, interpreted his anger as a continuation of 60s anti-establishment rage. True in part, but by America's bicentennial year that anger was finding its most acute audience on the right. Howard Beale portended Rush Limbaugh,

Gordon Liddy and Bob Bell. This movie really predicted the rise of what would eventually be known as the Angry White Male.

*   *   *

Meanwhile, there was still money to be made. During the 70s, it took the DC housing market only five years to double. That was just for starters. During the real estate boom, houses doubled or tripled, or even quadrupled in price within a few years. The average age of home ownership fell.

> ### *"Real Estate is the marijuana of the 70's."*
> ### —Sara Davidson

Boomers were out of college, into the job market, thirty-something and looking at their world through less rosy lenses. Paisley gave way to earth tones as boomers started to put down roots. Numbers alone would have caused a housing boom. Some boomers had the sense to get in early and made tidy fortunes because of it. Thousands got rich quick. Tens of thousands desperately sought to. Many others ended up "house-poor," but housed nonetheless. While it lasted the bubble meant boomers could add a third income to support their new addiction, material acquisition. We were becoming our parents. Writer Sara Davidson published a memoir in which she bemoaned the lost idealism while heralding the advent of the Yuppie (although the term was a decade away). "For years," she wrote, "I felt I had blown it, my generation had blown it, the Sixties had blown it, and we would never again see the heights."

Although the heights of togetherness and hope were re-captured briefly during the country's bicentennial celebration, she was right. The thrill was gone. In its place, alarmingly premature nostalgia provided an excuse for the continuing generational shift in focus.

Now it was about home and money. Typically post-war World War II America added half a million new households every year. In the 70s, with boomers coming of middle-age (so to speak), that number shot up to a priapic one and a half million. Boomers waited an extra few years to go house-shopping. But when they did, they did so all at once.

The explosion in housing prices—they climbed twelve percent a year—occurred as boomers began to realize their own mortality, as usually happens in the late 20s or early 30s. Suddenly the dusty crash pad was about as homey as a raft on the high seas. Woodstock was muddy and damp. Enough already. Gimme shelter—with a fireplace and a soft shag carpet for my full body massage. Throw in the spread of unconventional living arrangements and you get the spike in the market. One third of the new households were traditional. The other two-thirds were non-family group houses and the like. Many traditional households were financed on two-incomes.

The boom allowed the fortunate to trade up into ever larger homes, or acquire multiple dwellings at enormous profits. The rush drove up prices, fifty-three percent on average from 1973 to 1978. The effects were as intoxicating as any drug high, but ultimately not as defining as Sara Davidson expected. Apartments converted into condominiums, many with young adults in mind—no kids, singles preferred.

   *   *   *

But ferment rose under the firmament. Second wave boomers were now into their teens and full of blunted, hormonal angst. The first wave had protested against the establishment and now seemed to care more about fine wine. Their younger brothers and sisters had all that alienation, all that technique and no where to go with it.

No Future for You

—punks

So, up your BMW, up your skiing vacation in Aspen, which became the 70s version of the Haight. Up your pseudo-liberalism. No co-ops, no duplexes, no lofts. No pretense. They challenged the rock establishment, bands like Pink Floyd, Journey, Foreigner, Kansas, Fleetwood Mac and any number of arena rock groups and their show-biz orientation. When the Sex Pistols swaggered onto the scene, rejection of big time rock 'n' roll turned big time. Punks came from the English lower classes that saw nothing but life's grime and misery. They wore black leather, pierced their skin, and defiantly spit on hippies (and each other). 'Tudes this cool couldn't be long from pop culture's mainstream. Sure enough, Doc Martens, spiked hair and leather became, like, totally hip. The band itself didn't survive its first American tour. Sid Vicious eventually OD'd and Johnny Rotten went on the talk shows. Punk and its American counterpart that followed half a decade later shook the rock world to its roots—for about five minutes, before it went the way of all things countercultural and was co-opted.

Punks may have been nothing more than indoor hippies. But they sure hated hippies, and perhaps with reason. Hippies were supposed to offer an alternative to hypocrisy. When second wave boomers raised their heads and looked beyond their apartment complexes, they looked to their progenitors and saw a generation selling out.

Chapter 33

"May the Force Be With You."

1977. Hippies were distrustful of more than hypocrites. Hippies—indeed, perhaps most baby boomers—also held a deep distrust of technology. A decade—and an era ago, Stanley Kubrick's seminal *2001: A Space Odyssey* defined the evils of computers, technology, and the establishment. All that was about to change. George Lucas' labor of love gutted the old fears. R2D2 and the persnickety C3PO made the perfect goof-ball anodynes for the button-down malevolence of HAL 9000. In terms of public reception, the hi-tech future began with this movie. In the process childhood got a reprieve.

> *"May the Force be with you."*
>
> **—Han Solo**

And not a minute too soon. At last some optimism. George Lucas' wondrous space opera humanized computers and provided an encouraging take on the possibilities of technology. Conceived as nine movies, divided into three trilogies, *Star Wars'* innovative special effects and optimistic plot (that appeared to be a take on the Vietnam War) changed popular culture. This movie, which was later re-titled to *Episode Three: A New Hope*, injected a much-needed sense of hope to the sagging American spirit. Lucas' film allowed Americans to look at the future—to look at themselves—with renewed expectations. In the process, a generation known for its anti-technology bent began to embrace it with the fervor of religious converts. In the end *Star Wars*, supplemented by Steven Spielberg's ingenious science fiction epics *Close Encounters of the Third Kind* and *E.T.*, restored pride in what it meant to be an American.

Not bad for a B movie.

*   *   *

Some of us were unable to proceed into that future without making some sort of affirmation of the past. Americans, blacks most especially, warmed to the warmed-over "history" of author Alex Haley's ancestry. He claimed to have researched his forebears back to the West African village of Juffure, ultimately relying upon a griot (or native oral historian) to name his ancestor kidnapped into slavery,

"My name is Kunta Kinte."

—LeVar Burton in *Roots*

Roots: The Saga of an American Family came to TV the year after it was published. It won the National Book Award and a "special" Pulitzer. One hundred thirty million viewers watched the week-long miniseries in late January 1977, through a blizzard in parts of the country. It was the first time ever black Americans and many whites willingly, if all too briefly, came to grips with their slavery heritage.

The fact that Haley plagiarized parts of the book made little difference to the public. Readers bought a million copies the first year. Its message was too important. He ended up paying $650,000 to folklorist and writer Harold Courlander for stealing scenes from him. Some historians called *Roots* a novel, others a "fictionalized genealogy." The best way to look at it was the way Haley himself finally had to consider it—as "symbolic." He admitted his work was not so much history as an account of mythmaking. "What *Roots* gets at in whatever form, is that it touches the pulse of how alike we human beings are when you get down to the bottom, beneath these man-imposed differences."

Few American blacks knew who their forebears were, let alone much about their West African origins. The miniseries stirred popular interest in black history. The series held viewers as spellbound in Europe as in America.

*   *   *

In July the now faded memories of the Long Hot Summers received a jolt when a power failure in New York City produced several days of rioting.

Life during wartime

—Talking Heads

Though not specifically about the blackout riots, this lively, apocalyptic tune by David Byrne foreshadowed urban chaos of the 80s, as indeed did the riots. Half an hour after the lights went out for nine million residents of New York City and Westchester County, thousands of people took to the streets in a delirious spree of looting, arson and smash and grab thievery. By contrast, during the more pervasive and lengthier East Coast blackout of 1965, people stayed home and made babies. This time they were "mad as hell" and roaring anarchy from hastily thrown up barricades. Whatever community spirit had existed before had depleted. The downward spiral into self-absorption and mayhem was complete. "They're crazy," one man told *The New York Times*. "They're

taking their shoes and breaking windows. They're animals."
Another commented, "It's a lot different from 10 years ago. Last
time people were helpful."

Chapter 34

Revolutionary Suicide

1978. The self-centeredness of the Me Decade intensified and began to mutate towards the politics of the right. The blackout riots in the Big Apple revealed a rising frustration, due most likely to the faltering economy and a glaring lack of leadership at the top. As the country seemed to be coming unglued, the personal, to its own bemusement, was embracing physical fitness.

> *"Fewer and fewer people these days argue that running shortens lives, while a lot of people say that it may strengthen them. If that's all we've got for the time being, it seems a good enough argument for running. Not airtight, but good."*
>
> **—Jim Fixx, *The Complete Book of Running***

The fitness craze began with jogging. At first it seemed pure compensation. Our first military defeat, the abandonment of social responsibility in favor of individual growth had people out there chugging away in hopes of a better self, if not a better day. And that meant health foods, vitamins and all manner of fad diets in addition to pounding the pavement. The greatest boon to working out was the invention of Nautilus equipment. These counter-weighted and well padded machines promised to make muscle tone easier to re-acquire.

Perhaps muscle tone was the real reason baby boomers jogged, to get back to the way they used to be. Our generation, after all, made youth the eighth sacrament. There was something spiritually lifting (and comical) about not quite so young boomers flocking into newly constructed health spas, still smelling of cement dust and naugahyde, decked out in colored-coordinated nylon workout togs. Companies such as Nike became multi-million dollar concerns creating scientifically designed sports shoes for running, working out, hiking, cross training. It didn't take long for the boomer-driven health craze to create a new fashion trend, faux warm-up suits and sports clothes. The Nike ad campaign that first featured the amazing Bo Jones and later the super-human Michael Jordan sold America not only exercise garb but a new ethic, a culture of vigorous bodies that sought to capitalize on the protest spirit of an era gone by with "Just do it."

*   *   *

While some exercised, others got exercised. In California, another revolution was brewing. Also based in part on some of the same selfish passions that fueled the fitness boom, this one heralded the resurgence of the country's dominant political ethic, conservatism. Boomers, indeed a growing number of Americans, were sick of reforms dictated by the federal government and funded with their tax dollars. People felt put upon by self-righteous liberals and their relentless programs. It was as though Howard Beale's lament finally produced concrete action.

Proposition 13

—Howard Jarvis

The 75 year old retired school teacher Jarvis urged citizens to "take control of the government again or it will control you." Plenty of people agreed. Despite objections from state leaders, California voters rolled back their property taxes 57%, to mid-60's—pre-Great Society—levels and blocked future increases. Carter's pollster Pat Caddell called Proposition 13 the "primal scream of the people against Big Government." The referendum also sought to block unfunded federal mandates to the states that had caused taxes to go up in the first place. Predictably these cuts resulted in the reduction in public services such as libraries, sanitation, parks, and public health facilities. As the Jarvis-led tax revolt spread across the country, it became the forefront of a grass-roots uprising against "wasteful" and unwarranted government programs to help blacks and the poor.

High taxes were nothing compared to Affirmative Action directives forcing employers to hire minorities and women. Begun under LBJ, Affirmative Action had grown from a program to give a boost to qualified blacks into a massive leveling scheme based on hiring, admitting and promoting everyone but white men.

"some attention to numbers"
—Justice Lewis Powell in the *Bakke* case

The *Bakke* decision marked the end of public support for attempts to bring about "equality as a fact of life" that LBJ first spoke about in 1965. Deepening resentment against quotas, time tables and set asides that did in fact discriminate now and then against white men and women coalesced into full-fledged opposition. Baby boomers entered college or the work force during the heyday of Affirmative Action. And while it seemed that every white boomer had a story to tell about a less qualified minority being hired or promoted over them, on the whole, they had not been inconvenienced by Affirmative Action. Still, cases of reverse discrimination that violated the spirit and often the letter of the Civil Rights Act of 1964 and the 14th Amendment suggested that the government was using heroic medicine on an extremely reluctant patient. A patient that refused to believe he was even sick.

In *the University of California vs. Bakke,* the Supreme Court noted as much with its curious 5-4 split decision that outlawed quotas but upheld the use of Affirmative Action in the name of diversity. It appeared to acknowledge the continuing problem of entrenched inequality while agreeing with the growing anger at the color conscious nature of once "color blind" policies.

The Civil Rights Era ended when the Supreme Court ordered Alan Bakke, a white applicant who'd been rejected by a quota system, admitted to medical school. His grades and MCATs had been higher than most of the sixteen minorities for whom places were automatically reserved. The Supremes ruled that schools could consider the number of minority students currently enrolled in admitting the less qualified but could not set quotas in doing it. After this case, judicial and legislative activism on behalf of equal rights for all citizens began to succumb to an onslaught of counter-suits and conservative legislation. The era of activist governmental intervention to end racism began that began with *Brown vs. Board of Education* began to taper off.

    *   *   *

Strong feelings held the government had gone too far to promote racial equality, while others believed the government couldn't go far enough to overcome centuries of discrimination. Such growing divergences were a sign of the times.

In a backwater country along the northern tip of South America, a cult once dedicated to racial harmony went a couple extra miles to avoid what they thought was government invasiveness.

> *"...revolutionary suicide protesting against the conditions of an inhumane world."*
>
> **—Jim Jones**

Jim Jones, the mad leader of People's Temple cult, had dedicated his organization to ending racial prejudice and discrimination. He enforced monogamous relationships and encouraged inter-racial couples. In the end he called upon his followers, most of whom were black, to drink cyanide and tranquilizer-laced strawberry Flavour-aide. They lined up and obeyed.

Jones and many of his followers fled their home-base in San Francisco for Jonestown, Guyana, over issues of religious freedom. In reality its founder and leader had gone insane. He'd defrauded and abused the devout, ordering they worship him as God, as he confiscated their property and income. They called him "Father" or "Dad" and went along with him.

Peoples Temple was one of a growing number of religious, quasi-religious and non-religious cults that proliferated during the Me Decade's extravaganza of self-indulgence. Oddly, legions of lost souls, hell-bent on self-fulfillment, enlightenment and self-actual-ization, flocked to these groups or became Jesus Freaks, eager, it seems in retrospect, to toss away the free agentry that the Sixties had given them. Thousands of bright people were drawn into the debasement of cults, which were, after all, communes where zealots replaced hippies and conformity was often violently enforced. Deprogrammers tried to rescue members from these often-prison-like organizations. But they had to resort to kidnapping to do so.

Former alcoholic Charles Dederich transformed Synanon from an effective voluntary treatment program for drug addicts and alcoholics into an apparently malevolent cult: "We will do your thinking for you." Ultimately, he forced his followers to shave their heads and swap spouses. He ordered vasectomies for men (excluding himself) and abortions for women. Unproven rumors persisted he ordered the murder of several renegade cult members.

Far more visible, Hare Krishnas—the International Society of Krishna Consciousness—followed A. C. Bhaktivedanta Swami Prabhupada, who brought a little known version of Hindu to the U.S. in 1965. His followers shaved their heads, donned saffron robes, walked the streets in small groups chanting and dunning passers-by for money, all the while preaching inner peace. Their leader died in 1978 and though less visible Krishnas remained peaceful if annoying.

A similar cult, at least in its requests for money, was the Unification Church. The Moonies, some 37,000 of them, were an offshoot Christian sect led by South Korean evangelist Sun Myung Moon. They were just as persistent in street corner hawking of flowers. Dominated by boomers, like the Krishnas, their average age was twenty-four, Moonies dressed conventionally. Men wore coats and ties and obeyed Moon's home-brew blend of Christianity, eastern Mysticism and Puritan morality. Moonies also obeyed Reverend Moon's orders to sever ties with their families. Ensconced in a $625,000 estate in New York, he also decreed that all the world's religions should merge under his control. Not that his followers questioned him. They were so devoted that thousands married, often to people they'd never met. In a mass wedding in Madison Square Garden on September 18, 1974 some 18,800 couples were "married." In 1984 he went to prison for income tax evasion.

Far more dangerous was the Army of God led by David (Moses) Berg. This prominent doomsday cult inhabited various communes connected by its leader through rambling "Mo Letters." Berg encouraged his female followers to seduce prospective adherents as a way to increase membership.

These were some of the more prominent cults of the era. As pervasive as they were, none approached Peoples Temple in extremes of action.

Nine hundred fifteen men, women and children obeyed Jim Jones' crazed call to mass suicide. They forced poison into their children, then drank it themselves. Jones ordered his followers to kill Congressman Leo Ryan who'd come to Guyana to investigate them. Despite Manson's murderous antics a decade earlier, Jonestown called attention to a widespread phenomenon. People were so spiritually adrift they were easily seduced by the protective embrace of cults run by autocratic leaders promulgating bastardized forms of Christianity and eastern religions.

   *   *   *

Although discos were not cults, not exactly anyway, these tawdry dens offered similar promises of fulfillment. They were the cult's secular and eerie cousins. Home to people just as lost though not quite as desperate, they may have been tacky, but they were a whole lot safer. (It's surprising no enterprising disco king ever thought to call his emporium of glitz Jonestown.) Disco music—the dominant pop music format of the 70s—got a singular boost from a movie about discos featuring a rather cartoonish TV star.

Saturday Night Fever

—starring John Travolta

Disco was the soundtrack of the Me Decade. The clubs offered faux urban sophistication. The sleazy sophistication exemplified by Barry White provided an explicit alternative to anything the least bit socially aware, whether it be rock or soul. White invented disco by putting the bass line up front and de-emphasizing melody and lyric. It was the first commercially successful music to depend upon such electronic instruments as drum machines and synthesizers. Much of it was programmed and sequenced through MIDI.

Disco relieved its devotees from the heavy chore of thinking. Discos themselves were refuges from thought. The Village People's satiric *YMCA* and *Macho Man* offered the only hint of intelligence in what was otherwise mindless, beat-heavy music with a pronounced dearth of soul. With a few exceptions, such as the sumptuous Donna Summer, most disco acts did not perform live—because they couldn't. They were studio creations. In her biggest hit *Love to Love You Baby*, Summers repeated the title line twenty eight times while simulating the sounds of orgasm twenty-two times over the seventeen-minute duration of this interminable tune.

*   *   *

Maybe what was needed was a lesson in civility.

"Dear Miss Manners, Please list some tactful ways of removing
a man's saliva from your face.
Gentle Reader, Please list some decent ways of acquiring
a man's saliva on your face."

—Miss Manners

Those at the disco should have read Miss Manners. To help all those suffering from saturday night fever, *Washington Post* reporter Judith Martin started her thrice-weekly column in 1978. The columns and nine etiquette books presented a fresh way to deal in a civil way with the new and often confusing alterations in social and sexual mores. Beginning with the correct way to handle cohabiting unmarried couples and cohabiting unmarried same-sex couples, the issues facing "polite-society" were alien to the white-gloved worlds of Dear Abby and Amy Vanderbilt. Miss Manners became the perfect how-to guide for socially aggressive boomers.

*   *   *

Oddly, enough, signs of hope for the future were visible, even in these times that at best could be called vexing. Jimmy Carter was able to broker a world-changing treaty between bitter enemies, Egypt and Israel. The deeply religious Carter's persistent goodwill was the major factor in cementing the deal. The call for it originated with Egyptian president Anwar Sadat, who recognized the fruitlessness of continuing a war with a people who had legitimate, historic claims to the land where they lived.

Camp David Accords

—Carter–Sadat–Begin

Sadat changed history in November 1977 when he flew to Jerusalem to make peace with Israel. Addressing the Israel Knesset, he offered to end their thirty-year struggle. When the peace talks stalled, Jimmy Carter intervened and brought Sadat and Israeli Prime Minister Menachem Begin together at Camp David. Negotiations lasted thirteen days and resulted in an Israeli-Egyptian peace treaty that was signed in a joyous White House ceremony. It was the high point of Carter's presidency.

*   *   *

Science also made the sort of breakthrough that brought hope, this time to infertile couples. As remarkable an event as the Camp

David Accords, this advance brought revolutionary change to all humans. Nature suddenly didn't seem quite as inevitable.

First Test Tube Baby

—Louise Brown

Louise Brown became the first human being conceived outside the womb, via *in vitro fertilization* (in glass). Our Brave New World began in England on July 25, 1978, with a blue-eyed blond baby dubbed by the AP "a truck driver's miracle child." Today three hundred fifty clinics perform 40,000 procedures a year. IVF is expensive and has a one in four failure rate, but it hasn't been the moral horror that religious skeptics predicted. Instead, it has proven to be God's gift to childless couples.

Chapter 35

The Moral Majority

1979. Such a fitting start to the final year of the decade. Had the system finally broken down? For a moment people wondered.

Three Mile Island
—damaged nuclear power station

A cooling valve jammed and the reactor core overheated, producing a near meltdown. In the resultant panic 100,000 people fled the Harrisburg, Pennsylvania, area. According to one member of the commission appointed to study the event, "No one knew what was going on at the time, and it scares the hell out of me." For the first time Americans faced the reality of devastation from nuclear energy. Little radioactive material actually escaped into the atmosphere and no one was threatened. To prove this, Jimmy Carter and his wife, wearing hard hats and covers over their shoes that looked like bunny slippers, toured the plant. It calmed few and brought a lot of ridicule on the president and first lady.

Three Mile Island increased the credibility of the "No Nukes" movement that had been percolating along during the 70s, warning about plant safety, environmental damage, the difficulty of safely disposing of nuclear waste—and the potential cost in human lives.

Events at the plant gave these issues immediacy. Even without the activists, the near tragedy shifted public opinion against nuclear energy. Suddenly the promises of cheap, safe and plentiful energy weren't quite so certain. The costs had become prohibitive and local communities refused to countenance further plants, which went the way of rock festivals, as construction stopped.

Nuclear energy aside, technological innovations were beginning their futuristic onslaught. Besides, who needed festivals when you could carry around your own personal concert?

The Walkman

—personal music

Sony's innovation was just a tickling of the tidal wave to come. Until this hi-tech innovation, music had been a shared experience. Originally called the Sound About, the highly portable cassette player sold for $200 a unit. Sony's Akio Morita gambled and won. The Walkman caught on among Japan's strap-hangers. Boomers embraced them and soon watched their kids sink into sulking isolation in the back seat of the family car, shutting out their parents and the rest of the world, listening to music that was, ahem...increasingly incomprehensible and disconcertingly noisy. What can you say? We used our music to shut out our parents. Now our kids were shutting us out with theirs. And they didn't have to try hard to do it.

*   *   *

Indeed, the sensibility of the country had changed. Post-war, post oil-shock global economics were creating an annoying itch in the American way of living. Oil producing nations broke free of economic colonialism and began asserting themselves. Western Europe and Japan recovered and began to mount vigorous competition. All of this threatened every aspect of the once supreme and comfortable American society.

Raging double-digit inflation struck like a nuclear holocaust. The country's optimism went AWOL. Confidence in the future dropped as gas shot up to a dollar a gallon. Inflation peaked in 1980 at a painful 13.5%. Mortgage rates had been a tasty 7.5% in October 1970. In October 1981 they maxed out at a bitter 18.45%. So long housing boom. Inflation—too much money chasing too few goods—hit the middle class with such force people began to feel as though tough times and lowered prospects would never end. Bad enough you were supposed to keep your thermostat down to conserve energy. Continually rising prices was too much to put up with. People began buying in anticipation of higher prices. A very reckless way to live.

"Anticipatory buying"
—Secretary of the Treasury G. William Miller

Soaring oil prices and lax economic policies that held a little inflation would stimulate economic growth put the whammy on us. By 1979 a little inflation had become a lot of inflation. The economy stalled. Stagflation didn't. In August, in what became his wisest domestic act, Jimmy Carter asked the tough-talking, cigar smoking New York banker Paul Volcker to chair the Federal Reserve Board. Volcker began jacking up the interest rates to constrict the currency and squeeze inflation out of the economy. He believed long term inflation hurt the economy—at the time a somewhat contrarian philosophy. His policies proved tough medicine. Interest rates rose so sharply that by the early 80s the country had moved into the deepest recession with the highest unemployment since the Great Depression.

Slowly, painfully, unemployment increased as workers were laid off and weaker businesses closed. The housing industry was hit hardest. Potential homeowners couldn't pay the interest on mortgages and stopped buying. Irate builders sent Volcker two-by-fours with "We're mad as hell and we're not going to take it anymore" inscribed on them. Eventually the economy would sort itself out. In the meantime, employers began paying COLAs (cost-of-living-adjustments to wages) to counter inflation.

The uncertainty wasn't only the result of reduced circumstances, lowered expectations, and re-ordered geo-political relationships. It also resulted from fears of overpopulation and over-use of the world's natural resources. Americans comprised less than six percent of the world's population, yet, since the 50's had been using over a third of its resources. The warnings were dire.

Population Bomb

—Paul Erlich

Some people called him a doomsayer. Others took his predictions seriously enough that he appeared on Johnny Carson twenty-five times. He warned about the famine, disease and apocalypse that would ride across our planet as the direct result of overpopulation. Erlich and others preached family planning and contraceptives as a way to ward off what he considered inevitable disaster.

The world was producing far too many people to be sustained by its shrinking natural resources.* He turned out to be over-zealous in his forecasts of doom. Still, his warnings joined the chorus of despair wailing in the outer darkness.

| * | * | * |

*   Earth's 6 billionth person was born two minutes after midnight October 12, 1999, in Sarajevo, a boy

When President Carter spoke to the public about the failings of his administration, it played as if he were tendering his resignation. He might just as well. You can applaud the man's sincerity. But this speech was exactly what the country did *not* need to hear. Jimmy Carter gave them honesty when they wanted leadership.

National Malaise

—Jimmy Carter

Although the phrase came from pollster Patrick Caddell and journalist Joseph Craft, it characterized Carter's assessment of the psychological state of the union. The sense of failure, of lost opportunity without a real sense of crisis or impending danger was pervasive. Optimism faded to lassitude. Energy lapsed into indolence. A perilous state of affairs for a democracy. In his July 15 address he admitted his own shortcomings and vowed to stop managing the nation and start leading it. He removed five cabinet officers and attempted to re-order his administration. It was a wasted effort. National fatigue after years of chaos was too much for him to overcome.

     *   *   *

Carter couldn't have known at the time. Few saw it. But the conservative counter-revolution was accelerating. Though still formless, it had been underway for some time. Outraged by secularization of society, disgusted by gay rights, abortion and feminists, people turned to fundamentalist Christianity, which itself turned to politics. The result was the Fourth Great Awakening.

Americans have always been a religious people. Boomers have flocked to church throughout their lives. As the 70s wore on, the essential conservatism of our generation began to assert itself over left wing activism and nonconformity, first through a generational turn to spiritualism, then to evangelical and fundamentalist Christianity. From their church pews a new tide of boomers made a narrow right turn into politics, and, "praise God," a new form of activism was born.

The Moral Majority

—Jerry Falwell

Dominated by baby boomers new to political protest and a few who arrived here on a journey from the New Left of their college days, the Moral Majority was conservative Christianity's cause and effect. Prompted by the Carter administration's decision to remove the tax exemption from segregated, church-run colleges and universities, Baptist minister Falwell founded it to promote a legislative agenda that would ban abortions, curtail pornography, restore school prayer and promote "pro-God, pro-family policies in government." The Moral Majority issued morality ratings for Congress similar to those issued by the liberal Americans for Democratic Action.

Televangelists took to the airwaves attacking big government liberalism of the Great Society for creating a permissive society. They blamed liberals for declining morals, abortion, pornography—all the nation's social ills. This despite the corruption of the Nixon administration and moral failure in Southeast Asia. Pentecostal Pat Robertson declared, "We have enough votes to run the country."

Despite the public dislike of Falwell himself—he was widely scorned for his harsh, wrathful and even hateful posturing—they rallied behind his cause. That people tended to view him as a clerical version of Richard Nixon only emphasized their growing concern about the moral state of the country. Jerry Falwell played a central role in conservatism's mighty rise. The Baptist minister was openly "mad as hell" and would gladly bring God's wrath down on his enemies. Which suited many voters just fine. His group became the brown shirts of the New Right. It was also an important aspect of the nationwide religious awakening that stressed strict Biblical morality, ardent religiosity and "traditional values." When liberal critics pointed out that racism was a traditional value, Falwell changed it to traditional *family* values.

*   *   *

Religion makes far stranger bedfellows than politics. In this case, two clerics from different parts of the world: Jerry Falwell and the Ayatollah Khomeini. In truth, they weren't bedfellows. But, their complaints about American decadence were strikingly similar. Falwell, like Khomeini, represented the worldwide rise of religious fundamentalism in reaction to the spread of American secular culture. For America's Christian right, Satan was at play in the fields of the Lord. For Khomeini, America was

The Great Satan
—Ayatollah Ruholla Khomeini

When Khomeini's student followers seized the U.S. Embassy in Iran and made hostages of the Americans there, our entire nation rose up in righteous indignation. Americans wanted revenge. They never got it. In 1904 when a Moroccan strongman took an American citizen, Ion Pedicaris, hostage, President Theodore Roosevelt said, "This government wants Pedicaris alive or Rasuli dead." In 1979, receiving word of the hostage taking, Jimmy Carter went the Washington's National Cathedral to pray. Upright and sincere, it was not what Americans wanted or needed. They cried out for forceful action.

The Iranian revolution culminated with the November 4 seizing of 52 Americans in the US embassy in downtown Teheran. For 444 days America was held hostage by a theocracy that blamed American decadence and imperialism for Iran's problems. Our anger was surpassed only by our shame. Had we become the pitiful, helpless giant Nixon warned against? The failure of the rescue mission at Desert One in April, 1980, where American military men died, said yes. It also sealed the fate of the Carter presidency. As a nation we were more humiliated by the hostage crisis than the loss in Vietnam. Every weeknight ABC aired a half-hour news show, "America Held Hostage," that emphasized it. The show combined expert commentary and sage if pompous questioning and in 1980 became a permanent fixture under its new name "Nightline." The Ayatollah was responsible for making newsman Ted Koppel's career.

*　　　　　　　　　　*　　　　　　　　　　*

Carter's world—and the country he led—seemed to be unraveling. The Soviet invasion of Afghanistan (a reprise of its abortive 1947 invasion) was as great a shock as the hostage crisis. Yet another sign of what was becoming the Great Unraveling.

The Soviet Vietnam

—Afghanistan

During the early stages of the Iran Hostage Crisis, Soviet tanks rolled across its southern borders into Afghanistan. The brazen action caught America unawares. Worldwide it offered another sign of American weakness and incompetence. Six months earlier Leonid Brezhnev pledged peace and received pecks on his flabby cheeks from Jimmy Carter. It didn't take. Tensions between the superpowers returned to early 60's levels. The helpless president could only respond by withdrawing from the Moscow Olympics. Later, the U.S. gave the Afghan mujahidin Stinger missiles with which they neutralized Soviet helicopters. In 1988 Mikhail Gorbachev cited high costs and withdrew his troops.

*   *   *

> ### *"I can't lie to you about your chances, but you have my sympathies."*
> ### —Ian Holm in *Alien*

This scary movie actually caused a few heart attacks. At the time the sentiments of Ash, the android science officer, was a secular warning about imminent death from an indestructible alien creature. Its sacred equivalent had been around since 1970. At over fifteen million copies Hal Lindsey's *The Late Great Planet Earth* was the best selling book of the decade. This was "end-time prophecy" with detail as mortifying as any horror flick. The apocalypse was headed our way long about 1988. Millions and millions would die. How did Lindsey and the cohort of doomsayers know for sure? The Book of Revelations as supported by the Book of Daniel and other parts of the Bible told them so. The 1948 return of the Jews to Israel set in motion "the time of the end." For devout Christian Fundamentalists, Evangelicals and Pentecostals, whose secular influence was skyrocketing, this was far more enthralling than any celluloid product from the secular humanists on the Left Coast.

Why were Christian fundamentalists so anxious for Armageddon? After all, we're talking about the end of the world as we know it. Why feel fine about that? For the same reason so many others loved science fiction. Both are essentially optimistic— millions and millions may die, but we won't be among them.

Religious doomsayers have a built-in escape clause known as the Rapture. As the end nears, God's chosen will be swept up into Heaven. For the devout, it amounted to walking out on the movie. It made no difference that *The Late Great Planet Earth* was based upon half-baked Biblical exegesis that had no more basis in reality than *Alien*. At the tired end of a rough decade, it was hard to dispute either secular or sacred predictions for the fate of either the crew of the Nostromo or space ship America.

Chapter 36

"Are You Better Off?"

1980. Ronald Reagan was The Man on Horseback. The retired actor performed his way through eight years in the White House to wild applause, escorting baby boomers into middle age. Unintentionally picking up on boomer themes, this magnificent speechmaker told a seemingly leaderless, directionless nation its government was as corrupt and anti-American as protesters in the streets a decade earlier had said it was.

His solution, in its way as misleading as anything Timothy Leary ever advocated, was to embrace good old-fashioned materialism. He promised to bring back the Golden Age of the 1950's. Exhausted by nearly two decades of turmoil, the country fell for it. Boomers flocked to Reagan with a fervor that betrayed a deep desire to forget. Led by the Gipper, conservative politicians co-opted the anti-establishment rhetoric of the 60s and hurled it back at liberals and what was left of the counterculture with unfettered glee. Wealth, material acquisition, with a tip of the hat to Christian morality offered the true route to self-fulfillment and national salvation. Boomers embraced the culture of consumption as though we'd invented it—just as in the Sixties we thought we invented sex. Conspicuous Consumption, Laissez Faire and Social Darwinism became the new Holy Trinity.

"Are you better off than you were four years ago?"
—Ronald Reagan

That was easy. No, Hell no! We didn't feel better off, thank you very much. And most of us weren't. Inflation, de-industrialization, competition from Europe and the Japanese—not to forget the Ayatollah—were taking their toll. The consensus mourned the loss of the old American spark, the can-do spirit we'd once taken for granted. Not that we trusted the man who posed the question. Not just yet.

"There you go again."
—the Gipper

Reagan's cool performance in debate with Carter convinced the public that well…maybe he wasn't a mad bomber after all. He came off as personable, genteel and sensible. By contrast Carter seemed like a stick-in-the-mud, burdened by four years of history largely beyond his grasp. So was re-election. The dour man looked and sounded whipped. Reagan won in a landslide that extended to GOP control of the Senate. Middle America stepped up and shouted from the rooftops, "Goodbye to all of that!" Goodbye to liberalism. Goodbye to American defeatism, to the Iranians. Goodbye to the bad economy. Wimpy leadership. The counterculture. The Great Society. Protesters. Young people. Blacks. Feminists. Poor people. Goodbye, goodbye, goodbye, and, please—stay gone. The revenge was sweet.

*　　　　　*　　　　　*

Voodoo Economics

—George Bush's critique of Reaganomics

George, Sr. had a telling point, not that the electorate was listening. Supply-side economics' Laffer Curve proved exactly that. During the primaries Bush warned there was no way Reagan could increase defense spending, cut taxes and still balance the budget, no matter how much he promised to cut social spending. Reagan said, "Way."

Bush changed his tune after Reagan asked him to be vice president. The voters didn't care. Something for nothing promises worked like fool's gold. Disgust was so pervasive there was a general agreement to worry about the inconsistencies tomorrow. The sun was gonna come up tomorrow. Bet your bottom dollar.

    *   *   *

Who Shot J.R.?

—*Dallas* TV series

Power and greed became the national pastimes. They joined forces in this number one rated show and its bizarre values and dubious morality. The November episode of the prime time soap opera was one of the most widely watched shows in history. Eighty million people tuned in from all over the world to discover that Kristin was the one. The following year *Dynasty* premiered with its story line also celebrating glamour and greed. Still later chipmunk diva and sex goddess Madonna entered popular culture as the Material Girl. All the glitz bore an official imprimatur from the Reagan Administration, which, according to Johnny Carson, was "the first administration to have a premiere" instead of an inauguration.

The Second Gilded Age descended upon America with all the devil-may-care heedlessness of a costume ball in the Bowery. While those fortunate sons and daughters in the top ten percent bade goodbye to all the rest, the middle struggled to maintain and, as the saying goes, the poor got poorer. Reagan called them the "truly needy" and gently squeezed them from sight.

*   *   *

Little Havana

—Mariel Boat Lift

Cubans watched television, too. Miami already had well over 300,000 Hispanic residents when Castro allowed thousands more Cubans to flee his dictatorship. Actually, he dumped multiple boatloads of undesirables onto our shores. Ten years after the boat lift almost half of the city's two million people were Hispanic, the fastest growing minority in the country. Boat people from Southeast Asia had been immigrating since 1975. Later, Haitian boat people created "Little Haiti" with a population of 60,000. By the 1990's Miami had become a microcosm of our diverse and ethnically troubled nation.

Diminishing Anglo domination and aggressive minorities clamoring for their share of the American Pie would shade the political and cultural debate of the next several decades. Despite the ugliness of the reaction, America was well on the way to becoming truly multicultural and pluralistic, like it or not—and most native born whites (and a surprising number of native born blacks) didn't like it at all.

*   *   *

MADD

—Mothers Against Drunk Driving

Candi Lightner founded this seminal neo-reform group after one of her twin daughters was killed by a drunk driver who turned out to be a repeat offender. Focusing on public education and stiffened sentencing guidelines, MADD's mission was "to stop drunk driving and to support victims of this violent crime." It grew to a membership of over three million with 400 chapters. MADD represented a new type of boomer-led reform that sought to build a culture to counter the excesses of drug and alcohol abuse and sexual promiscuity.

"Neo-Prohibitionism" led by organizations such as MADD spread into a crusade against tobacco, of all things, and Nancy Reagan's "Just Say No" campaign against drugs. These were the heirs to the tradition stretching all the way back to Rosa Parks, who also just said, "No." It seemed as though boomers would forever be saying 'No,' or insisting others do. As we entered the 80s, reform moved from left to right and took on an ugliness unknown to the rambunctious idealism of days gone by. It was as though the right wing embraced the worst elements of the left's mistrust of government and corporate America, while holding none of its idealistic impulses.

*   *   *

Mount St. Helens

—Mother Nature's empire strikes back

When it blew its top on May 18, we saw nature in a way we weren't used to. The eruption blanketed Washington State with volcanic ash and altered national weather patterns. The twenty-four megaton blast created the largest known landslide in history, travelling a distance of fifteen miles in ten minutes, killing fifty-seven people. Mother Nature was no one to fool with. When we did the results could be disastrous.

Three days after Mount St. Helens, Jimmy Carter had to declare a state of emergency for the second time at a man-made disaster known as Love Canal. Nature wasn't always an agreeable dumping ground for our refuse. For three decades an unfinished canal near Niagara Falls served as a latrine for chemical wastes. The Hooker Chemical and Plastics Corporation unloaded something like 352 million pounds of hazardous materials, then covered the trench to hide the evidence. The chemicals leeched through the soil and into the ground water and basements of nearby homes. Not until 1976 did environmental tests reveal this as an industrial Mt. St. Helens.

The toxic wastes made the community uninhabitable. The local elementary school closed; families relocated. Hooker's parent company, Occidental Petroleum, eventually paid $150 million to cover clean-up and damages. As years passed without any illnesses, people began moving back, although some areas remained uninhabitable. The Love Canal area is now Black Creek Village. Mt. St. Helens is a major tourist attraction. The beat went on as though life had no consequences that couldn't be ignored.

Except that from now on we wouldn't be able to ignore anything. Beginning June 1, whatever was happening, whenever and wherever it was happening, an unblinking eye would be trained on it. Less than a month after Mount St. Helens blew off its tranquil past, nonstop news barged in, along with its devious partner the twenty-four hour news cycle.

CNN

—the global village

Information is power. Those controlling it determine the issues. The Cable News Network altered the equation by adding immediacy. Network news was still a corporate product. But the simple demands of filling airtime brought more news, less filtered. The result was greater access to information, hence greater power for a greater number of people.

Cable News Network was as much Marshall McLuhan's test tube baby as millionaire entrepreneur Ted Turner's. (In this case, the test tube was a cathode ray tube.) It was a birth every bit as dramatic as Louise Brown's. Yet viewers marveling at the breathtaking scope of information now illuminating their living rooms were unable to avoid the equally breathtaking scope of human misery.

Ugly reality had been hovering around the neighborhood like a peeping tom. With cable the hoary gent finally found a way to hop the backyard fence, slip past the now rusted brick barbecue, through the screen door and into the living room. Despite the democratizing effects of nonstop news, it had its negative aspects. It meant news runoff and historical amnesia: too much to process, too much to remember. Information, materialism and suffering now came wrapped in the same bite-sized packages—jump-cut bits of contextless information formatted like commercials. News brought power but it also increased the white noise.

World-wide coverage of the human condition changed the way our government did business, forcing leaders to react to a public outcry about a disastrous monsoon in Bangladesh, a ruthless warlord in Somalia or ethnic oppression in the Balkans. Some critics dubbed it the "CNN Effect." Melodrama became a major player in foreign and domestic policy. Public opinion forced the government to dispatch soldiers to out-of-the-way places because of an isolated horror people happened to catch on TV. National interest now came second, if it came at all. CNN caused a fundamental change in the way the average citizen related to the rest of the world. For isolationist America, it amounted to an altered state of being.

*   *   *

As if there were any doubt, the Sixties and our youth were about to bid their final adieu.

> *"All we are saying, is give peace a chance."*
>
> **—John Lennon**

On December 8 a psychotic fan, Mark David Chapman, shot and killed John Lennon outside his New York apartment. He was forty years old when he died. Peace had become a cliché. As though to emphasize this, it was Howard Cosell, at his most unctuous, who announced Lennon's death to the television audience watching *Monday Night Football*. Popular culture couldn't have designated a more fitting spokesman to mark the transition to dissatisfaction, recrimination and violence. John's murder presaged a wave of mass murders, serial killings and attacks on the rich and famous that would stretch into the millennium. The era was dead and gone. A new one was on its way.

It was time to grow up.

> ****** Inside every Baby Boomer is a child wondering what the hell happened. ******

Acknowledgements

First and foremost, I want to thank my friends on the Well for their suggestions and insights. I first presented the idea for this book in the Baby Boomer Conference on the Well and received exactly the sort of encouragement I was looking for. The Boomer Conference is home to many wise and knowledgeable baby boomers and a few precocious GenXers as well. It's the world's best forum for boomer issues. I asked many a stupid question on the "Experts on the Well" topic, and got many incisive answers. I especially want to thank and pay tribute to my friend Mark McDonough, who suggested the phrase (if not the entire idea) that the 60s set out to "re-wire the culture." Beyond that, Mark's voracious reading, pointers and insights which he enthusiastically passes along, and his tireless hosting of the Well's History Conference have made him an inspiration to me since we met online in 1993.

Thanks as well to Shirley Trostle for her editorial assistance, and a tip of the hat to those four historians who rendered great service in critiquing an earlier version of this book. My gratitude to Ed Schamel for the last minute use of his laptop, and for his steady friendship over the years. I also want to thank Kele Sante for ferreting out obscure facts (such as the color of the tablecloth at the Japanese surrender on the Battleship Maine) and other odd bits of information that I had given up on. She is a genius at these things. Nadia Singh turned out to be a better line editor than many people who get paid a lot more money that she did. Neither of these two is a boomer, which means they will have to take the blame for their mistakes. As a baby boomer, you can bet I will find someone else to blame for this book's many shortcomings. Here are two likely suspects from Generation X.

Finally, I must give special thanks to the most patient person I know, Kris Ecker. I owe you more than I can ever say.

About the Author

Howard Smead is the author of *Blood Justice, The Lynching of Mack Charles Parker*, an account of the last classic lynching in American History, which took place in Poplarville, Mississippi in 1959. He is the author of three novels: *The Redneck Waltz* about the effects of violence in a small town. *Kak Drenner*, a murder mystery about a violent struggle for control of a family fortune. And a cyberthriller, *My Name is Zed* in which hackers track two children kidnapped by a cyberstalker. He was on the staff at *The Washington Post* and currently teaches history at The University of Maryland.

Index

A

B

C

D

E

G

H

I

L

M

N

O

Q

R

S

U

V

W

Y

Z